LETTERS OF

JAMES RUSSELL LOWELL

EDITED BY

CHARLES ELIOT NORTON

VOLUME II.

NEW YORK

HARPER & BROTHERS PUBLISHERS

1894

CONTENTS OF VOL. II

VIII

1877–1880

IX

1880–1885

X

1885–1889

XI

1889–1891

RETURN TO ELMWOOD. — DECLINING HEALTH. — VISIT FROM LESLIE STEPHEN.—THE END.

LETTERS OF
JAMES RUSSELL LOWELL

VI
1868–1872

LIFE AT ELMWOOD. — "UNDER THE WILLOWS AND OTHER POEMS."—"MY STUDY WINDOWS."—"AMONG MY BOOKS," FIRST SERIES.—"THE CATHEDRAL."—VISIT FROM THOMAS HUGHES.

LETTERS TO C. E. NORTON, R. W. EMERSON, E. L. GODKIN, LESLIE STEPHEN, J. B. THAYER, W. D. HOWELLS, J. T. FIELDS, MISS NORTON, MISS CABOT, T. B. ALDRICH, THOMAS HUGHES, R. S. CHILTON, F. H. UNDERWOOD.

TO C. E. NORTON

Elmwood, Oct. 7, 1868.

... "The summer is past, the harvest is ended," and I have not yet written to you! Well, I was resolved I would not write till the printers had in their hands all the copy of my new volume of old poems. And that has taken longer than I expected. I have been Marthaized by many small troubles. But last night I fairly ended my work. ... I had decided to put the "June Idyl" in the forefront and call it "A June Idyl, and Other Poems." But Fields told me that Whittier's new volume was to be called "A Summer Idyl"—so I was

II.—1

blocked there. Then I took "Appledore," merely because it was a pretty name, though I did not wish to put that in the van. So it was all settled for the second time. Then I was suddenly moved to finish my "Voyage to Vinland," part of which, you remember, was written eighteen years ago. I meant to have made it much longer, but maybe it is better as it is. I clapt a beginning upon it, patched it in the middle, and then got to what had always been my favorite part of the plan. This was to be a prophecy by Gudrida, a woman who went with them, of the future America. I have written in an unrhymed alliterated measure, in very short verse and stanzas of five lines each. It does not aim at following the law of the Icelandic alliterated stave, but hints at it and also at the *asonante*, without being properly either. But it runs well and is melodious, and we think it pretty good here, as does also Howells. Well, after that, of course, I was all for alliteration, and, as I liked the poem, thought no title so good as "The Voyage to Vinland, and Other Poems." But Fields would not hear of it, and proposed that I should rechristen the Idyl "Elmwood," and name the book after that. But the more I thought of it the less I liked it. It was throwing my sanctuary open to the public and making a show-house of my hermitage. It was indecent. So I fumed and worried. I was *riled*. Then it occurred to me that I had taken the name of "June Idyl" as a *pis-aller*, because in my haste I could think of nothing else. Why not name it over? So I hit upon "Under the Willows," and that it is to be. . . . But it is awfully depressing work. They call back so many moods, and they are so bad. I think, though, there is a suggestion of something good in them at least, and they are not silly. But how much the public will stand! I sometimes wonder they don't drive all us authors into a corner and make a *battue* of the whole concern at once. . . .

TO R. W. EMERSON

Elmwood, Oct. 14, 1868.

My dear Sir,—If you had known what a poem your two tickets contained for me, how much they recalled, how many vanished faces of thirty years ago, how much gratitude for all you have been and are to us younger men (a debt I always love to acknowledge, though I can never repay it), you would not have dreamed of my not being an eager hearer during the whole course. Even were I not sure (as I always am with you) of having what is best in me heightened and strengthened, I should go out of loyalty to what has been one of the great privileges of my life. I, for one,

"Obey the voice at eve obeyed at prime,"

and you may be sure of one pair of ears in which the voice is always musical and magisterial too. . . .

I am gratefully and affectionately

Your liegeman,

J. R. LOWELL.

TO E. L. GODKIN

Elmwood, Nov. 20, 1868.

. . . The cause you advocate in the *Nation* is not specially American—it is that of honest men everywhere, and acknowledges no limits of nationality. And let me say for your comfort, that while I have heard the *criticism* of the *Nation* objected to as ill-natured (though I naturally don't think it so), I have never heard its political writing spoken of but with praise. The other day at a dinner-table some of its criticisms were assailed, and I said that I might be suspected of partiality if I defended them (though I *think* I am not [open to the charge]), but that "I deliberately thought that its discussions of politics had done more good and influenced opinion more than any other agency, or all others combined, in the country." This, so far as I could judge, was unanimously assented to. At any rate, one of my antagonists agreed with me entirely, and no one else dissented. The criticisms in the *Nation* often strike me as admirable. I sometimes dissent, but I am getting old and good-natured, and know, moreover, how hard it is to write well, to come even anywhere near one's own standard of good writing. . . .

. . . For my own part I am not only thankful for the *Nation*, but continually wonder how you are able to make so excellent a paper with your material. I have been an editor and know how hard it is. . . .

I had forgotten the financial question. I insist on my own view of it. I shall write from time to time till I think we are square. What Fields pays me, I doubt if anybody else would. He has always been truly generous in his dealings with me. If you feel any scruples, you can make matters even by sending the *Nation* for a year to John B. Minor, Professor in the University of Virginia, Charlottesville. Accident has lately put me in correspondence with him and given me a strong feeling of respect for his character. He lost everything by the war, but was and is a Union man, though he went with his State. I have often wished the *Nation* might have some circulation at the South, and here is a good chance to get at *one* sensible man there at any rate. I don't wish him to know where it comes from. Perhaps it would be better to send him a number now and then at first, till he got used to it, omitting numbers that might startle his natural prejudices in any way. I think it would do good. I confess to a strong sympathy with men who sacrificed everything even to a bad cause which they could see only the good side of; and, now the war is over, I see no way to heal the old wounds but by frankly admitting this and acting upon it. We can never reconstruct the South except through its own leading men, nor ever hope to have them on our side till we make it for their interest and compatible with their honor to be so. At this moment in Virginia, the oath required by the new Constitution makes it impossible to get a decent magistrate. . . .

TO LESLIE STEPHEN

Elmwood, Thanksgiving Day, 1868.

My dear Stephen,—I hope that while I am writing this, with my pipe in my mouth, you and Mrs. Stephen are not suffering those agonies that come from being rocked in the cradle of the deep. You are wallowing along through this dreary rain towards drearier Halifax, and I wish instead you were going to eat turkey with us. I am truly glad to hear that Mrs. Stephen is so much better, and that she could find something to like among us. I don't wonder that she thought America dull, if she judged it by Elmwood. It *was* dull, but I couldn't help it, for I am as stupid as a public dinner. A host should have nothing on his mind.

Had I known where, I should have sent you my book. You will get it before long in London, and may like it as little as you please, if you will keep on liking *me*.

M—— was delighted with her gift from England, and has written to say so. She was especially pleased to get a package from London addressed to herself and not to my care. I immediately seized the last volume (which I had not read) and went through it before I " retired," as Mrs. Stowe would say. I was amazingly taken with it, and am not ashamed to confess that I blubbered over " Beauty and the Beast," and gulped my heart down several times in " Little Red Riding-hood." I am no great judge, but the book struck me as simply delightful, which, after all, is something of a literary merit. As for Mabel, her conceit is intolerable. The books stand on her shelves, and when her young friends come to see her she turns the conversation adroitly upon Miss Thackeray, and then exhibits her prize. I gave her *my* book, and she has not read it yet. At so low an ebb is taste in a democracy! I begin to suspect an immoral tendency in " The Story of Elizabeth."

I was very much amused with your picture of those wretched British swells in Washington. If it is dull during the recess, what must it be when Congress gathers into one focus the united rays of boredom from every corner of the country? I am thankful that we can revenge ourselves on part of the British race for the wrongs of the *Alabama*. You gave us the heroic Semmes, and we let loose Sumner upon your embassy. I was not sorry you should say a kind word for poor old Johnson. I have never thought so ill of him as becomes an orthodox Republican. The worst of him was that he meant well. As for Chase, he is a weak man with an imposing presence — a most unhappy combination, of which the world has not wanted examples from Saul and Pompey down. Such men as infallibly make mischief as they defraud expectation. If you write about American politics, remember that Grant has always chosen able lieutenants. My own opinion is (I give it for what it is worth), that the extreme Republicans will be wofully disappointed in Grant. At any rate, if he should throw away his opportunity to be an independent President, he is not the man I take him to be. No man ever had a better chance to be a great magistrate than he. If he shouldn't prove to be one—well, a democracy can bear a great deal. . . .

It is raining drearily to-day, but my sister and a nephew and niece and Rowse are to keep festival with me, and I shall be quite patriarchal. It is by such fetches that I supply the want of grandchildren. However, I have grand-nephews, and so am a kind of grandfather by brevet.

1870, my dear boy, is a far cry, but I shall look forward to it as the bringer of good gifts, if it bring you back to me. You know the way to my door and my heart, and won't stupidly go to the Tremont House again. Perhaps I shall keep a coach by that time, who

your friendly warmth, I have expatiated into a letter. Forgive me, and set it down to your own friendly warmth.   It will be a warning to you in future.   Meanwhile, it is some consolation that I am cheating dear Gurney, for I ought to be doing the politics of the next *North American Review.*

I remain very cordially yours,

J. R. LOWELL.

P. S.   Since this was written (for it was written last Sunday, and I have rewritten it to get rid of some too *expansive* passages) Motley has given me the beginning of one of my poems, which I had lost.   I thought you might like to have it, so I copy it on the next leaf that you may paste it in before the poem called " A Mood," where it belongs.   Hamilton Wild wrote it down for Motley from memory, and as it has stuck in his head so many years I think it must have some good in it. I rather like it myself.   I found the poem as it stands in an old note-book.   I knew that it had been printed (part of it), and that it did not begin rightly—but could not remember where to look for it.

I go to the ridge in the forest
  Which I haunted in days gone by;
But thou, O Memory, pourest
  No magical drop in mine eye,
Nor the gleam of the secret restorest
  That has faded from woodland and sky.
A presence more sad and sober
  Invests the rock and the tree;
And the aureole of October
  Lights the maples, but darkens me.

TO J. T. FIELDS

Elmwood, Dec. 20, 1868.

My dear Fields,— . . . I read your advertisement in
the *Nation*, and discovered with some surprise what a
remarkable person I was.   It is lucky for Dante and
them fellers that they got their chance so early.   I hope
I shall still be able to meet my friends on an easy footing.   I trust I can unbend without too painful an air of
condescension.   But make the most of me, my dear
Fields, while you have me.   I begin to fear an untimely
death.   Such rare apparitions are apt to vanish as unexpectedly as they come.   There is no life-insurance for
these immortals.   They have their length of days on
t'other side.   For my part I don't understand how Bryant
holds out so long.   Yet it was pleasant to see him renewing his youth like the eagles, in that fine poem
about the trees.   He deserves to have a tree planted
over his grave, which I wouldn't say of many men.   A
cord of wood should be a better monument for most.
There was a very high air about those verses, a tone
of the best poetic society, that was very delightful.
Tell Mrs. Fields that I think they justify his portrait.

Your January *Atlantic* was excellent.   O. W. H. never
wrote more to my mind, so genial, so playfully tender.
And Howells.   Barring a turn of phrase here and there,
I think that as good a thing as you ever printed.*   It
had the uncommon merit of being interesting.   That
boy will know how to write if he goes on, and then we
old fellows will have to look about us.   His notice (I

* A paper entitled " Gnadenhütten."

suppose it was his) of Longfellow's book was a masterpiece of delicate handling.   How fair it was, and yet
what a kindly discretion in turning all good points to the
light!   Give my love to him, and tell him I miss him
much.   Also, in noticing my book, to forget his friendship, and deal honestly with me like a man.

With kind regards to Mrs. Fields and a merry Xmas
to both of you (you have made more than one of mine
merrier before now),

Yours ever,

J. R. L.

TO E. L. GODKIN

Elmwood, New Year, 1869.

My dear Godkin,—Thinking you might not otherwise
see it, I enclose you a paragraph from an harangue of Miss
Dickinson's at the Boston Music Hall last night—31st
December.   I don't send it because you will care for
what she says about the *Nation*—which is weak enough
—but because it will give you a chance to say a timely
word on an important subject.   This theory of settling
things by what anybody may choose to consider " humanity," instead of trying to find out how they may be
settled by knowledge, is a fallacy too common in this
country.   When one recollects that the Scythians (whoever they were) used to eat their grandfathers out of
humanity, one gets a little shy of trusting himself to it
altogether, especially as one grows older.   It is awful
to contemplate—and yet profoundly instructive—that,
when we talk of the "moral nature of man," we mean
the disposition that has been bred in him by habit—that
is, by respect for the opinion of others become a habit:

ἦθος, *mores, mœurs, costumbri, costumi, sitte* (connected, I
suppose, with the *suet* in *suetus*)—it is so in all tongues.
One must swallow the truth, though it makes one's eyes
water. Nor does this hinder one from believing in the
higher Reason, as I for one firmly do. We have an instinct to prefer the good, other things being equal, and
in exact proportion to our culture we know better what
is good, and prefer it more habitually.

For your guidance, I add that there were some very
good points in the lecture — better, indeed, than I expected. But it is very droll to me that Miss Dickinson
shouldn't see that her " humanity " style of setting things
right (by instinct, namely) is the very shillelah method she
condemns so savagely in the Irish. Is it not?

The *Nation* continues to be a great comfort to me. I
agree so entirely with most of its opinions that I begin
to have no small conceit of my own wisdom. You have
made yourself a Power (with a big p), my dear Fellow,
and have done it honestly by honest work, courage, and
impartiality. . . .

Yours always,

J. R. LOWELL.

TO THE SAME

Elmwood, Jan. 8, 1869.

My dear Godkin,—Don't think I have gone mad that
I so pepper you with letters—I have a reason, as you
will see presently. But in the first place let me thank
you for the article on Miss Dickinson, which was just
what I wanted and expected, for (excuse me) you preach
the best lay-sermons I know of. I know it is a weakness and all that, but I was born with an impulse to

tell people when I like them and what they do, and I
look upon you as a great public benefactor. I sit
under your preaching every week with indescribable
satisfaction, and know just how young women feel towards their parson—but let Mrs. Godkin take courage, I
can't marry you! . . .

My interest in the *Nation* is one of gratitude, and
has nothing to do with my friendship for you. I am
sure, from what I hear said against you, that you are
doing great good and that you are respected. I may
be wrong, but I sincerely believe you have raised the
tone of the American press.

I don't want to pay for the *Nation* myself. I take a
certain satisfaction in the large F. on the address of my
copy. It is the only thing for which I was ever dead-
headed. But I wish to do something in return. So I
enclose my check for $25, and wish you to send the pa-
per to five places where it will do most good to others
and to itself. Find out five College reading-rooms, and
send it to them for a year. Those who read it will want
to keep on reading it. I can think of no wiser plan.
Send one to the University of Virginia and one to
the College of South Carolina. One, perhaps, would do
good if sent to Paul H. Hayne, Augusta, Georgia. He
was a rebel colonel, I believe, but is in a good frame
of mind, if I may judge from what he has written to
me. . . .

TO W. D. HOWELLS

Elmwood, Under the Rain, 1869.

My dear Boy,—You know very well that I would

rather have you fond of me than write the best essay
that ever Montaigne conceived as he paced to and fro in
that bleak book-room of his.   But for all that, I am
grateful for what you say, since a gray beard brings self-
distrust—at least in my case, who never had any great
confidence in anything but Truth.

But what I write this for is only to say that to be sure
I knew who the "young Vermont sculptor" was,* and
pleased myself with alluding to him for your sake; for
when my heart is warm towards any one I like all about
him, and this is why I am so bad (or so good) a critic,
just as you choose to take it.   If women only knew how
much woman there is in me, they would forgive all my
heresies on the woman-question — I mean, they would if
they were not women.

But then I am a good critic about one thing, and I
see how you have mixed *me* and my essay.   Why, I
was thinking only this morning that if I could have you
to lecture to I could discourse with great good-luck, for
you always bring me a reinforcement of spirits.

Well, whatever happens, you can't be sorry that I
thought so much of you as I do.

With kindest regards to Mrs. Howells,

Always affectionately yours,

J. R. L.

TO J. T. FIELDS

Elmwood, March 23, 1869.

My dear Fields,—I don't see why the New York poets
should have all the sonnets to themselves, nor why

---

* Mr. Larkin G. Mead, the brother-in-law of Mr. Howells.

II.—2

we shouldn't be littery now and then as well as they.
With the help of Walker's "Rhyming Dictionary"
and Lemprière, I have hammered out fourteen lines
to you, which I honestly think are as much like Shakespeare's sonnets as some others I have seen.   Your
name does not consent so kindly to an invocation as
Stoddard or Taylor or Boker or Richard or Bayard,
which, albeit trochees, may well displace an iambus
in the first foot.

"Richard, thy verse that like molasses runs," launch-
es your sonnet without a hitch.   I tried at first to evade
the difficulty by beginning boldly,

> James T., the year, in its revolving round,
> Hath brought once more the tributary pig—

but it wants that classical turn which lends grace to
your true sonnets as shaped by the great masters in this
kind of writing.   So I have hit on another expedient,
which I think will serve the turn.   As I find some of
my critics blame me as too scholarly and obscure because I use such words as microcosm—which send even
well-read men to their dictionaries—I have added a
few notes:

> Poseidon[1] Fields, who dost the[2] *Atlantic*[3] sway,
> Making it swell, or flattening at thy will!
> O glaucous[4] one, be thou propitious still
> To me, a minnum[5] dandled on thy spray![6]
> Eftsoons[7] a milk-white porkerlet[8] we slay.
> No sweeter e'er repaid Eumæus'[9] skill;
> A blameless Lamb[10] thereon might feed his fill,
> Deeming he cropped the new-sprung herb[11] of May.

Our board do thou and Amphitrite[12] grace;
Archbishop[13] of our literary sea,
Lay by thy trident-crozier for a space,
And try our forks; or, earless[14] to our plea,
Let this appease thee and the frown displace:
The Gurneys come and John[15]—then answer, *Oui!*[16]

[1] "Poseidon," a fabulous deity, called by the Latins Neptunus; here applied to Fields as presiding over the issues of the *Atlantic*.

[2] "the Atlantic," to be read " th' Atlantic," in order to avoid the *hiatus* or gap where two vowels come together.   Authority for this will be found in Milton and other poets.

[3] "*Atlantic*," a well-known literary magazine.

[4] "Glaucus," between blue and green, an epithet of Poseidon, and an editor who shows greenness is sure to look blue in consequence.

[5] "Minnum," vulgo pro *minnow*, utpote species *minima* piscium.

[6] "Dandled on thy spray."—A striking figure.   Horace has *piscium et summa genus haesit ulmo*, but the poverty of the Latin did not allow this sport of fancy with the double meaning of the word *spray*.

[7] "Eftsoons."—This word (I *think*) may be found in Spenser.   It means soon after, i. e., before long.

[8] "Porkerlet," a pretty French diminutive, as in *roitelet*.

[9] "Eumæus," the swineherd of Ulysses, a character in Homer.

[10] "Lamb," a well-known literary character of the seventeenth century, chiefly remembered for having burnt his house to roast a favorite pig.   He invented mint-sauce.

[11] "Herb"—grass.—Borrow a Bible, and you will find the word thus used in that once popular work.

[12] "Amphitrite," the beautiful spouse of Poseidon.

[13] "Archbishop."—This is the Elizabethan style.   (N. B., the play is upon *sea* and *see*.)   This term is beautifully, may I not say piously, appropriate, since the Grecian gods have all been replaced by Christian saints, and St. Anthony of Padua converted the finny nomads of the deep.   He found a ready *herring*, I suppose.

[14] "Earless."—This is not to be taken literally, as in the case of Defoe, or as Hotspur misinterprets Glendower's " bootless."   It means simply *deaf*.

[15] "John."—It is hardly necessary to say that there is but one John— to wit, J. Holmes, Esq., of Holmes Place.

[16] "*Oui*," a neat transition to the French tongue, conveying at once a compliment to the learning of the person addressed and an allusion to his editorial position.   Editors and kings always say *We*.

There! I think I have made that clear enough except in one particular, namely, its meaning. I don't admit that a sonnet needs anything so vulgar—but this one means that I want you and Mrs. Fields to eat a tithe-pig ('tis an offering of William's) with us in about ten days from now. I will fix the day as soon as I find out when the fairy creature will be ripe.

I have corrected nearly all of one volume, and dreary work it is. I know nothing more depressing than to look one's old poems in the face. If Rousseau's brats had come back upon his hands from the *Enfans Trouvés*, he would have felt just as I do.

Always yours,

J. R. L.

TO THE SAME

Elmwood, April 1, 1869.

My dear Fields,—The late Governor Gore, of pious memory, having issued his proclamation for a fast, incontinently thereafter sent out invitations for a dinner upon the same day, and thereby lost as much credit for piety as he gained praise for hospitality. As a politician, the balance was clearly against him in a community whose belief in immortality was not based upon material nutriment. But as a man, it may be suspected that he lost nothing except in the opinion of those who were not invited. If Governor Claflin (if I am right in the name of our present illustrious chief magistrate) had known that my pig would have been exactly ripe on the 8th day of April, and that twenty-four hours (not to speak of forty-eight) would convert him into vulgar pork, he would have doubtless chosen another occasion for proving his devotion to the principles of our Puritan forefathers. That sense of culinary propriety which led Moses to forbid the seething of a kid in its mother's milk would have induced *him* to spare my suckling the vulgarization of a single day longer amid the multitu‑ dinous temptations of the sty. Fancy that object of our tender solicitude exposed, like Eve, to the solicita‑ tion of an apple, still worse of some obscener vegetable! I will not even suggest a turnip, for that were too hor‑ rible. Even an unbeliever in the literal inspiration of Scripture would reject such an hypothesis with disgust. Deeply revolving these things, and also the fact that Gur‑ ney can't come either on Wednesday or Friday, I must fix on Thursday next as the day of consummation.

Those who have read the excellent Claflin's proclama‑ tion (I have not) can take their measures accordingly. They can deny themselves the second helping. They can leave a bit of untasted *cracklin* on their plates, or, defying the wrath of an offended deity with a *tant de bruit pour une omelette,* they can eat their fill. At any rate, Thursday the 8th is the day — if I have a house over my head.

I say this because we have been April-fooled with an alarm of fire to-day. The house was thick with smoke to the coughing-point, and I sent for a carpenter to rip up here and there. We were undoubtedly afire, but, thank God, we went out. It was not pleasant while it lasted, but Vulcan showed a consideration I can't thank him too much for in coming by daylight. But fancy seeing smoke come up through the chinks of your gar‑ ret-floor in a house like this! Yet this we saw. I con‑

fess I expected to spend the night at my sister's in Rox-
bury, and even now I am almost afraid to go to bed lest
it may begin again.   I had a vision of our two chimneys
standing like the ruins of Persepolis.

Therefore, if we don't burn down, we shall expect you
on Thursday; and if we *do*, why, then we will invite ourselves to dine with you.

Yours always,

J. R. L.

TO THE SAME

Elmwood, April 5, 1869.

My dear Fields,—If it had been as hard for Eve to eat
her apple as for me to get my pig eaten, we should all
be at this moment enjoying an income of a million a
minute and our expenses paid—with roast pig growing
on every bush.   The Greeks thought a great man struggling with the storms of fate the sublimest spectacle
offered to mortal eyes; but if Œdipus begging a meal's
meat be an awful sight, is there not even something
more pathetic in the case of him who strives in vain to
give away a dinner?   The pleasure of eating roast pig
on Fast Day, in such company as I reckoned on, could
only have been increased by adding a stray Jew to our
commensals.   But, alas, "What is this life?   What asken
man to have?"   Our cook is gone!   And though Le-
nore's mother said many sensible things to console her
for a far lighter loss—that of a dragoon—yet the answer
was conclusive,

"O Mutter, Mutter, hin ist hin!"

If hin isn't hin, what is?   In short, we must postpone

our dinner.   That pig, like Hawthorne's youth asleep by
the fountain, will never know how near Fate came to
him and passed on.

I hope by Thursday week to have supplied the place
of the delinquent—perhaps to our common advantage.
Mary was a cook merely by a brevet conferred by herself, and I doubt whether she had the genius for that
more transcendental touch which such a subject of un-
fallen innocence demands.   The little creature might
have been heathenishly sacrificed instead of being served
up with that delicacy which befits Xtians.   In such
cases, a turn more or a turn less may lose all, and one
who might afterwards have grown up into a learned pig
(who knows but into a Professor!) is cut off untimely to
no good purpose.   Let us hope for the best—let us hope
that if *we* can't have him, the world may gain a Bacon
or a Hogg or a Pig-ault Lebrun.   If we get a cook—
and we already hear of one—our festival is but pro-
rogued; luckily, *he* will not be too old, even with an
added week.   I shall send word at once, so think of a
dinner being put off because there won't be a death in
the family!   My heart feels like a pig of lead;

But I am always affectionately yours,

J. R. L.

Don't think I have had a paralysis; I have only
bought a gold pen.

TO MISS NORTON

Elmwood, April 6, 1869.

. . . Authors, my altogether dear woman, can't write
letters.   At best they squeeze out an essay now and

then, burying every natural sprout in a dry and dreary
sand-flood, as unlike as possible to those delightful fresh-
ets with which your heart overflows the paper. *They*
are thinking of their punctuation, of crossing their *t's*
and dotting their *i's*, and cannot forget themselves in
their correspondent, which I take to be the true recipe
for a letter. . . . Now, you know that the main excel-
lence of Cambridge is that nothing ever happens there.
Since the founding of the College, in 1636, there has
been, properly speaking, no event till J. H. began to
build his shops on the parsonage-lot. . . . Elmwood is
Cambridge at the fifth power, and indeed one of the
great merits of the country is that it narcotizes instead
of stimulating. Even Voltaire, who had wit at will,
found Ferney an opiate, and is forced to apologize to
his cleverest correspondent, Mme. du Deffand (do you
remark the adroitness of the compliment in my italicized
pronoun?) for the prolonged gaps, or yawns, in his letter-writing. Cowper, a first-rate epistolizer, was sometimes driven to the wall in the same way. There is
something more than mere vacancy, there is a deep
principle of human nature, in the first question of man
to man when they meet — "What is the news?" A
hermit has none. I fancy if I were suddenly snatched
away to London, my brain would prickle all over, as a
foot that has been asleep when the blood starts in it
again. Books are good dry forage; we can keep alive on
them; but, after all, men are the only fresh pasture. . . .

We have had a very long winter with very little snow.
It is still cold, but the birds are come, and the impatient lovers among them insist on its being spring. I

heard a bluebird several weeks ago, but the next day came six inches of snow. The sparrows were the first persistent singers, and yesterday the robins were loud. I have no doubt the pines at Shady Hill are all a-creak with blackbirds by this time. . . .

I have nothing else in the way of novelty, except an expedient I hit upon for my hens who were backward with their eggs. On rainy days I set William to reading aloud to them the Lay-sermons of Coleridge, and the effect was magical. Whether their consciences were touched or they wished to escape the preaching, I know not. . . .

TO LESLIE STEPHEN

April 24, 1869.

My dear Stephen,—By what system of mnemonics you contrived to remember those melon-seeds, I can't conjecture. I was glad to find that they were " Queen Anne's pocket-melons," because I was a subject of her most gracious majesty. I had not then established my independence. It pleased me also to have the fruit associated with some definite name. The former vagueness evaporated imagination (as Dr. Johnson might say) into a mere mist of conjecture. Now I can fancy Miss Hyde's august daughter pacing the gardens at Kensington, her pockets graced with the fruit which bore her name, and giving one to Harley or Bolingbroke or whatever purse-proud aristocrat happened to be the moment's favorite.

Within an hour after the seeds arrived they were in the ground, and already I watch with an almost paternal solicitude the gradual expansion of their leaves. Thus far they are doing well, and if they escape the diseases of infancy, I hope you will sit down at table with their children's children. It was very good of you to remember them, and therefore just like you. They came like a fairy godmother's gift just as I was wishing I had them.

The great sensation of the day is Sumner's speech on the rejection of the treaty with Great Britain. I think he has expressed the national feeling of the moment pretty faithfully. Mind, I say of the moment. The country was blushing at the maudlin blarney of Reverdy Johnson, and that made the old red spot, where we felt that our cheek had been slapped, tingle again. If Mr. Adams had remained in England, I believe the whole matter might have been settled to the satisfaction of both parties. Now for some time to come that will unhappily be impossible. But our soberest heads do not think that Sumner is right in his statement of the law, and I think that the discussion which is likely to follow will clear the way for some reasonable settlement of the difficulty. That there is any annexation-cat under Sumner's meal I, for one, do not in the least believe. The absorption of Canada would be simply the addition of so much strength to the Democratic party—no bad thing in itself, by the way, but certainly not to the taste of the party now in power. Meanwhile, fools talk as glibly of a war with England as if it would not be the greatest wrong and calamity to civilization in all history. But I will not suffer myself to think of such an outrage. If the English government behave with discretion and show a kindly feeling towards us whenever they have a chance, I think all will come out right. It was the *tone* of Palmerston's cabinet, more than anything else during the war, that made the sore. The speech of Chandler of Michigan, by the way, is a sample of our folly in the same way. It may do harm in England—*here* it has no significance whatever. . . .

In certain respects you can say nothing worse of us than we deserve. The power of "Rings" in our politics is becoming enormous. Men buy their seats in the Senate, and, of course, expect a profit on their investment. This is why the Senate clung so to the Tenure-of-Office bill. Grant means well, but has his hands tied. We are becoming a huge stock-jobbery, and Republicans and Democrats are names for bulls and bears. Pitch into us on all these matters as you will. You will do us good, for English papers (except by a few barbarians like me) are more read here than ever before, and criticism—no matter how sharp if it be honest—is what we need.

Whatever happens, my dear Stephen, nothing can shake or alter the hearty love I feel for you. I was going to say *affection*, but the Saxon word has the truer flavor. If you should ever be called upon to receive my sword hilt foremost, I am sure you will share your tobacco-pouch and canteen with me; and if ever I should take you prisoner, the worst you will have to fear will be to be made to eat too many pocket-melons. . . .

Always yours,

J. R. L.

TO E. L. GODKIN

Elmwood, May 2, 1869.

My dear Godkin,— . . . I note particularly (as merchants say) your remarks on British manners and our opinion of them. I would have said it myself—if only I had thought of it! A frequent cause of misapprehension is their not being able to understand that while there is no caste here, there is the widest distinction of classes. O my dear Godkin, they say we don't speak English, and I wish from the bottom of my heart we didn't—that we might comprehend one another! Impertinence and ill-will are latent in French—the Gaul can poison his discourse so as to give it a more agreeable flavor; but we clumsy Anglo-Saxons stir in our arsenic so stupidly it grits between the teeth. I wrote the essay you allude to, mainly with the hope of bringing about a better understanding. My heart aches with apprehension as I sit here in my solitude and brood over the present aspect of things between the two countries. We are crowding England into a fight which would be a horrible calamity for both—but worse for us than for them. It would end in our bankruptcy and perhaps in disunion. (When I remember that both Ireland and Scotland have been the allies of France, I don't feel sure which side the South would take.) As for Canada—I doubt if we should get by war what will fall to us by natural gravitation if we wait. We don't want Canada; all we want is the free navigation of the St. Lawrence, and that England will yield us ere long. We have no better ground of action than Dr. Fell would have had because people didn't like him. It is not so much of what England *did* as of the *animus* with which she did it that we complain — a matter of sentiment wholly incapable of arbitration. Sumner's speech expressed the *feeling* of the country very truly, but I fear it was not a wise speech. Was he not trying rather to chime in with that feeling than to give it a juster and manlier direction? After all, it is not the *Alabama* that is at the bottom of our grudge. It is the *Trent* that we quarrel about, like Percy and Glendower. That was like an east wind to our old wound and set it a-twinge once more. Old wrongs are as sure to come back on our hands as cats. England had five thousand Americans (she herself admitted that she had half that number) serving enforcedly aboard her fleets. Remember what American seamen then were, and conceive the traditions of injustice they left behind them with an *exoriare aliquis !* That imperious despatch of Lord John's made all those inherited drops of ill blood as hot as present wrongs. It is a frightful tangle — but let us hope for the best. I have no patience with people who discuss the chances of such a war as if it were between France and Prussia. It is as if two fellows half way down the Niagara rapids should stop rowing to debate how far they were from the fall. As for Butler's " Wait till I catch you in a dark lane !" I have no words for it.

I could not at first think *what* book about Rome you meant. At length I recollected Duppa's " Papal Subversion." This, I take it, is the passage you mean. 'Tis a note on p. 79. " Such was the mild, or rather corrupt, state of the Roman government, that during the late pontificate culprits were rarely punished with death for any crime: hence the slightest offence between individuals was a sufficient plea to justify any atrocity, and each often became avenger of his own wrong by assassination. [Hang the fellow! what a talent of prolongation he has!] To such an excess was this arrived that, during twenty-two years of the late reign, not less than eighteen thousand persons were murdered in public and private quarrels in the Ecclesiastical State alone, according to the bills of mortality in the governor's office, where from every district a return was annually made.

"It was a common opinion that it was the Pope's particular aversion to capital punishment that produced this laxity in the administration of justice, but I have it from high authority that he never saved any man from death who had been condemned by the law. Justice, indeed, would seem not to have been worse administered by the officers of the State in this reign than in that of his penultimate predecessor Rezzonico, in whose pontificate, which comprehended a period of little more than eleven years, ten thousand murders were committed in the papal dominions, of which at least one third were perpetrated in the city of Rome."

That is all I find to your purpose. Is this what you meant? While I am copying, I send you an extract from the "Letters of an American Farmer" (1782), by H. St. John Crèvecœur—dear book, with some pages in it worthy of Selborne White. . . . Perhaps it will help you to a paragraph. 'Tis a consolation to see that the gloomy forebodings of the Frenchman have not yet been realized.

"Lawyers . . . are plants that will grow in any soil that is cultivated by the hands of others, and, when once they have taken root, they will extinguish every vegetable that grows around them. The fortunes they daily acquire in every province from the misfortunes of their fellow-citizens are surprising! The most ignorant, the most bungling member of that profession will, if placed in the most obscure part of the country, promote litigiousness, and amass more wealth without labor than the most opulent farmer with all his toils. They have so dexterously interwoven their doctrines and quirks with the laws of the land, or rather they are become so necessary an evil in our present constitutions, that it seems unavoidable and past all remedy. What a pity that our forefathers, who happily extinguished so many fatal customs, and expunged from their new government so many errors and abuses, both religious and civil, did not also prevent the introduction of a set of men so dangerous! . . . The nature of our laws, and the spirit of freedom, which often tends to make us litigious, must necessarily throw the greatest part of the property of the colonies into the hands of these gentlemen. In another century the law will possess in the north what now the Church possesses in Peru and Mexico."—There's a gloomy prospect for us! We have only thirteen years' grace, and the century of prophecy will have dribbled away to the last drop.

Pray give Henry Wilson a broadside for dipping his flag to that piratical craft of the eight-hour men. I don't blame him for sympathizing with his former fellow-craftsmen (though he took to unproductive industry at the first chance), but I have a thorough contempt for a man who pretends to believe that eight is equal to ten, and makes philanthropy a stalking-horse. Jove! what a fellow Aristophanes was! Here is Cleon over again with a vengeance.

It troubles me to hear that you of all men should be in low spirits, who ought to have store of good spirits in the consciousness that you are really doing good. The *Nation* is always cheering to me; let its success be a medicine to you. . . .

Affectionately yours,

J. R. L.

TO W. D. HOWELLS

Elmwood, May 12, 1869.

My dear Howells,—I have just got a letter from Miss Norton, in which she says, "What an enchanting little paper that is on 'My Doorstep Acquaintance,' by Mr. Howells! The pretty pictures in it come up before me as I write, and I am not quite sure whether Cambridge is in Italy—though, now I think of it, I know Italy is sometimes in Cambridge! When you see Mr. Howells, please tell him how much we all liked his sketches of our old friends."

There's for you! Put that in your pipe and smoke it! I liked it as much as they did.

Always affectionately yours,

J. R. L.

TO E. L. GODKIN

Elmwood, July 16, 1869.

My dear Godkin,—I have long been of that philosopher's opinion who declared that "nothing was of much consequence"—at least when it concerned only ourselves, and certainly my verses were of none at all. I copied them for *you*, not for myself.

But the *Nation* is of consequence, and that's the reason I am writing now, instead of merely melting, to which the weather so feelingly persuades. You have never done better than in the last six months. Indeed, I think that you have improved with your growing conviction of your own power—a fact which has, if possible, increased my respect for you. At any rate, it proves that you are to be counted among the strong and not the merely energetic. Most editors when they feel their power are like beggars on horseback. *I* don't see why everybody doesn't take the *Nation*. I always read it *through*, and I never read the editorials in any other paper. My opinion is worth as much as the next man's, at least, and I see no paper that is so uniformly good. I was looking over some numbers of the *Pall Mall* yesterday, and didn't think it at all up to your (I mean E. L. G.'s) standard. This is not loyalty, but my deliberate opinion. Your reception * the other day should show you (and that is all I value it for) that your services to the cause of good sense, good morals, and good letters are recognized. You have *hit*, which is all a man can ask. Most of us blaze away into the void, and are as likely to bring down a cherubin as anything else. Pat your gun and say, "Well done, Brown Bess!" For 'tis an honest, old-fashioned

* At the Commencement Dinner at Harvard University.

piece, of straightforward short-range notions, and carries an ounce ball.

And in other respects the *Nation* has been excellent lately. I haven't seen a better piece of writing than that French *atelier*. It is the very best of its kind. Cherish that man, whoever he is. Whatever he has seen he can write well about, for he really *sees*. Why, he made me see as I read. The fellow is a poet, and all the better for not knowing it.

It is the unsettled state of affairs that is hurting you, if anything, though your advertising pages look prosperous. Wells, I am told, prophesies a crash for 1870, and fears that Congress will be weak enough to water the currency again—in other words, the national stock. I am not yet cured of my fear of repudiation, I confess. Democracies are kittle cattle to shoe behind. It takes men of a higher sense of honor than our voters mostly are to look at national bankruptcy in any other than a business light— and whitewash of all kinds is *so* cheap nowadays. Still, in spite of my fears, I think we shall come out all right, for a country where everybody does something has a good many arrows in its quiver. And though I believe that property is the base of civilization, yet when I look at France, I am rather reconciled to the contempt with which we treat its claims. There are, after all, better things in the world than what we call civilization even.

Always yours,

J. R. L.

TO W. D. HOWELLS

Elmwood, Aug. 11, 1869.

My dear Howells,—Up to time, indeed! The fear

is not about time, but space. You won't have room in your menagerie for such a displeaseyousaurus. The verses if stretched end to end in a continuous line would go clear round the Cathedral they celebrate, and nobody (I fear) the wiser. I can't tell yet what they are. There seems a bit of clean carving here and there, a solid buttress or two, and perhaps a gleam through painted glass—but I have not copied it out yet, nor indeed read it over consecutively.

As for the poem you sent me, I should have printed it when I sat in your chair. I will not criticise it further than to say that there is a great deal too much epithet. The author has wreaked himself on it. I should say *her*self, for I guess 'tis a gal.

Here was I, who have just written an awfully long thing,* going to advise the shortening of this other. But such is human nature, capable, I am thankful to say, of every kind of inconsistency. However, I am always consistently yours,

J. R. L.

TO THE SAME

Elmwood, Thursday.

. . . Thank you from the bottom of my heart, old fellow, for your note. If I divine that it is partly *me* that you like in the poem, I am all the more pleased. I don't care how much or how long we mutually admire each other, if it make us happier and kindlier, as I am sure it does. No man's praise, at any rate, could please me more than yours, and your affectionate messages will

* "The Cathedral."

send me to my college lecture this afternoon with a better heart. God bless you! Keep on writing, and among other things billets-doux like this, which made my eyelids tremble a little with pleasure.

Always affectionately yours,

J. R. L.

P. S. I haven't a minute to spare, but I am just going to read it over again, lest I missed any of the sweetness.

TO MISS NORTON

Elmwood, Sept. 6, 1869.

1. You order me, dear Jane, to write a sonnet.
2. Behold the initial verse and eke the second;
3. This is the third (if I have rightly reckoned),
4. And now I clap the fourth and fifth upon it
5. As easily as you would don your bonnet;
6. The sixth comes tripping in as soon as beckoned,
7. Nor for the seventh is my brain infécund;
8. A shocking rhyme! but, while you pause to con it,
9. The eighth is finished, with the ninth to follow;
10. As for the tenth, why, that must wedge between
11. The ninth and this I am at present scrawling;
12. Twelve with nine matches pat as wings of swallow;
13. Blushingly after that comes coy thirteen;
14. And this crowns all, as sailor his tarpauling.

I confess that I stole the idea of the above sonnet from one of Lope de Vega's, written under similar circumstances. Now, in that very sonnet Lope offers you a bit of instruction by which I hope you will profit and never again ask for one in twelve lines. He says, in so many words,

" *Catorce* versos dicen que es soneto,"

one more than even the proverbial baker's dozen, which shows the unthriftiness of poets in their own wares—or, perhaps you will say, their somewhat tiresome liberality. I dare say most sonnets would be better if cut off, like the cur's tail, just behind the ears. Having given you this short and easy lesson in the essential element of Petrarch's inspiration, I now proceed to do another sonnet in the received sentimental style of those somewhat artificial compositions.

> Ah, think not, dearest Maid, that I forget!
> Say, in midwinter doth the prisoned bee
> Forget the flowers he whilom held in fee?
> In free-winged fantasy he hovers yet
> O'er pansy-tufts and beds of mignonette.
> And I, from honeyed cells of memory
> Drawing in darkened days my stores of thee,
> Seek La Pacotte on dream-wings of regret.
> I see thee vernal as when first I saw,
> Buzzing in quest of sugar for my rhyme;
> And this, my heart assures me, is Love's law,
> That he annuls the seasons' frosty crime,
> And, warmly wrapped against Oblivion's flaw,
> Tastes in his garnered sweets the blossoming thyme.

Perhaps the eighth verse would be better thus,

> Fly on dream-wings to La Pacotte, you bet!

That, at least, has the American flavor, which our poetry is said to lack. . . . I do not mean by the twelfth verse to insinuate anything unfeeling. It is merely to be in keeping with the laws of the sonnet, and to bring the thought back to where it set out, like a kitten playing with its own tail. But I will confess to you that I am getting so gray that *I* see it; so you may be sure there is not much to choose between me and the traditional badger. Happily, I am grown no stouter, though already " more fat than bard beseems."

But why have I not written all this while? . . . For all August I have a valid excuse. First, I was writing a poem, and second, a pot-boiler. The poem turned out to be something immense, as the slang is nowadays, that is, it ran on to eight hundred lines of blank verse. I hope it is good, for it fairly trussed me at last and bore me up as high as my poor lungs will bear into the heaven of invention. I was happy writing it, and so steeped in it that if I had written to you it would have been in blank verse. It is a kind of religious poem, and is called " A Day at Chartres." I remember telling Charles once that I had it under my hair. . . . I can't tell yet how it will stand. Already I am beginning to—to—you know what I mean — to taste my champagne next morning. However, you will see it in the January *Atlantic*, and you must try to like it and me. I can't spare either. . . .

TO MISS CABOT

Elmwood, Sept. 14, 1869.

. . . The advantage of study, I suspect, is not in the number of things we learn by it, but simply that it teaches us the one thing worth knowing—not *what*, but *how* to think. Nobody can learn that from other people. Apart from the affection I feel for you, I have always

liked in you a certain independence of character and a
tendency to judge for yourself. Both these are excellent
if kept within bounds, if you do not allow the one to degenerate into insubordination of mind and the other into
hastiness of prejudice. Now, I am inclined to think that
one may get a reasonably good education out of any first-
rate book if read in the right way. Take Dante or Milton,
for example. If you like or dislike a passage, insist with
yourself on knowing the reason why. You are already unconsciously learning rhetoric in the best way. Then ask
yourself what is contemporary and what perdurable in his
theology and the like. You are not only studying the
history of his time, but also, what is vastly more important, [learning] to look with deeper insight at that of your
own time. You see what I mean. If all roads lead to
Rome, so do all roads lead out of Rome to every province
of thought. What one wants is to enlarge his mind, to
make it charitable, and capable of instruction and enjoyment from many sides. When one has learned that, he
has begun to be wise—whether he be *learned* or not is of
less consequence. How is it possible, I always ask myself in reading, that a man *could* have thought so and so,
and especially a superior man? When I have formed to
myself some notion of that, I understand my contemporaries better, for every one of us has within ten miles'
circuit specimens of every generation since Adam.

But I am preaching, my dear Lilla, and you don't like
any preaching but Dr. Clarke's perhaps? What I mean
is that our aim should be not to get many things into
one's head, but to get *much*, and one gets that when he
has learned the relations of any one thing to all others;

because in so doing he has got the right way of looking at anything. I have no fear that your education will be neglected, because I am sure that you will look after it yourself—because, moreover, you have an alert nature and a scorn of ignoble things. . . .

TO THOMAS HUGHES

Elmwood, Cambridge, Sept. 18, 1869.

My dear Hughes,—We are all very well satisfied with the result of the match.* For my own part, I have always thought that "magnis tamen excidit ausis" was not a bad kind of epitaph. I should only be sorry if our defeat were attributed to want of bottom. Our crew had already pulled a four-mile race on their own water and won it against a crew of professional oarsmen. I think that in private we may claim a little on the score of change of climate, though, of course, they had to take their chance of that. I am particularly glad to know that you thought it a good pull, because you have a right to an opinion. I did not expect them to win, though I hoped they would. Especially I hoped it because I thought it would do more towards bringing about a more friendly feeling between the two countries than anything else. I am glad to think it has had that result as it is. It isn't the *Alabama* claims that rankle, but the tone of the English press, or the more influential part of it. There is a curious misapprehension about us over there, as if we had been a penal colony. For example:

* The race between an Oxford and a Harvard four-oar crew, on the Thames, of which Mr. Hughes was the umpire.

when Longfellow was in Rome he drove out to some
races on the Campagna.   There his carriage chanced to
be abreast of one in which two English ladies were dis-
cussing the manners of American girls.   At last one of
them summed up thus: " Well, you know, what can be
expected of people who are all descended from laboring
men or convicts?"   Now, between ourselves, one of the
things that has always amused me in my brother New-
Englanders is their fondness for family trees.   You will
remember that I made a little fun of it in the introduction to the first series of the " Biglow Papers."   It is a
branch of arboriculture in which I take no great interest
myself, but my father was as proud of his pedigree as a
Talbot or a Stanley could be, and Parson Wilbur's gene-
alogical mania was a private joke between us.   Now, you
can understand how the tone I speak of would be resented.   I think Sumner's speech as an argument a mere
colander, but it represented the temper of our people
pretty exactly.   On your side, it was all along assumed
that England had a point of honor to maintain, and all
along implied that this was something of which we naturally had no conception, and to which, of course, our side
could lay no claim.   Don't you see?   Now, our point of
honor runs back to the *Little Belt* and the *President*, as
long ago as 1809 or so.   In those days American seamen belonged to the very best class of our population,
and there were five thousand such serving enforcedly
on board your ships-of-war.   Put it at half the number
(which was admitted on your side), and fancy what a
ramification of bitter traditions would thread the whole
country from these men and their descendants.   You

know that such little chickens always come home to roost, and these are just beginning to flock in now. I am writing all this that you may understand something of the feeling here.

I think that all we want is to be treated in a manly way. We don't want to be flattered, and some of us thought your newspapers went quite far enough in that direction just after the war. Tell us the truth as much as you like, it will do us good; but tell it in a friendly way, or at least not quite so much *de haut en bas*. Your letter in accepting the umpireship in the race hit precisely the right key. There are plenty of sensible men on this side of the water (more, I think, than I have found in any other country)—men, I mean, who are governed rather more, in the long run, by reason than by passion or prejudice. I did not like Sumner's speech, nor did the kind of men I speak of like it (and their opinions, though less noisily expressed, have more influence on our politics than you would suppose); but I am inclined to think it has done more good than harm. It served as a vent for a great deal of fire-damp that might have gone off with an explosion, and satisfied that large class who need the "you're another" style of argument. If only some man in your government could find occasion to say that England had mistaken her own true interest in the sympathy she showed for the South during our civil war! No nation ever apologizes except on her knees, and I hope England is far enough from being brought to that—no sane man here expects it—but she could make some harmless concessions that would answer all the purpose. I have pretty good authority for thinking that Motley was instructed to make no overtures on the *Alabama* matter, and perhaps it is as well to let things subside a little first. Still, I dread to have the affair left unsettled a moment longer than can be helped. Your greatest safeguard against us would be a settlement of the Irish land question. It is a heroic remedy, but you must come to it one day or other. I never believed in the efficacy of disestablishment. Arthur Young told you where the real trouble was eighty odd years ago. My fear is (as things stand now) that if England should get into a war, we could not (with our immense length of coast) prevent privateers from slipping out, and then! It would be a black day for mankind.

You ask me who "Bob Wickliffe" was. He was a senator from Kentucky, and Kentucky undertook to be neutral. It was a bull I thought we should take by the horns at once, as we had at last to do.

I have been writing a poem which I think you will like. It will be published in the *Atlantic Monthly* for January, and I shall send you a copy. I did not send you my last volume, because I knew you would get it earlier from Macmillan, and you did not need it to assure you of my friendship. Mabel gives us hope of a visit from you next year. I need not say how welcome you will be.

Always heartily yours,

J. R. LOWELL.

TO W. D. HOWELLS

Elmwood, Sept. 22, 1869.

My dear Howells,—Forgive this purple ink. It was

palmed upon me the other day, who in my simple conservatism thought all the ink in the world was made by
Maynard & Noyes, as it used to be. I have a horrible
suspicion that it may be a "writing fluid"—still worse,
that it may treacherously turn black before you get this,
and puzzle you as to what I am driving at. It is now,
on my honor, of the color of pokeberry juice, whereof we
used to make a delusive red ink when we were boys. I
feel as if I were writing ancient Tyrian, and becoming
more inscrutable to you with every word. Take it for
"the purple light of love," and it will be all right.

I have a great mind (so strong is the devil in me, despite my years) to give you an awful pang by advising
you not to print your essay. It would be a most refined
malice, and pure jealousy, after all. I find it delightful,
full of those delicate touches which the elect pause over
and the multitude find out by and by—the test of good
writing and the warrant of a reputation worth having.
As Gray said of the romances of Crébillon *fils*, I should
like to lie on a sofa all day long and read such essays.
You know I would not flatter Neptune for his trident—
as indeed who would, that did not toast his own bread?
—but what you write gives me a real pleasure, as it
ought; for I have always prized in you the ideal element, not merely in your thought, but in your way of
putting it.

And one of these days, my boy, you will give us a little volume that we will set on our shelves, with James
Howell on one side of him and Charles Lamb on the
other—not to keep *him* warm, but for the pleasure *they*
will take in rubbing shoulders with him. What do you

say to that? It's true, and I hope it will please you to read it as much as it does me to write it. Nobody comes near you in your own line. Your Madonna would make the fortune of any essay—or that pathetic bit there in the graveyard — or your shop of decayed gentilities—or fifty other things. I do not speak of the *tone*, of the light here and shade there that tickle *me*.

You were mighty good to procure me that little accession of fortune.* It will give Madam a new gown—a luxury she has not had these three years—and will just make the odds between feeling easy and pinched. It may be even a public benefaction—for I attribute the late gale in large part to my frantic efforts at raising the wind in season for my autumnal taxes. Yet a dreadful qualm comes over me that I am paid too much. When a poet reads his verses he has such an advantage over types! You will gasp when you see me in print. But never fear that I shall betray my craft. Far from me the baseness of refunding! Indeed I seldom keep money long enough for Conscience to get her purchase on me and her lever in play. What a safety there is in impecuniosity! And yet—let me read Dryden's Horace's "Ode to Fortune," lest if a million come down upon me I should be so in love with security as to put aside the temptation.

Now to the important part of my note. I want you to eat roast pig with me on Saturday next at half-past four P. M. Your commensals will be J. H., Charles Storey, and Professor Lane—all true blades who will sit till Mon-

---

* An additional payment for "The Cathedral."

day morning if needful.   The pig is just ripe, and so
tender that he would drop from his tail if lifted by it,
like a mature cantaloupe from its stem.   With best
regards to Mrs. Howells,

Affectionately yours,

J. R. L.

TO MISS NORTON

Elmwood, Sept. 28, 1869.

My dearest old Friend,— . . . I am very busy.   It is
a lovely day, cool and bright, and the Clerk of the
Weather has just put a great lump of ice in the pitcher
from which he pours his best nectar.   Last night, as I
walked home from Faculty Meeting, the northern lights
streamed up like great organ-pipes, and loveliest hues of
pink, green, and blue flitted from one to another in a
silent symphony.   To-day, consequently, is cold and
clear, with a bracing dash of north-west.   Cutler is ill,
and I am shepherding his flocks for him meanwhile—now
leading them among the sham-classic pastures of Cor-
neille, where a colonnade supplies the dearth of herb-
age; now along the sunny, broad-viewed uplands of
Goethe's prose.   It is eleven o'clock, and I am just back
from my class.   At four I go down again for two hours
of German, and at half-past seven I begin on two hours
of Dante.   Meanwhile I am getting ready for a course
of twenty University lectures, and must all the while
keep the domestic pot at a cheerful boil.   I feel somehow as if I understood that disputed passage in the
"Tempest," where Ferdinand says,

"Most busy least when I do it"—

for I am busy enough, and yet not exactly in my own
vocation. . . . As for the Rousseau article, I was looking it over a few days ago—I am going to make a volume this fall, and it is not one of my best. I have not
confidence enough in myself to write my best often.
Sometimes in verse I forget myself enough to do it,
but one ought to be popular. If ever I become so, you
shall see a better kind of J. R. L. To me Rousseau is
mainly interesting as an ancestor. What a generation
lay hidden in his loins! and of children so unlike as
Cowper and Wordsworth and Byron and Chateaubriand
and Victor Hugo and George Sand! It is curious that
the healthier authors leave no such posterity. . . .

Your ever constant

J. R. L.

TO T. B. ALDRICH

Elmwood, Nov. 30, 1869.

My dear Aldrich,—It is a capital little book*—but I
had read it all before, and liked it thoroughly. It has
been pretty much all my novel reading all summer. I
think it is wholesome, interesting, and above all, natural.
The only quarrel I have with you is that I found in it
that infamous word "transpired." E-pluribus-unum it!
Why not "happened"? You are on the very brink of
the pit. I read in the paper t'other day that some
folks had "extended a dinner to the Hon." Somebody
or other. There was something pleasing to the baser

* "The Story of a Bad Boy."

man in fancying it held out in a pair of tongs, as too many of our Hon'bles deserve—but consider where English is going!

I know something about Rivermouth myself—only before you were born. I remember in my seventh year opening a long red chest in the "mansion" of the late famous Dr. Brackett, and being confronted with a skeleton—the first I had ever seen. The "Mysteries of Udolpho" were nothing to it, for a child, somehow, is apt to think that these anatomies are always made so by foul means, a creed which I still hold to a certain extent.

However, I am not writing to tell you about myself —but merely to say how much I like your little book. I wish it had been twice as large! I shall send you a thin one of my own before long, and shall be content if it give you half the pleasure. Make my kind remembrances acceptable to Mrs. Aldrich, and tell the twins I wish they may both grow up Bad Boys.

Cordially yours,
J. R. LOWELL.

TO E. L. GODKIN

Elmwood, Dec. 3, 1869.

. . . I think the article in the last *Quarterly* settles the Byron matter—and settles it as I expected. After this, any discussion of the particular charge in question seems to me a mere waste of pen and ink, perhaps (worse) of temper too. I doubt, even if this were not so, if I could at present treat it with the all-roundness it deserves. With four lectures a week, I am as busy as I can bear just now.

But I write to ask a favor of you. I read in my newspaper this morning that the dramatic critic of the *Daily News* has been giving a list of John Kemble's odd pronunciations. I should much like to see it, and thought it not unlikely that you might have a copy of the paper which you could spare me. If not, could you not get me one? I should be greatly obliged. . . .

TO C. E. NORTON

Elmwood, Dec. 10, 1869.

. . . My vacation was pretty well occupied with writing and rewriting my new poem, and then as usual coming back to the first draught as by far better than any after-thought. Those who have seen it think well of it. I shall contrive to send it you, and beg you not to read it in the *Atlantic*—for I have restored to it (they are printing it separately) some omitted passages, besides correcting a phrase here and there whose faultiness the stronger light of print revealed to me. How happy I was while I was writing it! For weeks it and I were alone in the world, till Fanny well-nigh grew jealous. You don't know, my dear Charles, what it is to have sordid cares, to be shivering on the steep edge of your bank-book, beyond which lies debt. I am willing to say it to you, because I know I should have written more and better. They say it is good to be obliged to do what we don't like, but I am sure it is not good for me—it wastes so much time in the mere forethought of what you are to do. And then I sometimes think it hard that I, who have such an immense capacity for happiness, should so often be un-

II.—4

happy. I recoil, to be sure, with a pretty good spring, but I have learned what it is to despond. You know I don't sentimentalize about myself or I would not write this. You used to laugh when I told you I was growing dull, but it was quite true. A man is dull who can't give himself up without *arrière-pensée* to the present. I *do* lose myself (to find myself) in writing verse, and so I mean in some way to shape myself more leisure for it, even if I have to leave Elmwood. . . . I agree with Euripides that it is fitting—

Σοφὸν δὲ . . .
τόν θ' ὑμνοποιὸν, αὐτὸς ἂν τίκτῃ μέλη,
χαίροντα τίκτειν· ἢν δὲ μὴ πάσχῃ τόδε,
οὔτοι δύναιτ' ἂν, οἴκοθέν γ' ἀτώμενος,
τέρπειν ἂν ἄλλους· οὐδὲ γὰρ δίκην ἔχει.*

You will find this amplified in Juvenal's Seventh Satire. You see I am suffering a professor change! No; the truth is, I read Euripides through very carefully last winter, and took a great fancy to him. Æschylus for imagination (perhaps 'twas his time did it for him), Sophocles for strength, and Euripides for facility, invention, and *go*. I guess him to be the more simply poet of the three. Anyhow, he delights me much as Calderon does, not for any power of thought, but for the perhaps rarer power of pleasing. As one slowly grows able to think for himself, he begins to be partial towards the fellows who merely entertain. Not that I don't find thought too in Euripides. . . .

* "It is well that the poet, if he produce songs, should produce them with joy, for if, being troubled in himself, he felt it not, he could not delight others — the means would not be his." — *The Suppliants*, 182–85.

I sometimes feel a little blue over the outlook here, with our penny-paper universal education and our workingmen's parties, with their tremendous lever of suffrage, decrying brains. . . . But the more I learn, the more am I impressed with the wonderful system of checks and balances which history reveals (our Constitution is a baby-house to it!), and the more my confidence in the general common-sense and honest intention of mankind increases. When I reflect what changes I, a man of fifty, have seen, how old-fashioned my ways of thinking have become, that I have lived quietly through that awful Revolution of the Civil War (I was cutting my hay while such a different mowing went on at Gettysburg); in short, that my whole life has been passed in what they call an age of transition, the signs of the times cease to alarm me, and seem as natural as to a mother the teething of her seventh baby. I take great comfort in God. I think he is considerably amused with us sometimes, but that he likes us, on the whole, and would not let us get at the match-box so carelessly as he does, unless he knew that the frame of his Universe was fire-proof. How many times have I not seen the fire-engines of Church and State clanging and lumbering along to put out—a false alarm! And when the heavens are cloudy what a glare can be cast by a burning shanty! . . .

Our new President* of the College is winning praise of everybody. I take the inmost satisfaction in him, and think him just the best man that could have been chosen. We have a real Captain at last.

* President Eliot.

I was very glad to get your account of Ferney. No, I never was there. I was too foolishly true to my faith in the blessing of Unexpectedness to visit many shrines. If I stumbled on them, well and good. But I would give a deal now that I had seen old Michel Eyquem's château—the first modern that ever confronted those hectoring ancients without casting down his eyes, bless his honest old soul! Yes, and Ferney, too. For we owe half our freedom now to the leering old mocker with an earnest purpose in spite of himself.

I wish, with all my heart, I *could* see you for a moment! For a while last spring I thought it possible I might be sent abroad. Hoar was strenuous for it, and I should have been very glad of it then. . . . However, it all fell through, and I am glad it did, for I should not have written my new poem, and I hope to go abroad on my own charges one of these days, if I can only sell my land before I am too old. . . .

Well, I have been getting on with my University lectures as well as I could. Cutler was ill, and I had to take his classes in French and German — losing five weeks thereby. And then I worried myself out of sleep and appetite—and then I concluded to do the best I could under the circumstances. So I have been reading to my class with extempore commentary. I wrote out four lectures on the origin of the romance lingo and romantic poetry, and then took up Ferabras and Roland, and am now on the Trouvères. Twenty lectures scared me, and now my next is the sixteenth and I am not half through! . . .

We are having the most superb winter weather—

though I have lost two of the noblest days of it before
my fire. (I am burning Goody Blake fuel, by the way;
supplied by the new September gale.) I do not envy you
your olive-trees, nor even your view of Florence, when
I look out on the smooth white of my fields, with the
blue shadows of the trees on it.   Jane's feeling allusion
to the Perseus gave me a twinge, though.   I should like
to see the lovely arches of that loggia again!   Tell her
not to turn up her dear nose at a statue the story of
whose casting is worth half the statues in the world—
yes, and throw in the poems too. . . .

TO CHARLES NORDHOFF

Elmwood, Dec. 15, 1869.

. . . You cannot set too high a value on the *character*
of Judge Hoar. The extraordinary quickness and acute-
ness, the *flash* of his mind (which I never saw matched
but in Dr. Holmes) have dazzled and bewildered some
people so that they were blind to his solid qualities.
Moreover, you know there are people—I am almost inclined to call them the majority—who are *afraid* of wit,
and cannot see wisdom unless in that deliberate movement of thought whose every step they can accompany.
I have known Mr. Hoar for more than thirty years, intimately for nearly twenty, and it is the solidity of the
man, his courage, and his integrity that I value most
highly.   I think with you that his loss would be irrep-
arable, if he should leave the cabinet for a seat on the
bench.   But I do not believe this to be so probable as
the Washington correspondents would persuade us.   I

do not speak by authority, but only upon inference from what I know. If any change take place, it will be one in which Judge Hoar heartily concurs and which he is satisfied will be for the good of the country. If any one is the confidential adviser of the President, I *guess* it is he. . . .

TO E. L. GODKIN

Elmwood, Jan. 24, 1870.

. . . I am very glad you found anything to like in my poem, though I am apt to be lenient with my friends in those matters, content if they tolerate *me*, and leaving what I write to that perfectly just fate which in the long run awaits all literature. The article of Renan I had not then read, but have read it since with a great deal of interest. I think I see what you mean.

I should have written you long ago but for the scrap I enclose—which may now come too late to be of any use. But after writing that, it occurred to me that a somewhat longer article, giving some account of the different theories as to what the *Grail* was, might be interesting. For that I wanted a book which I had sent as a pattern to the binder, and which he had promised me on Friday last. Of course it did not come, and so I send my correction of Sir G. B.'s nonsense as it stands.

You cannot choose a subject into which you will not infuse interest by thought and knowledge. The one you mention seems to me a remarkably good one, and I hope I shall be here to see and hear you. A Boston

audience is like every other in this—that they like a
serious discussion of any topic, and have an instinct
whether it will be well handled or no. We have had a
course of mountebanks this winter, and people will be
all the more hungry for something serious and instructive. That I am sure you will give them, whatever you
talk about. . . .

Many thanks for the cutting from the *Daily News*. It
was just what I wanted. Every one of Kemble's pronunciations is a Yankeeism, confirming me in my belief
that these are mostly archaisms and not barbarisms. . . .

TO R. S. CHILTON

Elmwood, March 17, 1870.

. . . I had no notion what a conundrum I was making
when I used the word " decuman "*—or decumane, as I
should have spelt it. Where I got the word I am sure
I don't know, nor had I the least doubt that it was to
be found in all the dictionaries, till some one asked me
what it meant. " Oh," I said, " you'll find it sure
enough in Ovid somewhere." But no : Ovid speaks
only of the tenth wave. " Well, then," I insisted, "try
Lucan." He said ditto to Ovid. *Then* I hunted it up,
and my Ducange defines it *fluctus vehementior sic nude
dictus*, citing examples from Festus and Tertullian.
Perhaps neither a lexicographer nor a Father of the
Church is very good authority for Latin, but in Eng-

---

* In " The Cathedral,"

> " . . . shocks of surf that clomb and fell,
> Spume-sliding down the baffled decuman."

lish I have my right of common, and I wanted the word
for its melodic value. So I used it. I don't write
verses with the dictionary at my elbow—but I think I
shall probably come across the word somewhere in English again, where I no doubt met with it years ago. A
word that cleaves to the memory is always a good
word—that's the way to test them. . . .

TO LESLIE STEPHEN

Elmwood, March 25, 1870.

My dear Stephen,—Your letter found me with a pipe
in my mouth and a quarto volume containing *La Che-
valerie Ogier l'Ardenois* on my knee—a mediæval cu-
cumber from which I hope to extract more sunbeams
than from many others on which I have experimented.
The fields all about us are white with snow (thermometer 18° this morning), and the weather is paying us off
for the violets we had in blossom on the 6th January.
We are all well and unchanged. Mrs. Lowell and I
have been gadding as far as Washington—our business
being to deliver some lectures in Baltimore. In Washington we spent three days—quite long enough—and if
the country depended on its representatives for its sal-
vation, I should despair of it. I liked Grant, and was
struck with the pathos of his face; a puzzled pathos, as
of a man with a problem before him of which he does
not understand the terms. But Washington left a very
bad taste in my mouth, and I was glad to be out of it
and back again with pleasant old Mrs. K—— in Baltimore. Of course, I had a good time with Judge Hoar.

He and Mr. Cox struck me as the only really strong men in the Cabinet.

I am glad you liked " The Cathedral," and sorry for anything in it you didn't like. The name was none of my choosing. I called it "A Day at Chartres," and Fields rechristened it. You see with *my* name the episode of the Britons comes in naturally enough (it is historical, by the way). The truth is, I had no notion of being satirical, but wrote what I did just as I might have said it to you in badinage. But, of course, the tone is lost in print. Anyhow, there is *one* Englishman I am fond enough of to balance any spite I might have against others, as you know. But I haven't a particle. If I had met two of my own countrymen at Chartres, I should have been quite as free with them. . . .

How I should like to come over and pay you a visit! But it seems more and more inaccessible, that other side of the water. Whenever I can turn my land into money I shall come across, but at present it is all I can do to pay the cost of staying where I am. What with taxes and tariffs, and the general high prices induced by the vulgar profuseness of my countrymen, a moderate income is fast becoming a narrow one in these parts. If I only had a few cadetships to sell! However, maybe one of these days a gray old boy will be trying to make out through his double eye-glass which is No. 16 in Onslow Gardens, and about half an hour thereafter Mrs. Stephen will be wondering whence comes that nasty smell of tobacco.

Affectionately ever,

J. R. L.

TO W. D. HOWELLS

Elmwood, Friday.

My dear Howells,—Who writes to me casts his bread on the waters. The carrier handed me your note on the road. I put it into my pocket and straightway forgot all about it.

We are told in a book (which I still look on as quite up to the level of any that have come out in my time) to do whatever we do with all our might. That's the way I forget my letters, and I hope I shall find my reward in the next world, for I certainly don't in this.

On the contrary, happening to thrust my hands into my pockets (I don't know why—there is seldom anything in them), I found your note, and it stuck into me like an unexpected pin in the girdle of Saccharissa. If you didn't want our company, you might want our room! Therefore, to be categorical, *I* am coming, as I said I would.

Mrs. Lowell has unhappily an inflamed eye, and is very sorry (for she prefers " My Summer in a Garden," I fear, to some more solid works done under her immediate supervision), and Miss Dunlap is in Portland. So the whole of our family can sit in one chair, like St. Thomas Aquinas's angels.

With kind regards to Mrs. Howells,

Affectionately yours always,

J. R. LOWELL.

TO THOMAS HUGHES

Elmwood, June 11, 1870.

My dear Hughes,—The papers tell me you are coming hither, but I fear the news is too good to be true. But if you are, you know who will be delighted to take you by the hand and to say "*Casa usted*" with more than Spanish sincerity.

If this reaches you in time, pray let me hear from you as to your plans.

Our newspapers read like an old-fashioned Newsletter with their rumors of war. The spirit of all the defunct quidnuncs seems to have entered the man who makes up the telegrams for the American press. But what an impudent scoundrel Louis Napoleon is, to be sure!

Come early and come often, as they say to the voters in New York.

In great haste

Affectionately yours,

J. R. LOWELL.

TO THE SAME

Elmwood, July 18, 1870.

My dear Hughes,—I hope you will come hither as early as you can, for it will be vacation, and I can see more of you. And I want you to see my trees with the leaves on—especially my English elms, which I think no small beer of. I hope by the middle of August our worst heats will be over, for they began early this year. As I write the thermometer is 92 deg.

Already I have an invitation for you from a friend of mine at Newport (our great watering-place) whom I would like you to know. It is a good place to see our people—"shoddy" and other. While you are here, I will take you to Concord and show you such lions as

we have. We shall be delighted to see you and keep
you as long as you can stay.

By the way, I was truly sorry not to see your friend
Mr. Lawson again. He interested me very much with
his simple sincere ways. I owe you a great deal also for
letting me know Stephen, whom I soon learned to love.

This war in Europe shocks me deeply. But I can
now understand better than before, perhaps, the feeling of so many Englishmen about "our" war. However, I never quarrelled with the feeling, but with the
brutal way in which it was expressed.

" This" war seems begun in the most wanton selfishness, and I hope that the charlatan who has ridden
France for so many years will at least get his quietus.
I have never credited him with any greatness but un-
scrupulousness, an immense advantage with five hundred thousand bayonets behind it.

I have been deeply interested in your Irish Land bill.
It concerns us also, for one of the worst diseases we
have to cure in the Irish who come over here is their
belief that the laws are their natural enemies. Give
them property (or a chance at it) in the land, " coûte
qu'il coûte." Fixity of tenure is only a palliative. It
won't stand against the influences that are in the air
nowadays. It was tried here on the Van Rensselaers'
property in New York, and led to the " Anti-rent war."
You are doing noble things, and in that practical and
manly way which must always make England respectable in the eyes of foreigners. England is the only
country where things get a thorough discussion before
the people and by the best men.

Good-by and God bless you till I take you by the hand.

Always heartily yours,

J. R. LOWELL.

TO THE SAME

Elmwood, Aug. 13, 1870.

My dear Hughes,—On one account alone can I say I am glad you are coming later. I hope by the time you get here it will be cooler. The three children in the furnace never saw anything worse than we have had for a month.

Of course, you must suit your plans to your change of route. All I ask is to have you here before vacation is over, 29th Sept. As to lecturing—the only argument in its favor is that it is the easiest way of turning an honest penny for a man who is used to speaking in public. If you should look at it from this point of view, you might easily make an interesting and instructive lecture on the labor-reform movements in England. But I would not do it under five hundred dollars a night.

I enclose a letter for you which came this morning from Mr. Forbes,* whom perhaps you saw in England. At any rate, he is a man worth knowing in every way.

It is very pleasant to be writing to you on this side of the water.

Quebec, by the way, is better than most things in Europe by its startling contrast. A bit of Louis Qua-

* Mr. John M. Forbes.

torze set down bodily in the middle of the nineteenth century.

The sooner you come the better, is all I have to say.

Yours always,

J. R. Lowell.

TO C. E. NORTON

Elmwood, Aug. 28, 1870.

. . . I had hoped during vacation to fill some gaps in my "Cathedral," but work has been out of the question. I have read a good deal of mediæval French poetry in the way of business—and nothing more. But my hopes of freedom brighten a little. Already there are inquiries after my land, and whenever I can sell it for enough to live on modestly I shall do it. One can't write poetry unless he give his whole life to it, and I long to do something yet that shall be as good as I can. Now and then I get a bit impatient, and I fear I wrote you last winter in some such mood. But you know I am pretty reasonable, and always strive to look at myself and my fortune from another man's point of view. I do not think it so hard for a solitary to see himself as others see him—the difficult thing is to act in accordance with your knowledge, an art I have never acquired. I believe no criticism has ever been made on what I write (I mean no just one) that I had not made before, and let slip through my fingers. . . .

The war in Europe has interested me profoundly, and if the Prussians don't win, then the laws of the great game have been changed, for a moral enthusiasm

always makes battalions heavier than a courage that
rises like an exhilaration from heated blood. Moreover, as against the Gaul I believe in the Teuton.
And just now I *wish* to believe in him, for he represents civilization. Anything that knocks the nonsense
out of Johnny Crapaud will be a blessing to the world.
How like a gentleman the King of Prussia shows in
his despatches alongside of that *fanfaron* Napoleon!
It refreshes me wonderfully, also, to see that the
French don't show the quiet front under reverses that
we did, and our trial was one of years.

. . . My only news (we never have any in Cambridge, and my *cordon sanitaire* of trees secludes me
from such gossip as buzzes down in the village) is a
visit from Tom Hughes, who is as frank and hearty
and natural a dear good fellow as could be wished.
He is now at Naushon, and comes back to us on Tuesday. Wednesday we go to Concord, to dine with Hoar.
Hughes will leave us sooner than I like, in order to be
back here for the laying of the corner-stone of Memorial
Hall, 29th September. . . .

TO MISS NORTON

Elmwood, Oct. 14, 1870.

. . . We have been having a truly delightful visit
from Hughes, who was as charming as man can be—
so simple, hearty, and affectionate. He was with us a
fortnight, off and on, and we liked him better and better. His only fault is that he *will* keep quoting the
" Biglow Papers," which he knows vastly better than

I. I was astonished to find what a heap of wisdom was accumulated in those admirable volumes. There never was an Englishman who took this country so naturally as Hughes. I was really saddened to part with him—it was saying good-by to sunshine. We have had other agreeable Britons here this autumn. Bryce I especially liked, and Hughes brought with him a very nice young Rawlins.

All summer I have been studying old French metrical romances and the like, and have done an immense deal of reading—for which I have a talent, if for nothing else. During vacation—a good part of it—I must have averaged my twelve hours a day. And the use of it all? —for some lectures which I am reading to about a score of young women twice a week during the term. Think of *me* with thirty-six lectures on my mind, and you will understand why I am getting a little thin. . . . What good all this lumber will do me I find it hard to say. I long to give myself to poetry again before I am so old that I have only thought and no music left. I can't say, as Milton did, " I am growing my wings." I held back a copy of " The Cathedral," that I might write into it a passage or two, and now, after all, I have sent it by Theodora without them. My vein would *not* flow this summer. The heat dried up that with the other springs. . . .

TO C. E. NORTON

Elmwood, Oct. 15, 1870.

. . . Of course it could not but be very pleasant to me that Ruskin found something to like in " The Cathedral."

There is nobody whom I would rather please, for he is catholic enough to like both Dante and Scott. I am glad to find also that the poem *sticks*. Those who liked it at first like it still, some of them better than ever, some extravagantly. At any rate, it wrote itself; all of a sudden it was *there*, and that is something in its favor. Now Ruskin wants me to go over it with the file. That is just what I did. I wrote in pencil, then copied it out in ink, and worked over it as I never worked over anything before. I may fairly say there is not a word in it over which I have not thought, not an objection which I did not foresee and maturely consider. Well, in my second copy I made many changes, as I thought for the better, and then put it away in my desk to cool for three weeks or so. When I came to print it, I put back, I believe, *every one* of the original readings which I had changed. Those which had come to me were far better than those I had come at. Only one change I made (for the worse), in order to escape a rhyme that had crept in without my catching it.

Now for Ruskin's criticisms. As to words, I am something of a purist, though I like best the word that best says the thing. (You know I have studied lingo a little.) I am fifty-one years old, however, and have in some sense won my spurs. I claim the right now and then to knight a plebeian word for good service in the field. But it will almost always turn out that it has after all good blood in its veins, and can prove its claim to be put in the saddle. *Rote* is a familiar word all along our seaboard to express that dull and continuous burden of the sea heard inland before or after a great storm. The root of the word may

II.—5

be in *rumpere*, but is more likely in *rotare*, from the
identity of this sea-music with that of the *rote*—a kind
of hurdy-gurdy with which the jongleurs accompanied
their song.   It is one of those Elizabethan words which
we New-Englanders have preserved along with so many
others.   It occurs in the " Mirror for Magistrates," " the
sea's *rote*," which Nares, not understanding, would change
to *rore !*   It is not to be found in any provincial glos-
sary, but I caught it *alive* at Beverly and the Isles of
Shoals.   Like "mobbled queen," 'tis "good."

Whiff Ruskin calls " an American elevation of English
lower word."   Not a bit of it.   I have always thought
" the *whiff* and wind of his fell sword " in " Hamlet " rather fine than otherwise.   Ben also has the word.   " Down-
shod " means shod with down.   I doubted about this word
myself—but I wanted it.   As to "misgave," the older poets
used it as an active verb, and I have done with it as all
poets do with language.   My *meaning* is clear, and that is
the main point.   His objection to "spume-sliding down
the baffled decuman " I do not understand.   I think if he
will read over his "ridiculous Germanism " (p. 13 seq.)
with the context he will see that he has misunderstood
me.   (By the way, " in our life alone doth Nature live "
is Coleridge's, not Wordsworth's.)   I never hesitate to
say anything I have honestly felt because some one
may have said it before, for it will always get a new
color from the new mind, but here I was not saying the
same thing by a great deal.   *Nihil in intellectu quod non
prius in sensu* would be nearer — though not what I
meant.   Nature (inanimate), which is the image of the
mind, sympathizes with all our moods.   I would have

numbered the lines as Ruskin suggests, only it looks
as if one valued them too much. That sort of thing
should be posthumous. You may do it for me, my dear
Charles, if my poems survive me. Two dropt stitches
I must take up which I notice on looking over what
I have written. Ruskin surely remembers Carlyle's
"whiff of grapeshot." That is one. The other is that
rote may quite as well be from the Icelandic *at* hriota
= to *snore;* but my studies more and more persuade me
that where there is in English a Teutonic and a Romance root meaning the same thing, the two are apt to
melt into each other so as to make it hard to say from
which our word comes. . . .

TO THOMAS HUGHES

Elmwood, Oct. 18, 1870.

My dear old Friend,—Parting with you was like saying good-by to sunshine. As I took my solitary whiff
o' baccy, after I got home, my study looked bare, and
my old cronies on the shelves could not make up to
me for my new loss. I sat with my book on my knee
and mused with a queer feeling about my eyelids now
and then. And yet you have left so much behind that
is precious to me, that by and by I know that my room
will have a virtue in it never there before, because of
your presence. And now it seems so short—a hail at
sea with a God-speed and no more. But you will come
back, I am sure. We all send love and regret.

The day after you left us Rose discovered your thin
coat, which she called a " duster." I had half a mind

to confiscate it, it was such a good one; but on second thoughts concluded that that was, on the whole, as good a reason for sending it back as for keeping it.

Letters continue to pour in, and I enclose them with the coat to No. 9 Lexington Avenue. There came also a telegram from Montreal, which I felt justified in opening. From what you had told me, I had no doubt that you had already answered in a letter. It only said that they should expect you on Tuesday.

As you will no doubt see Bryce and Dicey in London, pray tell them how sorry I was not to see more of them. They left many friends in Cambridge. If all Englishmen could only take America so "naturally" as you did! I think, if it could be so, there would never be any risk of war. That reminds me that I am sure your address has done great good. It has set people thinking, and that is all we need. I enclose a little poem from to-day's *Advertiser* which pleased me. I do not know who "H. T. B." is, but I think his verses very sweet, and Mrs. Hughes may like to see them. I would rather have the kind of welcome that met you in this country than all the shouts of all the crowds on the "Via Sacra" of Fame. There was "love" in it, you beloved old boy, and no man ever earns that for nothing—unless now and then from a woman. By Jove! it is worth writing books for—such a feeling as that. . . .

I am holding "Good-by" at arm's length as long as I can, but I must come to it. Give my kindest regards to Rawlins, and take all my heart yourself. God bless you.   A pleasant voyage, and all well in the nest when you get back to it.

Always most affectionately yours,

J. R. LOWELL.

TO THE SAME

Elmwood, Feb. 7, 1871.

My dear Friend,—That friendship should be able to endure silence without suspicion is the surest touchstone of its sufficiency.   I did not expect to hear from you very soon after your return, for I knew how busy you must be in many ways.   But I was none the less glad to get your letter with assurance of your welfare. I should have written you, indeed, before this, but that I have been away from home three weeks reading some lectures in Baltimore.

We are all well except Mabel's Meg, who has fallen lame.   After our warm autumn, Winter, as usual, has put his screws on, and when I walk it is over five feet thick of cast iron—for we have little snow.   Several times within the last fortnight the thermometer has marked —8° Fahrenheit.   But Cambridge is odd in this respect.   Owing to our ice-trade the poorer people always bless a hard winter, which gives them work when other sources fail.   Mild weather is always looked on as a misfortune.

I was much interested in your mutual-enlightenment scheme, though I am not at all clear as to its doing good here—I mean, whether a similar committee would be advisable on this side.   Our people are so sensitively jealous just now that I fear it might arouse opposition of an ignorant sort, and so do more harm than good. I think they are settling down to a more rational view of the *Alabama* matter, and if you can keep the hotheads in Canada within bounds, all will go well. A very little more folly on their part would make "a pretty kettle of fish," if I know my countrymen. Even granting the claim of the Dominion to be legally admissible (which I doubt), you can no more persuade the bulk of our people of it than you were able to convince the English peasant of the righteousness of game laws. Moreover, and this heightens the danger, our fishermen are the class which among us most nearly resembles the borderers of the West, and they are the direct descendants of the men who suffered by British impressment before 1812. They have inherited a very bitter legacy of hatred, and might too easily be led by an unscrupulous demagogue like Butler to make reprisals. When I remember how like thunder out of a clear sky war comes nowadays, I wish to get drawn off from the atmosphere as much of the ominous electricity as may be.

I think it fortunate that Schenk (pronounced Skenk) is a Western man, because he will be free at least from any commercial animosity. He is said to be able, and he will represent an administration just now especially hostile to Sumner and his theory of constructive damages.

The Senate (who are the real arbiters after all) may be suspected of being in somewhat the same mood. Except for the fishery business, I am not inclined to agree with those who see danger in delay. Already the discussion of the law-points of neutrality has brought our people to a more reasonable frame of mind about the rights and duties of neutrals. The Irish element, I think, will never affect our foreign politics — nor our domestic, for that matter, except that through New York it may turn the scale of the next national election in favor of the Democrats; but the Democrats, once in power, will be in no more danger of rushing into a war with England than the Republicans—whom office has already largely corrupted. I still think (as I told you here) that a war would be more disastrous to us than to you, though the direst misfortune for both and for the advance of enlightened freedom.

As for the war in Europe, I am a Prussian, and believe it to be in the interest of civilization that a public bully (as France had become) should be soundly thrashed. The French will never be safe neighbors till the taint of Louis XIV. is drawn out of their blood. If the Prussian lancet shall effect this I shall rejoice. The misery I feel as keenly as anybody, but I remember that it might have been, but for German energy and courage, even worse on the other side of the Rhine. The Gaul has never been an amiable conqueror, and the Teuton has the longest historical memory among men. . . .

Elmwood expects you longingly again. With the heart's affection,

Yours always,

J. R. LOWELL.

TO J. T. FIELDS

Elmwood, Feb. 11, 1871.

. . . I am looking forward to your next installment of Hawthorne. I read the first with great interest, and wish you would give us more rather than less—especially in extracts from his letters. We don't seem likely to get a biography, and these in some sort supply it. . . . Be sure and don't leave out anything because it seems trifling, for it is out of these trifles only that it is possible to reconstruct character sometimes, if not always. I think your method is above criticism, and you have hit the true channel between the Charybdis of reticence and the Scylla of gossip, as Dr. Parr would have said. . . .

TO LESLIE STEPHEN

Elmwood, July 31, 1871.

. . . I have been selling my birthright for a mess of pottage, and find it so savory that I side with Esau more than ever. I don't know whether you ever suspected it (I hope you didn't—for I have noticed that you English use " beggar " as a clincher in the way of contempt), but I have been hitherto pretty well pinched for money. Our taxes are so heavy that nobody since Atlas ever carried such a burthen of real estate as I, and *he* wouldn't if he had been compelled to pay for it. Well, I have just (29th July was the happy date) been selling all that I held in my own right for enough to give me about $5000 a year and Mabel about $1400 more. This isn't much, according to present standards, but is as much as I want. It is a life-preserver that will keep my head above water, and the swimming I will do for myself. Then, I am going to have Elmwood divided. It is a bitter dose, but I have made up my mind to it, and make myself believe that I shall like

the house with a couple of acres as well as I do now
with twelve times as much. The city has crept up to
me, curbstones are feeling after and swooping upon
the green edges of the roads, and the calf I used to
carry is grown to a bull. I have gone over to the
enemy and become a capitalist. I denounce the Commune with the best of them, and find it extremely
natural that I should be *natus consumere fruges*—which
means that I shall now grow consumedly frugal. I have
weighed out the reasons (so far as I could decipher
them) which you give me for coming over, and think
them excellent—especially does your lavish offer of five
shillings to sit in a certain chair weigh with me, and I
shall certainly claim it. The reasons I couldn't read
(for you became particularly runic or cuneiform or
something worse in this passage) I took to be of some
loving sort or other, and reciprocate them heartily. If
everything goes well I mean to go abroad in a year
from last June—that is, at the end of our next college
year, and if I do, you will see a youth you never saw
before. Property, sir, is the Ponce-de-Leon fountain
of youth. I am already regenerate. I am the master
of forty legions. I will kick the vizier's daughter, my
wife, for a constitutional. And now cometh L. S. (I
relish your initials now, and mentally add a D. to
them), and prayeth that I would write some verses for
his magazine!* I am given to understand by several
gentlemen in easy circumstances (with whom I discuss
the prices of stocks and the dangers of universal suf-

* Mr. Stephen had lately become editor of the *Cornhill Magazine.*

frage) that poets are notorious for nothing so much as
the smallness of their balance at the banker's. Is there
no danger of my losing caste by meddling in such matters—I who am casting about where I can steal a railway and share with Jem Fisk the applauses of my
grateful countrymen? Bethink yourself, my dear Stephen. Put yourself for a moment in my position. I
have a great affection for you, and shall lay it to the
small experience of the world natural to the remote
corner in which you dwell. I have no doubt it was
kindly meant. A few Latin versicles, fruits of an ele-
gant leisure, I might send you perhaps—but English—
I must ask Vanderbilt's opinion. I will bear it in mind.

I should have sent "My Study Windows" (a hateful
name, forced upon me by the publishers), but was waiting for a new edition, in which the misprints are corrected. I quite agree with you about Carlyle, and
perhaps was harder on him than I meant, because I
was fighting against a secret partiality. I go off also
in a day or two on a fishing jaunt, to get rid of a pain
in the head that has been bothering me. . . .

TO C. E. NORTON

Elmwood, Sept. 5, 1871.

. . . Yesterday, as I was walking down the Beacon
Street mall, the yellowing leaves were dozily drifting from
the trees, and the sentiment of autumn was in all the air;
though the day, despite an easterly breeze, was sultry.
I enjoyed the laziness of everything to the core, and
sauntered as idly as a thistledown, thinking with a

pleasurable twinge of sympathy that the fall was beginning for me also, and that the buds of next season
were pushing our stems from their hold on the ever-
renewing tree of Life. I am getting to be an old fellow, and my sheaves are not so many as I hoped; but I
am outwardly more prosperous than ever before—indeed,
than ever I dreamed of being. If none of my stays
give way, I shall have a clear income of over four thousand a year, with a house over my head, and a great
heap of what I have always found the best fertilizer of
the mind—leisure. I cannot tell you how this sense
of my regained paradise of Independence enlivens me.
It is something I have not felt for years—hardly since
I have been a professor. . . . Meanwhile I am getting a
kind of fame—though I never valued *that*, as you know
—and what is better, a certain respect as a man of
some solid qualities, which I *do* value highly. I have
always believed that a man's fate is born with him, and
that he cannot escape from it nor greatly modify it—
and that consequently every one gets in the long run
exactly what he deserves, neither more nor less. At
any rate, this is a cheerful creed, and enables one to
sleep soundly in the very shadow of Miltiades' trophy.
What I said long ago is literally true, that it is only
for the sake of those who believed in us early that we
desire the verdict of the world in our favor. It is the
natural point of honor to hold our endorsers harmless.
. . . It is always my happiest thought that with all
the drawbacks of temperament (of which no one is
more keenly conscious than myself) I have never lost
a friend. For I would rather be loved than anything

else in the world. I always thirst after affection, and depend more on the expression of it than is altogether wise. And yet I leave the letters of those I love unanswered so long! It is because the habits of authorship are fatal to the careless unconsciousness that is the life of a letter, and still more, in my case, that I have always something on my mind—an uneasy sense of disagreeable duties to come, which I cannot shake myself free from. But worse than all is that lack of interest in one's self that comes of drudgery—for I hold that a letter which is not mainly about the writer of it lacks the prime flavor. The wine must smack a little of the cask. You will recognize the taste of my old wood in this! . . .

TO E. L. GODKIN

Elmwood, Dec. 20, 1871.

My dear Godkin,—I haven't looked into Taine's book since it first appeared seven years ago, and as I had no thought of reviewing it, I find that I did not mark it as I read. To write a competent review I should have to read it all through again, for which I have neither the time nor the head just now. I have just been writing about Masson's "Life of Milton," for the *North American*, and the result has convinced me that my brain is softening. You are the only man I know who carries his head perfectly steady, and I find myself so thoroughly agreeing with the *Nation* always that I am half persuaded I edit it myself! Or rather, you always say what I would have said—if I had only thought of it.

I am thinking of coming on to New York for a day or two next week, to see you and a few other friends. Somehow my youth is revived in me, and I have a great longing for an hour or two in Page's studio, to convince me that I am really only twenty-four, as I seem to myself. So get ready to be jolly, for I mean to bring a spare trunk full of good spirits with me and to forget that I have ever been professor or author or any other kind of nuisance. Just as I was in fancy kicking off my ball and chain, a glance at the clock tells me I must run down to College! But when I come to New York (since I can't get rid of them) I shall wear 'em as a breastpin. I have seen some near-ly as large. Dickens had one when I first saw him in '42. Give my kindest regards to Mrs. Godkin.

Always affectionately yours,
J. R. L.

Give Schenck another shot. Also say something on the queer notion of the Republican party that they can get along without their brains. "Time was that when the brains were out the man would *die*," but *nous avons changé tout cela.*

TO MISS NORTON

Elmwood, Dec. 21, 1871.

. . . You forget that I know Dresden better than any other city except Rome, and I wish to know whether you are in the Altstadt or the Neustadt, and in what part of either, that I may figure you to myself the more comfortably. Is the theatre rebuilt? Are the Schloss and the Japanische Palast in their old places? Does the sandstone statue of the reforming Elector still keep watch and ward at the corner of the little garden on which my room opened, where I heard the first European thrush, and had my daily breakfast-party of sparrows? Is there still a *Victoria regia* in the little greenhouse? Are there yellow-coated chairmen yet? And do the linkmen run before the royal coaches at night? And will the postman who brings you this wear a scarlet jacket as he should? And is it dreadfully cold, and do you worry yourself every morning by reducing Réaumur to Fahrenheit before you know how cold you can conscientiously feel? Dear me, how I should like to be over there just for an hour on Christmas eve, to stroll about with you and see again the prettiest sight I ever saw—the innocent jollity in the houses of the poor, and the dancing shadows of the children round the frugal Christmas-tree!

Here we are having winter in earnest. Thermometer four below zero this morning, and the whole earth shining in the sun like the garments of the saints at the Resurrection. Presently I shall walk down to the village to post this and drink a beaker full of the north-west—the true elixir of good spirits. . . .

George Curtis has just sent in his report on the Civil Service, and I expect much good from it. A man like him who knows the value of moderation, and who can be perfectly firm in his own opinions without stroking those of everybody else against the fur, was sure to do the right thing. I am glad his name will be associated with so excellent a reform. He deserved it. . . .

TO THE SAME

Elmwood, Feb. 17, 1872.

. . . Everything goes on here as usual. Three times
a week I have my classes, one in Nannucci, " Letteratura
del Primo Secolo," the other in Bartsch, " Chrestomathie
de l'Ancien Français." On Wednesdays I have besides a
University class, with whom I have read the "Chanson de
Roland," and am now reading the " Roman de la Rose."
On my off-days, the first thing in the morning I go over
my work for the next day, and then renew my reading
of Old French. The only modern book I have read for a
long while is Comte Gobineau's " La Philosophie et les
Religions de l'Asie Centrale," which I think one of the
most interesting works I ever read. It tells you a great
deal you did not know, and in a very lively way. If you
have not read it I advise you to do so forthwith. . . .

. . . As for my being in low spirits, I haven't been so
this long while. I thought it was constitutional with
me, but since I have had no pecuniary anxieties I am as
light as a bird. No, you are quite right; you wouldn't
suspect it from my letters. But, my dear Jane, it takes
a good while to slough off the effect of seventeen years
of pedagogy. I am grown learned (after a fashion) and
dull. The lead has entered into my soul. But I have
great faith in putting the sea between me and the stocks
I have been sitting in so long. . . .

TO F. H. UNDERWOOD

Elmwood, May 12, 1872.

. . . Don't bother yourself with any sympathy for me

under my supposed sufferings from critics. I don't need
it in the least. If a man does anything good, the world
always finds it out, sooner or later; and if he doesn't,
why, the world finds *that* out too—and ought to. . . .

> 'Gainst monkey's claws and ass's hoof
> My studies forge me mail of proof.
> I climb through paths forever new
> To purer air and broader view.
> What matter though they should efface,
> So far below, my footstep's trace?

TO MISS NORTON

Elmwood, July 2, 1872.

. . . We have had Commencement week, too, but I
saw little of it, being hard at work all the while upon
an article about Dante, with Miss Rossetti's book for
a text. I have not made so much of it as I should if
my time had been less broken. As it was, I had to keep
the press going from day to day. Charles will smile at
this, remembering his editorial experience of me. . . .

We sail in a week from to-day, and I have as yet no
plans. J. H. goes with us! Frank Parkman and Henry
Adams are also fellow-passengers, so that we shall have
a pleasant ship's company. We shall contrive to meet
you *somewhere*, you may be sure. Write to care of
Barings whether you are still at St. Germain. I associate the name pleasantly with the old homonymous
pear which used to be in our garden. . . .

VII

1872–1876

TO MISS GRACE NORTON

11 Down Street, Piccadilly, Aug. 4, 1872.

. . . Our voyage was as smooth as the style of the late Mr. Samuel Rogers of happy memory. . . . We landed at Queenstown on the morning of the eleventh day out. . . .

Dublin interested me much. I can describe it in one word by calling it Hogarthian. I walked pretty well over it while there, and was continually struck with its last-century look. I saw even a genuine Tom O'Bed-

II.—6

lam one day. Beggars are as thick as in Italy and quite as pertinacious. One pretty little scene I shall never forget. It was a drizzly day, and the sidewalks were covered with a slippery black paste. Near the Tholsel (City Hall) sat a woman on some steps nursing her baby, and in front of her a ring of barefoot children (the oldest not more than five years) were dancing round a little tot who stood bewildered in the middle, and singing as they whirled hand in hand. They were as dirty and as rosy and as ragged as could be, and as pretty as one of Richter's groups. The ballad-singer with her baby and lugubrious song I met several times. At the National Gallery we saw a portrait by Morone as good as anything south of the Alps, and at the National Exhibition lots of Irish portraits and other interesting things. I went to the library of Trinity College, where the librarian, Dr. Malet, was very civil, and promised to send some books to the good old Sibley.* I was interested in the College as being Godkin's, whom I celebrated to Dr. Malet, you may be sure. From Dublin to Chester, where we stayed five days, and where Charles Kingsley (who is a canon there) was very kind. We had the advantage of going over the Cathedral with him, and over the town with the chief local antiquary. We fell quite in love with it and with the delightful walk round the walls. We arrived in London night before last. . . .

Affectionately yours,

LLUMBAGO LLOWELL.

* The Librarian of Harvard University.

TO MISS NORTON

11 Down Street, Piccadilly, Aug. 19, 1872.

. . . I do not mean to say that I am not enjoying myself. I suppose I *am*, in an indolent kind of fashion, but I caught myself being homesick before I had been a week in England. Some little solace I got out of an Anglo-Norman poem which I picked up here, and I can't help laughing when I think of it. So, then, my nature, like a dyer's hand, *has* been subdued to what it has been working in, and the curious dulness I am sensible of in myself is a fair standard of how much there must be in the literature whence I drew it. It worries me, though, this slowness. You have always laughed at me when I talked about it, but what I said of myself years ago (I could not say anything so smart now)— that I had been altered from percussion to flint—is perfectly true.

Something you say in your letter puts me in mind of what I always thought one of the most truly pathetic passages in all literature. I mean that in which Froissart, after devoting a chapter to the praises of the Queen (I forget her name) who had been his patroness, seems to bethink himself, and rousing from his reverie with a sigh, begins his next chapter by saying, " There is no death which we must not get over," or something to that effect. Whether he meant just that or not, there is nothing sadder, nothing we resent so much, as the necessity of being distracted and consoled. I fear I have quoted this to you before, it comes up to my mind so often. I wish I could recollect the Queen's name.

But I never can. And this the more persuades me of
my unfitness to be a professor, whose main business it
is to remember names and to be cocksure of dates. I
can't for my life tell you (without going to my books)
who it was that first alternated male and female rhymes
in French alexandrine verse, nor whether he hit upon
this clever scheme for setting the French Muse in the
stocks towards the close of the twelfth or beginning
of the thirteenth century. Isn't there a pretty professor! Anyhow, the said Muse has sat there ever
since! Béranger cheered her up with a bottle of
claret, and de Musset gave her a kind of wicked inspiration with *absinthe*; but there she sits, and all
owing to this wretch whose name I can't recall. Am
I the right sort of man to guide ingenuous youth?
Not a bit of it! . . .

Tell Charles the article on Dante was written in all
the distraction of getting away, with the thermometer
at 95°, and keeping abreast of the printers, so that I
could not arrange and revise properly. I am glad he
found anything in it. . . .

Good-by, my dear woman, for a few days. By Jove,
isn't it pleasant to be able to say that? For a *few days*,
mind you. It was years, a month ago. . . .

Yours most everything always,

J. R. L.

TO C. E. NORTON

Hôtel de Lorraine, No. 7 Rue de Beaune,
Paris, Dec. 4, 1872.

. . . Oddly enough when I got your letter about

Tennyson's poem I had just finished reading a *real* Arthurian romance—"Fergus"—not one of the best, certainly, but having that merit of being a genuine blossom for which no triumph of artifice can compensate; having, in short, that *woodsy* hint and tantalization of perfume which is so infinitely better than anything more defined.   Emerson had left me Tennyson's book; so last night I took it to bed with me and finished it at a gulp—reading like a naughty boy till half-past one.   The contrast between his pomp and my old rhymer's simpleness was very curious and even instructive.   One bit of the latter (which I cannot recollect elsewhere) amused me a good deal as a Yankee.   When Fergus comes to Arthur's court and Sir Kay "sarses" him (which, you know, is *de rigeur* in the old poems), Sir Gawain saunters up *whittling a stick* as a medicine against ennui.   So afterwards, when Arthur is dreadfully bored by hearing no news of Fergus, he reclines at table without any taste for his dinner, and whittles to purge his heart of melancholy.   I suppose a modern poet would not dare to come so near Nature as this lest she should fling up her heels.   But I am not yet "aff wi' the auld love," nor quite "on with the new."   There are very fine childish things in Tennyson's poem and fine manly things, too, as it seems to me, but I conceive the theory to be wrong.   I have the same feeling (I am not wholly sure of its justice) that I have when I see these modern-mediæval pictures.   I am defrauded; I do not see reality, but a masquerade.   The costumes are all that is genuine, and the people inside them are shams—which, I take it, is just the reverse of what ought to be.   One special

criticism I should make on Tennyson's new Idyls, and
that is that the similes are so often dragged in by the
hair. They seem to be taken (*à la* Tom Moore) from
note-books, and not suggested by the quickened sense of
association in the glow of composition. Sometimes it
almost seems as if the verses were made for the similes,
instead of being the cresting of a wave that heightens as
it rolls. This is analogous to the costume objection and
springs perhaps from the same cause — the making of
poetry with malice prepense. However, I am not going
to forget the lovely things that Tennyson has written,
and I think they give him rather hard measure now.
However, it is the natural recoil of a too rapid fame.
Wordsworth had the true kind — an unpopularity that
roused and stimulated while he was strong enough to despise it, and honor, obedience, troops of friends, when the
grasshopper would have been a burthen to the drooping
shoulders. Tennyson, to be sure, has been childishly
petulant; but what have these whipper-snappers, who
cry "Go up, baldhead," done that can be named with
some things of his? He has been the greatest artist in
words we have had since Gray — and remember how
Gray holds his own with little fuel, but real fire. He
had the secret of the inconsumable oil, and so, I fancy,
has Tennyson.

I keep on picking up books here and there, but I
shall be forced to stop, for I find I have got beyond
my income. Still, I shall try gradually to make my
Old French and Provençal collection tolerably complete,
for the temptation is great where the field is definitely
bounded. . . .

TO GEORGE PUTNAM

Hôtel de Lorraine, No. 7 Rue de Beaune,
Paris, Dec. 12, 1872.

My dear Putnam,— . . . We are still at the same little
hotel, and like it better and better. It is really being
in foreign parts, for everybody is French but ourselves,
and we are become a part of the household, so that
night before last in the gale it was our *haut de cheminée*
that came rattling down.

We like the people very much. They are kindly and
honest, and we think we shall stay a month or two
longer. It will be wise, for if I stay so long my income will overtake me. It is a little out of breath just
now—but then I have got some books (all in Old French
and Provençal) which will be a revenue to me so long
as I live. We are too near the quais, where all the
bouquinistes spin their webs. We are threatened with
a kind of mild revolution (an inoculated one), but I
doubt. I think the Right must keep on with Thiers,
and that even had they the courage for a *coup-d'état*,
he would outgeneral them. But, after all, *en France
tout arrive*, and the French are the most wonderful
creatures for talking wisely and acting foolishly I ever
saw. However, I like Paris, and am beginning to be
glad I came abroad. . . .

TO C. E. NORTON

Paris, Jan. 11, 1873.

My dear Charles,— . . . I begin to foresee that I shall
not stay abroad so long as I expected. I thought I was

all right now, but as usual my income is never so large
as my auguries.   Fortunately, I like Cambridge better
than any other spot of the earth's surface, and if I can
only manage to live there, shall be at ease yet.   *Inveni
portum, spes et fortuna, valete ; sat me lusistis, ludite jam
alios !* That's what I *shall* say—at least I hope so. . . .

Paris, old Mr. Sales said, was not exactly the place
for deacons.   Nor is it for poets.   However, no place
is where one only perches.   I cannot contrive the right
kind of solitude, and if I compose as I walk about I
shall be run over.   I made out a sonnet day before yesterday, which, as I composed it expressly for you, I
shall send to its address—though its merit lies mainly
in the sentiment and not (as it should be with a sonnet)
in the execution.   But I am getting as bad with my
prelude as the band in a penny show, and you will
begin to expect something wonderful if I don't give
you the thing at once.

P. S.   I conceived it in Cumberland.

> As sinks the sun behind yon alien hills,
> Whose heather-purpled slopes in glory rolled
> Flush all my thought with momentary gold,
> What pang of vague regret my fancy thrills ?
> Here 'tis enchanted ground the peasant tills,
> Where the shy ballad could its leaves unfold,
> And Memory's glamour makes new sights seem old,
> As when our life some vanished dream fulfils.
> Yet not to you belong these painless tears,
> Land loved ere seen ; before my darkened eyes,
> From far beyond the waters and the years,
> Horizons mute that wait their poet rise ;
> The stream before me fades and disappears,
> And in the Charles the western splendor dies.

I have hardly expressed the strange feeling of ideal familiarity vexed with a longing for something visibly intimate. But I miss my *old* Solitude, and if Memory be the mother of the Muses, this lonely lady is their maiden aunt who always has gifts for them in her cupboard when they visit her. However, I have a poem or two in my head which I hope will come to something one of these days. The theme of one of them is pretty enough. To the cradle of Garin come the three fairies. One gives him beauty—one power—and the third misfortune. Grown an old, old man, he sits in the courtyard of the palace he has conquered from the Saracens, and muses over his past life to the murmur of the fountain, which sings to him as it did to its old lords, and as it will to the new after he is gone. As he reckons up what is left him as the result of the three gifts, what is really a possession of the soul, what has turned the soft fibre of gifts to the hard muscle of character, he comes to the conclusion that the third fairy, whom his parents would fain have kept away or propitiated, was the beneficent one.

I have seen nothing new except the Duc d'Aumale, whom I met the other night at the Laugels'. I had, of course, only a few moments' commonplace talk with him. As a general thing, I like men vastly better than dukes, though where the two qualities are united, as in him, I am willing to encounter the product. He is a *distingué* person in a high sense, with a real genius for looking like a gentleman. I was pleased to see how much might be done by *breeding*, and how effective the result is—greater in some respects than that of great natural parts. It was good to see so pure a face in the grandson of Egalité and great-grandson of the Regent. There is hope, then, for the most degraded races, and Whitefriars may contain the ancestors of saints and heroes. One thing struck me particularly, and made our Americanism (which weighs a man honestly, without throwing in the bones of his ancestors) dearer to me. Nobody, I could see, was quite at ease with the duke, nor he with anybody. There was something unnatural in the relation, a dimly defined sense of anachronism, something of what a dog might feel in the company of a tame wolf. The more I see of the old world, the better I like the new. I am disgusted to see how the papers are willing to overlook the crimes and the essential littleness of Napoleon III., simply because he has had the wit to die, a stroke of genius within reach of us all. However, I was long ago convinced that one of the rarest things in the world was a real opinion based on judgment and unshakable by events. The *clamor civium prava laudantium* is as bad as that of the *jubentium*. . . .

Always most lovingly yours,

J. R. L.

TO MISS NORTON

Hôtel de Lorraine, 7 Rue de Beaune,
Paris, March 4, 1873.

. . . We have enjoyed our winter here on the whole very much, and have really learned something of the French and their ways—more than ten years on the other side of the river would have done for us. The

French are fearfully and wonderfully made in some respects, but I like them and their pretty ways. It is a positive pleasure (after home experiences, where one has to pad himself all over against the rude elbowing of life) to go and buy a cigar. It is an affair of the highest and most gracious diplomacy, and we spend more monsieurs and madames upon it than would supply all the traffic of Cambridge for a half-century. It is a good drill, for I have always been of the mind that in a democracy manners are the only effective weapons against the bowie-knife, the only thing that will save us from barbarism. Our little hotel is very pleasant in its way, and its clientèle is of the most respectable. . . . I can't remember whether I told Charles that one of our convives turned out to be a gentleman who had lived many years in Finland, and had translated into French my favorite " Kalewala." He tells me that the Finns recite their poems six or seven hours on the stretch, *spelling* one another, as we say in New England. This would make easily possible the recitation of a poem like the " Roland," for example, or of one even much longer. . . .

TO C. E. NORTON

Hôtel de Lorraine, 7 Rue de Beaune,
Paris, March 18, 1873.

. . . The Emersons are back with us, to our great satisfaction, and yesterday I took him to the top of the tower of Nôtre Dame, and played the part of Satan very well, I hope, showing him all the kingdoms of this world. A very pleasant walk we had of it. He grows sweeter if possible as he grows older. He had a prosperous Egyptian journey. . . . He told us a droll story of Alcott last night. He asked the Brahmin what he had to show for himself, what he had *done*, in short, to justify his having been on the earth. " If Pythagoras came to Concord whom would he ask to see?" demanded the accused triumphantly. . . .

TO THOMAS HUGHES

Hôtel de Lorraine, 7 Rue de Beaune,
Paris, March 19, 1873.

My dear Friend,—First, of what interests me most. The day I got your book* the Emersons came back from the crocodiles and pyramids and fleas. So I could not get at it so soon as I would. But I began it in the hour before dinner, and at last, when everybody had gone to bed, I sat up (like a naughty boy) till half-past one and read every word of it, even including my own verses, which had a kind of sweetness for me because you liked them. It interested me very much, and I quite fell in love with your father, who seems to me to have been a model of good sense and that manliness which it is perhaps our weakness to limit by calling it gentle-manliness. I see where you got a great deal of what I love in you. I wish your brother had done more, and I confess (though it is awkward) that I would rather have had your life (but for a single tragic contingency) than his. I did, to be sure, get a part of it. But I was touched especially and inspired with the glimpse I got

* The book was " Memoir of a Brother."

of the affection and unity of your household. Your preface came to me just at the right moment, when I was saddened by the news from home, above all, with the fact that the average public opinion of the country did not seem to be higher than the personal sense of duty of its representatives. What you say of the quiet lives that would come to the front in England in a time of stress I believe to be true of us also. I cannot think such a character as Emerson's—one of the simplest and noblest I have ever known—a freak of chance, and I hope that my feeling that the country is growing worse is nothing more than men of my age have always felt when they looked back to the *tempus actum*. I think that this book of yours also, like all your others, will do a great deal of good and add to the number of honest men in the world. The longer I live (you will see or divine the subtle thread of association) the less I wonder that men make much of soldiers. The Romans were right when they lumped together manhood, courage, and virtue in the single word *virtus*. What profounder moral than that their descendants should express by the word *virtu* the contents of a shop where second-hand shreds and fragments of old housekeeping fashions are sold?

As for the degree, read Charles Lamb's sonnet on visiting Oxford and you will see how I feel. I would take a much longer journey for the sake of feeling even a son-in-law's right in that ancient household of scholarship and pluck. I believe I care very little for decorations, but I should prize this not only abstractedly, but because it would give more "power to my elbow," as Paddy says, at home. How it would have pleased my father! But I shall not be a bit disappointed if I do not get it, and shall always count myself a D.C.L. so far as you are concerned.

We had a good laugh over the woodcut on the cover of my book. The one inside is a very good copy of the photograph, though it does not, I fancy, look much like me. Madame pronounces it dreadful. Luckily, I have the skin of a rhinoceros in this regard, and have never sloughed off the wholesome effect of having been brought up to consider myself visible to the naked eye, in other words plain. What a frank creature the sun is, to be sure, as an artist! He would almost take the nonsense out of a Frenchman.

If I had dreamed you would have run over to Paris, wouldn't I have told you where I was! But, in fact, I have lingered on here from week to week aimlessly, having come abroad to do nothing, and having thus far succeeded admirably.

So far as I understood your "differ"* with your electors I thought you were right. I doubt if it be time yet to give up the Church of England or indeed to cut rashly any cable that anchors you to your historical past. If I am wanted in England I will be with you at Easter.

Always affectionately yours,

J. R. L.

* My supporters at Frome, which borough I then represented, had passed resolutions in favor of disestablishing the Church and against co-operation, having been visited by the agents of the Liberation Society and the Trades' Protection Society, and I had refused to vote for disestablishment or for any measure limiting the right to associate for any lawful purpose.—T. H.

TO LESLIE STEPHEN

Paris, April 29, 1873.

My dear Stephen,—Behold me now these six months, like Napoleon the First, buried here on the banks of the Seine, in the midst of that French people whom I love so well. I ought to have answered your kind letter long ago, but I have delayed from day to day till I could tell you something definite about my plans. But somehow or other I find it harder and harder to have any plans. Mine host has mixed nepenthe with his wine, or mandragora, that takes the reason prisoner. But I think I have made up my mind to run over to London for a day or two to bid the Nortons good-by, for I cannot bear to have the sea between us before I see them again. If I do, I shall arrive about the 7th of May, and I shall count on seeing you as much as possible. It will depend very much on whether I can find a good perch for Mrs. Lowell when I am gone, for she is not in condition just now for so long a journey, though not in any sense ill. As for me, I am grown more fat than bard beseems, but have had a continual bother with my eyes — now better, now worse, but on the whole staying worse. Three days ago I thought I was all right, and this morning my left eye is as bad as ever. A good reason this for going over to England, for you will always be to me as good a sight for sair een as anything I can think of. I have an eyeglass swinging at my neck like the albatross (indeed I am getting to be a tolerably ancient mariner by this time), but it is only a bother to me. So I have to give up the old-age theory and drift in the ocean of conjecture.

However, with all drawbacks I have had a pleasant winter, and have at least pretty well shaken myself clear of one of my pet antipathies. I have even learnt to like the French after a fashion, but it is curious to me that I like and dislike them with nothing of the intensity which I feel towards Americans and English. I feel, always unconsciously, that they are a different breed, for whom I am in no way responsible. In the other case, a sense of common blood and partnership makes attraction easier and repulsion more instinctive. I watch these people as Mr. Darwin might his distant relations in a menagerie. Their tricks amuse me, and I am not altogether surprised when they remind me of "folks," as we say in New England. I don't believe they will make their *République* (a very different thing from a republic, by the way) march, for every one of them wants to squat on the upper bar and to snatch the nuts from his fellows. *Esprit* is their ruin, and an epigram has with them twice the force of an argument. However, I have learned to like them, which is a great comfort, and to see that they have some qualities we might borrow to advantage.

I have read your "Are We Christians?" and liked it, of course, because I found *you* in it, and that is something that will be dear to me so long as I keep my wits. I think I should say that you lump *shams* and *conventions* too solidly together in a common condemnation. All conventions are not shams by a good deal, and we

should soon be Papuans without them.   But I dare say
I have misunderstood you.   I am curious to see your
brother's book, which, from some extracts I have read,
I think will suit me very well.   What I saw was good
old-fashioned sense, and would have tickled Dr. Johnson.   I should find it hard to say why I dislike John
Stuart Mill, but I have an instinct that he has done lots
of harm.

I hope you have seen something of Emerson, who is
as sweet and wholesome as an Indian-summer afternoon.   We had nearly three weeks of him here, to
my great satisfaction. . . .

I remain as always

Most heartily and affectionately yours,

J. R. L.

TO C. E. NORTON

Paris, May 1, 1873.

. . . I think I shall get some good out of it (my laziness) one of these days, for I am pleased to find that
my dreams have recovered their tone and are getting
as fanciful as they used to be before I was twenty-five.
So I don't mind the circumference of my waist.   The
other night I heard a peasant girl in the ruins of a castle
sing an old French ballad that would have been worth
a thousand pound if I could have pieced it together
again when I awoke.   What bit I could recall satisfied
me that it was not one of those tricks that sleep puts on
us sometimes.   I have seen the Delectable Mountains,
too, several times to my great comfort, for I began to
believe myself fairly stalled in the slough of middle age.

II.—7

Montaigne called himself an old man at forty-seven, and I am fifty-four!

Our last expedition was down the Seine in the steamboat to Suresnes, which despite a leaden day was delightful. Spring is a never-failing medicine with me. Something or other within us pushes and revives with the season, and the first song of a bird sums up all the past happiness of life, all its past sorrow too, with a passion of regret that is sweeter than any happiness. The spring here is very lovely. The tender and translucent green of the leaves, their dream of summer, as it were, lasts longer than with us, where they become mere business arrangements for getting grub out of the blue air before they are out of their teens.

I look forward to having two or three real days with you. I haven't got the groove of the collar out of my neck yet, but I am a little freer in mind than when you were here. However, we shall see. I *think* I am not so dull as then.

J. H. came back to us day before yesterday, after a month in Italy, where he did not much enjoy himself. He says that he has become a thorough *misoscopist*, or hater of sights. He goes home in June, and I shall miss him more than I like to think. . . .

TO T. B. ALDRICH

Paris, May 28, 1873.

My dear Aldrich,—I have been so busy lately with doing nothing (which on the whole demands more time, patience, and attention than any other business) that I have failed to answer your very pleasant letter of I don't know how long ago.

What you say about William amused me much.* You know there is a proverb that "service is no inheritance," but it was invented by the radical opposition— by some servant, that is, who was asking for higher wages. My relation with William realized the saying in an inverse sense, for I received him from my father, already partly formed by an easy master, and have, I think, pretty well finished his education. I believe I fled to Europe partly to escape his tyranny, and I am sure he is awaiting the return of his vassal to re-enter on all the feudal privileges which belong of right to his class in a country so admirably free as ours. He had all the more purchase upon me that his wife had been in our service before he was, so that he knew all my weak points beforehand. Nevertheless, he has been an excellent servant, diligent, sober, and systematic, and I have no doubt I shall end my days as his milch cow if the udders of my purse continue to have a drop in them. You would see his worst side. He has eyes all round his head for the main chance; but anybody would take advantage of *me*, and I prefer the shearer to whom I am wonted, who clips close, to be sure, but has skill enough to spare the skin. He saves me trouble, and that is a saving I would rather buy dear than any other. Beyond meat and drink, it is the only use I have ever discovered for money—unless you give it away, which is apt to breed enemies. You will for-

---

* Mr. Aldrich was occupying Elmwood during Lowell's absence. "William" was the old factotum of the place.

give my saying that I feel a certain grain of pleasure
(with the safe moat of ocean between) in thinking
of you in your unequal struggle with Wilhelmus Con-
questor.

It gives me a very odd feeling to receive a letter
dated at Elmwood from anybody whose name isn't
Lowell. I used to have a strange fancy when I came
home late at night that I might find my double seated
in my chair, and how should I prove my identity?
Your letter revived it. I can see my study so plainly
as I sit here—but I find it hard to fill my chair with
anybody but myself. By the way, the study table was
made of some old mahogany ones that came from
Portsmouth—only I gave it to be done by a man in
want of work, and of course the cheap-looking affair
which affronts your eyes. 'Twas too bad, for the wood
was priceless. You may have dined at it in some former generation. It is a pleasant old house, isn't it?
Doesn't elbow one, as it were. It will make a frightful conservative of you before you know it. It was
born a Tory and will die so. Don't get too used to it.
I often wish I had not grown into it so. I am not
happy anywhere else.

I am glad to hear you are writing a novel. Get it
all done before you begin to print. Serials have been
the bane of literature. There is no more good ship-
building. But I draw a good augury from your letter.
You had the strength of mind to leave off at the end
of your third page—though I would readily have for-
given you the fourth. This is a rare virtue, and if you
will but write your book on the same principle of leav-

ing off when you have done, I am sure I shall be glad to read it.

I shall stay out my two years, though personally I would rather be at home. In certain ways this side is more agreeable to my tastes than the other—but even the buttercups stare at me as a stranger and the birds have a foreign accent. I'll be hanged but the very clouds put on strange looks to thwart me, and turn the cold shoulder on me. However, I have learned to know and like the French during my nine months' stay among them.

I am sorry to hear they stole your fruit. It gave me a sensible pang, for the trees I have planted are part of myself, and I feel the furtive evulsion of every pear even at this distance. Get a dog. He will eat up all your chickens, keep you awake all moonlight nights, and root up all your flowers, but he will make you feel safe about your pears till they have been made booty of. Study the book of Job. It supplies one with admirable formulas of impatience, and in that way serves to reconcile one to his lot. To learn patience read the works of A. H. K. B.

Give my love to Howells when you see him, and tell him that as he is pretty busy he will easily find time to write to me. I suppose he is in his new house by this time. And Bartlett's house? I sha'n't know my Cambridge when I come back to it. Are you annexed yet? Before this reaches you I shall have been over to Oxford to get a D.C.L. So by the time you get it this will be the letter of a Doctor and entitled to the more respect. Perhaps, in order to get the full flavor, you had better read this passage first if you happen to think of it. Do you not detect a certain flavor of parchment and Civil Law?

Mrs. Lowell joins me in kind regards to Mrs. Aldrich and yourself—and I am always

Yours cordially,

J. R. L.

P. S. I have kept this back for the Brest steamer, which saves me fourteen cents postage. We leave Paris in a day or two. I have learned to like it and the French, which is a great gain. We have had a very pleasant winter here in the most French of hotels. But Cambridge is better, as the rivers of Damascus were better than Jordan. There is no place like it, no, not even for taxes! I am getting gray and fat—about $\frac{1}{2}$ as large as Howells.

TO THOMAS HUGHES

Paris, June 2, 1873.

My dear Friend,—If I am not wise enough for a Doctorate, the fault will be yours. The cap is about to fall on my head, and you are chiefly to be thanked for it. I am as pleased as Punch at the thought of having a kind of denizenship, if nothing more, at Oxford; for though the two countries insist on misunderstanding each other, I can't conceive why the sensible men on both sides shouldn't in time bring 'em to see the madness of their ways. Born on the edge of a University town, I have a proper respect for academical decorations, and I am provoked that I must wait till 1875 before I see myself in our triennial catalogue with "D.C.L. Oxon." at my tail. If I don't know much Roman law, I shall at least endeavor to do credit to my new title by being as civil as an orange to all mankind. Mr. Bernard has been good enough to invite me to stay with him during my visit to Oxford, so I am sure to be in good hands. I do not know whether you old Oxonians attend the University festivals or not, but I shall not feel properly Doctored unless you are to the fore. My visit will be a flying one at best, for I shall leave Mrs. Lowell at Bruges.

My last trip to England did me good. My eyes— whether it was the friends I saw or no I can't say—have been better ever since. England looked so lovely after France, though I can't yet quite make out why. But the land of the Gauls has the advantage that one can live on his income there.

We have had a revolution since I saw you—not so much of a one as your papers in England seem to think, however. The conservatives never had any intention of making a president of the Duc d'Aumale, and though I never make prophecies, yet I am sure their present intention (as it is their only good policy) is to keep things steady as they are. But you remember how the great Julius begins—" Omnis divisa est Gallia in partes tres." That is, into three parties—monarchists, Bonapartists, and republicans, who have to pull together for their own ends, and therefore, whether they will or no, must help the conservative republic. Henri V. is out of the question, and the radical republic equally so — I mean, as a thing that could endure. Meanwhile the legitimists are a drag on the Orleanists, and whatever Bonapartism there is among the masses means merely a longing for order and peace. Whatever government can secure these for a year or two will become the residuary legatee of the Empire.

I think it was the egotism of Thiers that overset him rather than any policy he was supposed to have, and I look on the peacefulness of the late change as a most hopeful augury for France. I believe in the bewildering force of names, but I believe also that things carry it in the long run. The French are a frugal, sensible, industrious, and conservative people, and if they can only keep the beggar prince out of the saddle, they won't be ridden to the devil so easily in future.

We shall leave Paris to-morrow or next day, stopping in Rheims to see the churches, at Louvain for the Town House, and so on to Antwerp, Ghent, and Bruges. If you write, address me " poste restante " at the last named.

I promised your little girl, when I was in London, to send her an autograph from Paris, so I have scribbled her a few nonsense-verses which I hope will serve her turn. If I don't see you in Oxford, I shall stop long enough in London to get a glimpse of you. Our plan is to go to Switzerland and Germany, and so down to Italy for the winter. Then back to Paris, and so over to England on our way home next year. I hate travelling with my whole soul, though I like well enough to " be " in places.

With kindest regards to Mrs. Hughes, I remain always

Affectionately yours,

J. R. L.

TO MRS. LEWIS A. STIMSON

Bruges, June 25, 1873.

My dear Mrs. Stimson, — Here are the poor little verses I wrote the night before we left Paris and promised to send you. They have been rattling about in Mrs. Lowell's portfolio ever since, but I cannot see that they are at all the wiser for their travels. This is the first chance I have had to copy them out for you.

"You may break, you may shatter the vase if you will,
The scent of the roses will hang round it still."

———

Lucretius first, as I suppose,
Ventured to fasten on the nose
A simile both rich and rare,
As savages hang jewels there;
Perhaps *he* stole it from some Greek
Whose poem lost 'twere vain to seek;
Perhaps he found it (if it were *was* his)
By simply following his proboscis;
At any rate 'tis no wise dim
That Tom Moore borrowed it of him,
And thinned it to the filagree
Which at my verses' top you see.

Some other poet 'twas, no doubt,
Who found a further secret out—
I mean, those intimate relations
'Twixt perfumes and associations;
Nay, 'twixt a smell of any kind
And the recesses of the mind,
Since Memory is reached by *no* door
So quickly as by that of odor.

Now, what do all these steps lead up to?
Why not speak frankly *ex abrupto?*
They lead to this—that when I'm gone,
And you sit trying fancies on,
Puzzling your brain with buts and maybes
About the future of your babies,
Planning some bow (Oh, sure, no harm)
To give your looks a heightened charm—
Sudden you'll give a little sniff
And say: "It surely seems as if
There was an odor in the room
Not just like mignonette in bloom,
Nor like the breeze that brings away
Sweet messages of new-mown hay:—
What? No! Why, yes, it is indeed
Stale traces of that hateful weed
The red man to his spoilers left,
Fatal as Nessus' burning weft."
And then with eyes still fixed in vision,
Unconscious of the least transition,
"I wonder what the ~~Lowells~~ Lowles are doing,
What bit of scenery pursuing.
Do they in Switzerland repent?
Or, o'er their guardian Murrays bent,
Do they endeavor to divine
Why they must needs enjoy the Rhine?
Count they the shocks the German kitchen
Is so incomparably rich in?
Do they across Lugano steer
In whose ethereal silence clear
It seems that one might hear a fin stir?
Or, in some grim and chilly minster,
Are they condemned to dog the Suisse
Through nasal rounds of that and this,
Till, to the very marrow chilled,
They wish men had not learned to build?

Or, bored with Tintorets and Titians
And saints in all the queer positions
They can be twisted to with paints,
Do they wish wicked things of saints?
Well, *she* was pleasant as could be,
So sweet and cheerful too—but *he!*
He left behind at every visit
Tobacco perfumes so explicit,
That in the night I often woke
Thinking myself about to choke.
I wish I had his pipe to throw it
Into the fire—a pretty poet!
Whene'er he's buried, those that love him,
Instead of violets sweet above him,
Should plant, to soothe his melancholy,
The poisonous herb brought home by Raleigh!"

Now, when such vixenish thoughts assail you,
And other lenitives all fail you,
Do like the children, who are wiser
And happier far than king or kaiser:
Play that a thing is thus or so,
And gradually you'll find it grow
The very truth (for bale or bliss)
Of what you fancy that it is;
Just call the weed, to try the spell,
Nepenthe, lotus, asphodel,
And say my pipe was such as those
The slim Arcadian shepherd blows
On old sarcophagi to lull
An ear these twenty centuries dull—
Pipe of such sweet and potent tone
It charmed to shapes of deathless stone
The piper and the dancers too
(As may mine never do for you,

But keep you rather fresh and fair
To breathe the sweetest mortal air).
Then, when your thought has worked its will,
And turned to sweetness things of ill,
Muse o'er your girlish smile and say,
"Well, now he's fairly gone away,
If on his faults one does not dwell,
There are worse bores than J. R. L."

There's an autograph for you! As long as one of Bach's fugues. Remember us to M. Garrier and Madame and Clarisse. Tell Baptiste (if he has not already boned it) that an old coat I left on a chair in my bedroom was meant for him. I have been over to Oxford to be doctored, and had a very pleasant time of it. You would respect me if you could have seen me in my scarlet gown. Kindest regards from both of us to both of you. We go from here in a day or two to Holland — then up the Rhine to Switzerland, where we join the Stephens and Miss Thackeray.

You must pardon the verses—my hand is out. The writing looks *something* like mine—not much.

Good-by; give an orange to each of the children for me, and believe me yours affectionately always,

J. R. L.

TO C. E. NORTON

Venice, Oct. 30, 1873.

. . . We made a pretty good *giro* in the Low Countries, going wherever there was a good Cathedral or Town Hall. Ypres charmed us especially, even after Bruges, which is always a Capua for me. The little town is so quiet and sleepy—no, not sleepy, but drowsy

and dreamy, and the walk round the ramparts looking
out over endless green and down upon the tranquil
moat, with its swans as still as the water-lilies whose
whiteness they tarnished, that I felt sure I was an
enchanted prince till I paid my bill at the inn. But
for that I should assuredly have stumbled upon the
Sleeping Beauty before long. But, alas and alas, the
only kiss that awakens towns that have dropt asleep
nowadays is that of Dame Trade, who makes bond-
slaves of all she brings back to life. We passed by
where Charlemagne (with Mr. Freeman's pardon) is said
to have been born, and by a little town that gave
me a pleasanter thrill—the birthplace of Dan Froissart.
It lay about half a mile away, cuddled among trees,
with its great hulk of a church looming up above the
houses like a hen among her brood. I did not choose
to see it nearer—it would have betrayed itself. As it
was, I must have seen it very much as it looked to the
dear old canon himself, when he used to play at all
those incomprehensible games of which he gives us an
inventory in his verses. . . .

I am more impressed by Tintoretto than ever before
—his force, his freedom, and his originality. I never
fairly *saw* the San Rocco pictures before—for one must
choose the brightest days for them. The "Annuncia-
tion" especially has taken me by assault. That flight
of baby angels caught up and whirled along in the wake
of Gabriel like a skurry of autumn birds is to me something incomparable. And then the Cimas and the Bel-
linis and the Carpaccios! I think I am really happy
here for the first time since I came abroad. . . .

I am looking forward now with compressed eagerness
to our coming home.   I shall not overstay my two years
by a single day if I can help it. . . . For myself I see
no result as yet but rest—which, to be sure, is a good
thing—but I suppose when I get back I shall find I
have learned something.   But habit is so strong in me
that I cannot work outside the reach of my wonted
surroundings. . . .

TO THOMAS HUGHES

Venice, Thanksgiving Day, 1873.

My dear Friend,—As you are one of the good things
I have to be thankful for in this life, I naturally think
of you to-day, when I am far from the roast turkeys
and plum-puddings of Elmwood.   It makes me a little sad to think that, if I were at home, this would have
been the first of these festivals that I should have celebrated in the true patriarchal way with a grandson at
my board.   It is a queer sensation when one begins to
put out these feelers towards the future that are to keep
us alive in a certain sense (perhaps to repeat us) after
we are gone.   It is a melancholy kind of meditation
this, but travelling is melancholy — a constant succession of partings like life.   To-day some very agreeable
Portuguese leave us whose acquaintance we made here,
the Viscount de Soveral, his wife, and daughter.   They
have lived much in England, and he, I suspect, must
have been either ambassador or attached to the Portuguese embassy there.   To-morrow two English ladies,
whom I had just learned to like very much, go off to
Cairo.   It is just like a constant succession of funerals

—only people are buried in distance instead of in earth. Nay, since the earth is round, they will be covered from us by that also as in the grave.

The truth is, my dear friend, I have just been trying to make up my accounts, and as I don't very well know how, I have got dumpy before them—for the mysterious is always rather a damper for the spirits. Moreover, I am bored. I can't "do" anything over here except study a little now and then, and I long to get back to my reeky old den at Elmwood. Then I hope to find I have learned something in my two years abroad. . . .

We have been through Switzerland, where I climbed some of the highest peaks with a spy-glass—a method I find very agreeable, and which spares honest sole-leathers. I am thinking of getting up an achromatic-telescope Alpine Club, to which none will be admitted till they have had two fits of gout, authenticated by a doctor's bill.

So far I wrote yesterday. To-day the weather is triumphant, and my views of life consequently more cheerful. It is so warm that we are going out presently in the gondola, to take up a few dropped stitches. Venice, after all, is incomparable, and during this visit I have penetrated its little slits of streets in every direction on foot. The canals only give one a visiting acquaintance. The *calli* make you an intimate of the household. I have found no books except two or three in the Venetian dialect. I am looking forward to home now, and shouldn't wonder if I took up my work at Harvard again, as they wish me to do.

We leave Venice probably to-morrow for Verona. Thence to Florence, Rome, and Naples. . . .

TO MISS NORTON

Florence, Jan. 7, 1874.

. . . You find our beloved country dull, it seems. With a library like that at Shady Hill all lands are next door and all nations within visiting distance—better still, all ages are contemporary with us. But I understand your feeling, I think. Women need social stimulus more than we. They contribute to it more, and their magnetism, unless drawn off by the natural conductors, turns inward and irritates. Well, when I come back I shall be a good knob on which to vent some of your superfluous electricity; though on second thoughts I am not so sure of that, for the Leyden jar after a while becomes clever enough to give off sparks in return. But, dear Jane, the world in general is loutish and dull. I am more and more struck with it, and a certain sprightliness of brain, with which I came into life, is driven in on myself by continual rebuffs of misapprehension. I have grown wary and don't dare to let myself go, and what are we good for if our natural temperament doesn't now and then take the bit between its teeth and scamper till our hair whistles in the wind? But indeed America is too busy, too troubled about many things, and Martha is only good to make puddings. There is no *leisure*, and that is the only climate in which society is indigenous, the only one in which good-humor and wit and all the growths of art are more than half-hardy exotics. It is not that one needs to be idle—but only to have this southern atmosphere about him. Democracies lie, perhaps, too far north. You were made—with your breadth of sympathy, the contagion of your temperament, and the social *go* of your mind—to drive the four-in-hand of a *salon*, and American life boxes us all up in a one-horse *sulky* of absorbing occupation. We are isolated in our own despite, the people who have a common ground of sympathy in pursuits (or the want of them) are rare, and without partnership the highest forms of culture are impossible. . . .

TO MISS GRACE NORTON

Florence, Jan. 27, 1874.

. . . We have been living very quietly here in Florence, which I find very beautiful in spite of the threnody Charles once wrote me about the loss of the walls. I hate changes in my familiar earth—they give me a feeling as if I myself had been transplanted and my roots unpleasantly disturbed ; but I was not intimate enough with Florence to be discomforted, and the older parts of the town, which I chiefly haunt, have a noble mediæval distance and reserve for me—a frown I was going to call it, not of hostility, but of haughty doubt. These grim palace fronts meet you with an aristocratic stare that puts you to the proof of your credentials. There is to me something wholesome in it that makes you feel your place. As for pictures, I am tired to death of 'em, and never could enjoy them much when I had to run them down. And then most of them are so bad. I like best the earlier ones, that say so much in their half-uncon-

II.—8

scious prattle, and talk nature to me instead of high art
—spell the last two words with capitals, if you please.
You see that they honestly mean to say something outside of themselves, and not to make you think about
themselves. Children talk so, whose want of language
often gives a pungency to their speech which the dictionary cannot give, but, alas, can take away. There is
an instructive difference between the simple honesty of
the earlier painters' portraits of themselves and the conscious attitudinizing of the later ones, which expresses
what I mean. But the truth is, as Northcote says the
choristers used to sing at St. Paul's, " I'm tired and want
to go home "! . . .

TO C. E. NORTON

Albergo del Norte, Firenze,
Feb. 2, 1874.

My dear Boy,— . . . I don't feel like going on with a
poem I am writing about Agassiz, whom I understood
and liked better as I grew older (perhaps less provincial),
and whom I shall miss as if some familiar hill should be
gone out of my horizon when I come home and walk
down the river-side to the village, as we used to call it; so
I am going to answer your letter, which came yesterday.
. . . I never was good for much as a professor—once a
week, perhaps, at the best, when I could manage to get
into some conceit of myself, and so could put a little of
my *go* into the boys. The rest of the time my desk was
as good as I. And then, on the other hand, my being a
professor wasn't good for me—it damped my gunpowder,
as it were, and my mind, when it took fire at all (which

wasn't often), drawled off in an unwilling fuse instead of leaping to meet the first spark.　Since I have discharged my soul of it and see the callus on my ankle, where the ball and chain used to be, subsiding gradually to smooth and natural skin, I feel like dancing round the table as I used when I was twenty, to let off the animal spirits.　If I were a profane man, I should say, "Darn the College!" . . .

TO THE SAME

> Palazzo Barberini, Rome,
> Feb. 26, 1874.

. . . I sent you the other day from Florence a long poem (*too* long, I fear), in the nature of an elegy on Agassiz.　His death came home to me in a singular way, growing into my consciousness from day to day as if it were a graft new-set, that by degrees became part of my own wood and drew a greater share of my sap than belonged to it, as grafts sometimes will.　I suppose that, unconsciously to myself, a great part of the ferment it produced in me was owing to the deaths of my sister Anna,* of Mrs. ——, whom I knew as a child in my early manhood, and of my cousin Amory, who was inextricably bound up with the primal associations of my life, associations which always have a singular sweetness for me.　A very deep chord had been touched also at Florence by the sight of our old lodgings in the Casa Guidi, of the balcony Mabel used to run on, and the windows we used to look out at so long ago.　I got sometimes into the mood I used to be in when I was always repeating to myself,

* Mrs. Charles R. Lowell.

"King Pandion he is dead;
    All *thy* friends are lapt in lead"—

verses which seem to me desolately pathetic. At last I
began to hum over bits of my poem in my head till it
took complete possession of me and worked me up to a
delicious state of excitement, all the more delicious as
my brain (or at any rate the musical part of it) had been
lying dormant so long. I couldn't sleep, and when I
walked out I saw nothing outward. My old trick of
seeing things with my eyes shut after I had gone to
bed (I mean whimsical things utterly alien to the train
of my thoughts—for example, a hospital ward with a
long row of white, untenanted beds, and on the farthest
a pile of those little wooden dolls with red-painted slip-
pers) revived in full force. Nervous, horribly nervous,
but happy for the first time (I mean consciously happy)
since I came over here. And so by degrees my poem
worked itself out. The parts came to me as I came
awake, and I wrote them down in the morning. I had
all my bricks—but the mortar wouldn't *set*, as the ma-
sons say. However, I got it into order at last. You
will see there is a logical sequence if you look sharp.
It was curious to me after it was done to see how flesh-
ly it was. This impression of Agassiz had wormed itself into my consciousness, and without my knowing it
had colored my whole poem. I could not help feeling
how, if I had been writing of Emerson, for example, I
should have been quite otherwise ideal. But there it is,
and you can judge for yourself. I think there is some
go in it somehow, but it is too near me yet to be
judged fairly by me. It is old-fashioned, you see, but
none the worse for that. . . .

TO MISS NORTON

Albergo Crocolle, Napoli,
Marzo 12, 1874.

My dear Jane,—If I should offer to explain any ec-
centricities of chirography by telling you my fingers
were numb, you would think me joking, and be much
rather inclined to account for it by the intoxication of
this heavenliest of climates as you remember it. But I
speak forth the words of truth and soberness when I
assure you that Vesuvius is hoary with snow to his very
roots, that Sorrento has just been hidden by a cloud
which I doubt not is bursting in hail, for we were
greeted on our arrival last night by a hailstone chorus
of the most emphatic kind, so that the streets were
white with it as we drove shiveringly along, and the
top of the 'bus rattled to the old tune of " Pease on a
Trencher." All the way from Rome I saw Virgil's too-
fortunate husbandmen (he was right in his parenthetic
sua si bona norint) working with their great blue cloaks
on, or crouching under hedges from the wire-edged
wind. The very teeth in their harrows must have been
chattering for cold. And this is the climate you so
rapturously wish us joy of! *Vedi Napoli, e poi morì* of
a catarrh. I envy you with your foot of honest snow
on the ground where it ought to be, and not indigested
in the atmosphere, giving it a chill beyond that of condensed Unitarianism.

We left Rome after a fortnight's visit to the Storys,
which was very pleasant *quoad* the old friends, but rather wild and whirling *quoad* the new. Two receptions
a week, one in the afternoon and one in the evening,

were rather confusing for wits so eremetical as mine. I am not equal to the *grande monde*. 'Tis very well of its kind, I dare say, but it is not *my* kind, and I still think the company I kept at home better than any I have seen—especially better in its simplicity. The Old World carries too much top-hamper for an old salt like me to be easy in his hammock. There are good things west of the ocean in spite of —— 's pessimism, and better things to come, let us hope. . . .

I had a great pleasure at Rome in seeing William's new statue of Alcestis, which I think is *di gran lungo* ahead of anything he has done. It is very simple and noble. She is walking as if in a dream. The right hand gathers the mantle about her head. The left hangs loosely at her side. The face has a lovely expression of awakening and half-bewildered expectation. The drapery is admirably graceful, and the gliding motion of the figure (seen from whichever point of view) gives a unity of intention and feeling to the whole figure which I call masterly. I know no satisfaction more profound than that we feel in the success of an old friend, in the real success of anybody, for the matter of that. It was so pleasant to be able to say frankly, "You have done something really fine, and which everybody will like." I wonder whether I shall ever give that pleasure to anybody. Never mind, it is next best to feel it about the work of another, and I never do care very long for anything I have done myself. But, as one gets older, one can't help feeling sad sometimes to think how little one has achieved.

It is now (as regards my date) to-morrow the 13th.

We have been twice to the incomparable Museum, which to me is the most interesting in the world. There is the keyhole through which we barbarians can peep into a Greek interior—provincial Greek, Roman Greek, if you will, but still Greek. Vesuvius should be sainted for this miracle of his—hiding Pompeii and Herculaneum under his gray mantle so long, and saving them from those dreadful melters and smashers, the Dark Ages. Now we come in on them with the smell of wine still in their cups—we catch them boiling their eggs, selling their figs, and scribbling naughty things on the walls. I do not find that they were much our betters in parietal wit, but in sense of form how they dwarf us! They contrived to make commonplace graceful—or rather they could not help it. Well, we are alive (after a fashion) and they dead. That is one advantage we have over 'em. And they could not look forward to going home to Cambridge and to pleasant visits at Shady Hill. On the whole, I pity 'em. They are welcome to their poor little bronzes and things. Haven't we our newspapers, marry come up! What did they know about the Duke of Edinburgh's wedding and all the other edifying things that make us wise and great, I should like to know? They were poor devils, after all, and I trample on 'em and snub 'em to my heart's content. Where were their Common Schools? They are dumb and cast down their eyes, every mother's son of 'em. Not a school-desk among all their relics! No wonder they came to grief.

It is now after dinner. I write this by installments, as the amiable bandits of this neighborhood send a man

they have caught home to his friends till they pay a
ransom—first one ear, then the other, and so on. I am
a little cross with the table-d'hôte, because I always
know so well what is coming—it is like the signs of the
zodiac. I think we should be bored to death with the
regular courses of the seasons were it not for the whim-
sicality of the weather. That saves us from suicide.
On the other hand, though depressed by the inevitable
rosbif and *pollo arrostito*, I am enlivened by a fiddle
and guitar, and a voice singing the Naples of twenty
years ago under my window. For Naples has changed
for the worse (shade of Stuart Mill! I mean for the
better) more than any other Italian city. Fancy, there
are no more lazzaroni, there is no more *corricolo*. The
mountains are here, and Capri, but where is Naples?
Italia unita will be all very well one of these days, I
doubt not. At present it is paper money, and the practical instead of the picturesque. Is the day of railways
worse than that of Judgment? Why could not one
country be taken and the other left? Let them try all
their new acids of universal suffrage and what not on
the tough body of the New World. The skin will heal
again. But this lovely, disburied figure of Ausonia—
they corrode her marble surface beyond all cure. *Panem et circenses* wasn't so bad after all. A bellyful and
amusement—isn't that more than the average mortal is
apt to get? more than perhaps he is capable of getting? America gives the *panem*, but do you find it
particularly amusing just now? My dear Jane, you see
I have had a birthday since I wrote last, and these are
the sentiments of a gentleman of fifty-five—and after

dinner. Change in itself becomes hateful to us as we grow older, and naturally enough, because every change in ourselves is for the worse. I am writing to you, for example, by lamp-light, and I feel what usèd to be a pleasure almost a sin. To-morrow morning I shall see that the crows have been drinking at my eyes. Fanny is wiser (as women always are), and is sound asleep in her arm-chair on the other side of the fire. The wood here, by the way, is poplar—good for the inn-keeper, but only cheering for the guest, as it reminds him of the Horatian *large super foco ligna reponens*, and the old fellow in Smollett, whom you never read. . . .

TO C. E. NORTON

Hôtel de Lorraine, 7 Rue de Beaune,
Paris, May 11, 1874.

. . . Hearty thanks for all the trouble you have taken about my poor old poem. I had quite got over the first flush by the time I saw it in print, and now it seems weary, stale, flat, and unprofitable enough, God knows! Well, I confess I thought it better till I saw it. . . .

TO W. D. HOWELLS

Paris, May 13, 1874.

My dear Howells,—I was very glad to get a line from you. I should have sent my poem directly to you (for it tickled me that our positions should be reversed, and that you should be sitting in the seat of the scorner where I used to sit); but I happened to see a number of the *Atlantic* in Florence, and in the list of contribu-

tors my name was left out. As the magazine had just
changed hands I did not know but it had changed minds
as well, so I would not put you in a position where your
friendship might come in conflict with some whimsey of
your publishers. Thank you heartily for the pleasant
things you say about the poem. I thought it very well
just after parturition, and explained any motives of aversion I might feel by that uncomfortable redness which is
common to newly born babes. But since I have it in
print I have not been able to read it through—but only
to dip in here and there on passages which C. E. N. had
doubts about. What a witch is this Imagination, who
sings as she weaves till we seem to *see* the music in the
growing web, and when all is done that magic has vanished and the poor thing looks cheap as printed muslin!
Well, I am pleased, all the same, with what you say,
because, after all, you needn't have said it unless you
liked.

Why, of course I went to see young Mead—am I not
very fond of his sister and her husband? I should have
gone again, but that poem got hold of me and squeezed
all my life out for the time and a good bit after.

Now a word of business. I wrote C. E. N. day before
yesterday, and of course forgot what I wished to say—
or a part of it. If Osgood still wishes to reprint the
Agassiz, pray make these further corrections—

"And scanned the festering *heap* we all despise."

I left out the word in copying. Instead of the "paler
primrose of a second spring," read "Like those pale
blossoms," etc., as I wrote at first. Why I changed it I

can't guess, for it makes an absurdity. I suppose I was misled by the alliteration. The verse is a better one as printed, but I couldn't have looked at the context. I mean those blossoms that come on fruit-trees sometimes in September. I have seen them once or twice in my own garden.

We have taken our passage for the 24th June, and shall arrive, if all go well, in time for the "glorious Fourth." I hope we shall find you in Cambridge. I long to get back, and yet am just beginning to get wonted (as they say of babies and new cows) over here. The delightful little inn where I am lodged is almost like home to me, and the people are as nice as can be.

Tell Mrs. Howells—with my kindest regards and Mrs. Lowell's too—that we are just going out shopping. The weather is infamous. Love to Winny and Boy, alias Booah.

> Always affectionately yours,
> J. R. L.

TO THOMAS HUGHES

> Hôtel de Lorraine, 7 Rue de Beaune,
> Paris, May 16, 1874.

My dear Friend,—Here we are back again in our old quarters, though not so soon by several weeks as I expected. But how get away from Rome, even though it be changed much for the worse so far as its outside is concerned? It is a providential arrangement that after fifty one hates improvement; it is the drag that hinders things from going too fast. In this respect Paris is comforting, for I find the French exactly where I left 'em a year ago, only more so.

In your revolution I took a personal interest, as I need not tell you. I happened to be where I saw the English papers at the time, and though I was disgusted that you should not have been returned, I was entirely pleased with the way in which you lost your election. It was like you, for it was honorable and magnanimous, and therefore a higher kind of success than winning the seat would have been. But men like you are wanted in Parliament, and so I feel sure that I shall have to write M. P. after your name again before long. Last year you said something about running over to Paris for a week. It would be very jolly if you would come, now that you have no Parliamentary duties to detain you.

I can't tell you how glad I am to be on my way home. I hope after I get there I shall find I have got something by my travels better than a grayer beard and the torments of what the doctors call "suppressed gout." It is suppressed after the fashion of the Commune, which has jumped from the Parisian great toe into every nerve and muscle of the body. . . .

TO LESLIE STEPHEN

Hôtel de Lorraine, 7 Rue de Beaune,
Paris, May 16, 1874.

Dear Stephen,—We have got thus far on our way home, and hope to arrive in England about the first of next month. I was on the point of writing you again from Florence when I was suddenly snatched up by a poem which occupied me wholly for some time, and left me, like a bit of rock-weed at low water, dangling helpless and waiting for the next tide.

I read your book * with great interest and, in the main, with great satisfaction, and gave it to Harry James, who liked it altogether. My only objection to any part of your book is, that I think our beliefs more a matter of choice (natural selection, perhaps, but anyhow not logical) than you would admit, and that I find no fault with a judicious shutting of the eyes. You would have shut yours tight before you finally let go at the end of your bad five minutes—and yet I fancy the descent would have been both interesting scientifically and morally picturesque. . . .

When I was with the Storys in Rome, I took down one day while waiting for my breakfast a volume of the *Living Age*, made up of articles from the English journals. I hit upon one entitled "In a Library," and liked it so much that I carried it to my room and read all the rest of the series I could find with equal interest. There were some more than odd coincidences with my own experience. You can fancy how tickled I was when I found I had been reading you all the while. I actually damaged my eyes over them — reading on after candle-light and when I ought to have been abed. There, you see, is perfectly disinterested testimony. The pills had no label. I tried one and then swallowed the box because they did me good.

I half feel at home now that I am back again in my little inn, with its household as simple and honest as if it were in Arcadia. It amuses me (I know it ought to sadden me, but I can't help it) to find the French in

* This book was "Essays on Free Thinking and Plain Speaking."

the same *cul-de-sac* where I left them a year ago, and saying helplessly, *C'est une crise très sérieuse, mais que voulez-vous? Nous sommes Français—voilà tout!* And yet the same Frenchmen have managed their finances in a way that ought to make *us* blush to the roots of our hair. . . .

TO GEORGE PUTNAM

Paris, May 19, 1874.

. . . I ought long ago to have answered your letter, received just before we left Florence. But somehow I could not. That long list of deaths, following so closely upon each other's heels, saddened me profoundly. I had a notion that as we grow older we get used to death, and in some sense it is true, but no habitude can make us less sensible to deaths which make us older and lonelier by widening the gap between our past and present selves. Our own lives seem to lose their continuity, and those who died long ago seem more wholly dead when some one who was associated with them and linked our memory more indissolubly with them goes out into the endless silence and separation. I was very much struck with this when I heard of the death of my cousin Amory Lowell. I had hardly seen her for many years, but she was closely intertwined with all the recollections of my early life. I can't tell how, but the thought of her kept Broomly Vale unchanged, and she brought my father and my uncle John before me as they were in those old days. A great part of my fairyland went to dust with her. . . .

For my own part, though I have had a great deal of home-sickness, I come back to Cambridge rather sadly. I have not been over-well of late. The doctor in Rome, however, gave my troubles a name—and that by robbing them of mystery has made them commonplace. He said it was *suppressed gout*. It has a fancy of gripping me in the stomach sometimes, holding on like a slow fire for seven hours at a time. It is wonderful how one gets used to things, however. But it seems to be growing lighter, and I hope to come home robust and red. . . .

TO LESLIE STEPHEN

Paris, May 27, 1874.

My dear Stephen,—I can't say that the sight of your handwriting again was good for *sair een*, for the force of mine is so far abated that I had to take your letter to the window—but it was just as good as if it had been.

I had thought about the white-choker business and all that, and from your point of view I liked your book altogether. My objection was a purely personal one. I shut my eyes resolutely (I confess) when I turn them in certain directions, and trust my instincts or my longings or whatever you choose to call them. For myself I hate to see religion compounded with police as much as you do, but I confess that my intimacy with the French makes me doubt, makes me ready to welcome almost anything that will save them from their logic and deliver them over, bound hand and foot, to anything that will give them a continuity that looks before

and after with as great a respect for facts as for syllo-
gisms. . . .

I hope whoever stole the *Atlantic* from you did it because of my poem. You shall have another copy one
of these days, but so long as you like me, you are welcome to think what you must of what I write. Besides,
this is an old story with me now. It should have some
virtue in it, to judge by what it took out of me.

If we had only got here as soon as I expected I
should have met you in Paris. I never saw my habit
of taking root in so ill a light before. It would have
been so jolly—for I know all the old nooks and corners
so well now that I should have been an admirable
guide, and these levels suit my elderly feet. It is too
bad, but our weaknesses always come home to roost at
last. . . .

Always affectionately yours,

J. R. L.

TO THOMAS HUGHES

Elmwood, July 11, 1874.

Dear Friend,— . . . We had a foggy and rainy passage, but the north-westerly and south-easterly winds
that made it disagreeable made it also short. . . . At
about 7 A. M. of the 4th we landed, and by half-past nine
I was at home again. . . .

This has been a rainy summer, so I found everything
as green as in the noble old island I had just left. The
birds have pretty much given over singing, but my im-
memorial cat-bird made music all dinner-time day before yesterday, and next morning in the early dawn

the Phœbe was calling her own name sadly, like one of
Ovid's metamorphosed ladies. . . .

TO MISS GRACE NORTON

Elmwood, July 21, 1874.

. . . It is so long since I have been able to send news
from Cambridge that I find a certain relish in it, and
begin again to think that it is as important as most
other domains of history. Was I not told yesterday
by Mrs. Mary Mullins that "Cambridge had seemed
kind o' lonesome without me"? and shall I not strive
to atone to her (Cambridge to wit) for this two years'
widowhood? I do not think, however, that the dear
soul missed me very much, nor that "every jow" the
bell of the First Parish gave sounded in her ear "Come
back, Russell Lowell!" These returns from the under-
world would be good medicine for one inclined to value
himself over-duly. Things seem to have got on very
well during our absence, and it is odds if nine tenths
of our fellow-citizens missed us from the customed
hill any more than they would if we had authentically
suffered obituary. I have sometimes had traitorous
surmises about Alcestis, as if she might have surprised
Admetus seated before a smoking joint of one of those
sheep Apollo once tended for him, and inarticulate for
more material reasons than joy. Our returns, whether
quick or slow, prove to us that we are small prophets
in our own country. I except All-of-you, who welcomed me better than I deserved.

I do not find so many changes as I expected. . . .

II.—9

TO MISS NORTON

Elmwood, Sept. 19, 1874.

. . . I have been at work, and really hard at work, in making books that I had read and marked really useful by indexes of all peculiar words and locations. I have finished in this way, since I came home, Golding's "Ovid," Warner's "Albion's England," Laing's and the Thornton "Metrical Romances," the *Chevalier au lion;* and yesterday, in eight unbroken hours, I did Barbour's "Brus." Then I have been reading many volumes of the Early English Text Society's series in the same thorough way. A professor, you know, must be learned, if he can't be anything else, and I have now reached the point where I feel sure enough of myself in Old French and Old English to make my corrections with a pen instead of a pencil as I go along. Ten hours a day, on an average, I have been at it for the last two months, and get so absorbed that I turn grudgingly to anything else. My only other reading has been Mr. Sibley's book of "Harvard Graduates," which is as unillumined, dry, and simple as the fourteenth-century prose of the Early English Texts. But it interests me and makes me laugh. It is the prettiest rescue of prey from Oblivion I ever saw. The gallant librarian, like a knight-errant, slays this giant, who carries us all captive sooner or later, and then delivers his prisoners. There are ninety-seven of them by tale, and as he fishes them out of those dismal *oubliettes* they come up dripping with the ooze of Lethe, like Curll from his dive in the Thames, like him also gallant com-

petitors for the crown of Dulness. It is the very balm
of authorship. No matter how far you may be gone
under, if you are a graduate of Harvard College you
are sure of being dredged up again and handsomely
buried, with a catalogue of your works to keep you
down. I do not know when the provincialism of New
England has been thrust upon me with so ineradicable
a barb. Not one of their works which stands in any
appreciable relation with the controlling currents of
human thought or history, not one of them that has
now the smallest interest for any living soul! And yet
somehow I make myself a picture of the past out of
this arid waste, just as the mirage rises out of the dry
desert. Dear old Sibley! I would read even a sermon
of his writing, so really noble and beautiful is the soul
under that commonplace hull!

Since I wrote you I have finished an autobiography.
Do not be frightened, dear Jane; it is only ten lines
long, and I plagiarized every word of it from Drake's
"American Biography," which was far better informed
than I found myself to be. Last night was our first
Whist Club since my return. I looked in the record,
found it was John's deal, and we began as if there had
been no gap. The club is now in its thirtieth year, and
I was saying last night that it was, I thought, both a
creditable and American fact that I had never heard a
dispute or even a difference at the table in all those
years. . . .

TO C. E. NORTON.

Elmwood, Oct. 7, 1874.

My dear Charles,—The nameless author of that de-

lightful poem, "The Squyr of Lowe Degree" (may God
him save and see!) gives a list of every bird he can
think of that sang to comfort his hero. Here they are:

1. Lavrock,
2. Nightingale,
3. Pie,
4. Popinjay,
5. Throstil,
6. Marlyn,
7. Wren,
8. Jay,
9. Sparrow,
10. Nuthatch,
11. Starling,
12. Goldfinch,
13. Ousel.

On Monday the 5th I walked up to the Oaks with Still-
man, and in a quarter of an hour had noted on a paper
the following birds (most of which counted by dozens):

1. Robin,
2. Wilson's thrush (singing),
3. Chewink,
4. Bluebird (warbling as in spring),
5. Phœbe (doing his best),
6. Ground sparrow (singing),
7. Tree   "   ("),
8. Nuthatch,
9. Flicker (laughing and crying like Andromache),
10. Chickadee (doing all he could),
11. Goldfinch,

12. Linnet,

13. Jay,

14. Crow (to balance his popinjay),

15. Catbird.

Thus I take down the gauntlet which you left hanging for all comers in your English hedge. I don't believe that hedge birds are a whit more respectable than hedge priests or hedge schoolmasters. All the while we were there the air was tinkling with one or other of them. Remember—this was in October. Three cheers for the rivers of Damascus!

Affectionately always,
HOSEA BIGLOW.

Et ego in Arcadia, says Mr. Wilbur.

TO E. L. GODKIN

Elmwood, Oct. 10, 1874.

Dear Godkin,— . . . I see they are driven at Washington to a reform of the office-holders at the South. It has always been my belief that if tenure of office had been permanent, secession would have been (if not impossible) vastly more difficult, and reconstruction more easy and simple. As it was, a large body of the most influential men in the discontented States knew that the election of Lincoln would be fatal to their bread and butter—and, after all, it is to this that the mass of men are loyal. It is well that they should be so, for habitual comfort is the main fortress of conservatism and respectability, two old-fashioned qualities for which all the finest sentiments in the world are but a windy substitute. . . .

By the way, I found a curious misprint in the new edition of Chapman (vol. ii., p. 159), which I thought might make a paragraph for the *Nation*.

> " *Caucusses*
> That cut their too large murtherous thieveries
> To their den's length still."

He means *Cacus*, of course, though the editor didn't see it, for the word doesn't occur in his index of proper names. It is a curious *sors castigatoris preli*, at any rate, and hits true, for the Caucus always cuts down its candidates to the measure of its robber's cave. It shows, too, that old Chapman pronounced *a au*.

And by this graceful transition I come to the reason why I write you to-day instead of in some indefinite future. In a sonnet printed in last week's *Nation* there is a misprint which it were well to correct. For "Nothing to *court*" *lege* "Nothing to *count*." I tried to think it made some better meaning than mine, but couldn't make it out. Thank the Power who presides over the *Nation* (who, I am given to understand, is the D—l) that I am of calmer temper than those are whom a misprint drives clean daft—I mean one in their own contribution to the general *tedium vitæ*. . . . Goodby, with gratitude always for the admirable work you are doing.

Affectionately yours,

J. R. L.

TO THOMAS HUGHES

Elmwood, Feb. 16, 1875.

My dear Friend,— . . . I [have been reading] Grote's "Greece," which I had never read before, and its prosy

good sense was medicinal to me. His honest incapacity
of imagination is singularly soothing. The curious political (not æsthetic) analogies struck me more forcibly
than ever. I have long thought, and Grote's book
confirmed me in it, that this history will first be ade-
quately written by a Yankee. Grote's Dutch blood
helped him a little, but the moment that panhellenism
(the need of which he could see plainly enough two
thousand odd years ago) showed itself in a million
armed men over here under his very nose, he fancied
them sprung from unblessed dragon's teeth,

> "And back recoiled, he knew not why,
> E'en at the sound himself had made."

The sentimentalist stood revealed under the imposing
outside of the banker. It is humorously sad to me.

As with you in the early part of the winter, our talk
now is wholly of the weather. So long as it was cold
with you (a fact I have observed before) it was excep-
tionally mild here. We had a true Indian summer,
and I heard birds singing by Beaver Brook in November. Being much of an hypæthral, I augured ill from
it, and was sure that Winter was waiting only to get a
better purchase on us. About Christmas he had got
everything ready in his laboratory and shut upon us
with the snap of a steel trap. Since then our thermom-
eters have skulked in the neighborhood of zero (Fahr.).
So continuous a cold has brought down the oldest in-
habitant to the wretched level of us juniors. Out of
doors, however, it has been noble weather, the most pi-
quant sauce for my walks to and from College—where,

by the way, I am installed again with a class in Old French and another in Dante. In my study sometimes of an evening, when the north-west took a vigorous turn at the bellows, and the thermometer in the back parts could not be coaxed above 42°, it has been more than invigorating. But I have not given in, nor once admitted the furnace, unknown to my youth and my progenitors. I always was a natural tory, and in England (barring Dizzy) should be a staunch one. I would not give up a thing that had roots to it, though it might suck up its food from graveyards. Good-by. God bless you! . . . .

TO T. S. PERRY

Elmwood, March 2, 1875.

My dear Perry,—I don't believe I ever wrote a line for the *Harvardiana* of 1836–37. I certainly did not write the poem you mention, and doubt if I ever saw it, for I was not a subscriber. For 1837–38 I was one of the editors, and scribbled some wretched stuff, which I hope you will be too charitable to exhume. I was in my nineteenth year, but younger and greener than most boys are at that age. In short, I was as great an ass as ever brayed and thought it singing.

I believe our volume was the worst of the lot, for nobody took much interest in it, and the editing was from hand to mouth. N. Hale, Jr., did the cleverest things in it, as indeed he was perhaps the cleverest man in the class.

I hope to see you before long, but have promised some copy for the *North American Review* for Wednesday and shall have to keep abreast of the press. Authorship is a wretched business, after all. . . .

TO W. D. HOWELLS

Elmwood, March 21, 1875.

Dear Howells,—There was one verse in the "Border" sonnet which, when I came to copy it, worried me with its lack of just what I wanted. Only *one?* you will say. Yes, all ; but never mind—this one *most*. Instead of "Where the shy ballad could its leaves unfold," read "dared its blooms." I had liefer "cup" —but cup is already metaphoric when applied to flowers, and Bottom the Weaver would be sure to ask in one of the many journals he edits—"How unfold a cup? Does he mean one of those pocket drinking-cups—leathern inconveniencies that always *stick* when you try to unfold 'em?" Damn Bottom! We ought not to think of him, but then the Public is made up of him, and I wish him to know that I was thinking of a flower. Besides, the sonnet is, more than any other kind of verse, a deliberate composition, and "susceptible of a high polish," as the dendrologists say of the woods of certain trees. Or shall we say "grew in secret bold"? I write both on the opposite leaf, that you may choose one to paste over and not get the credit of tinkering my rhymes.

Yours always,

J. R. L.

dared its blooms
grew in secret bold.

Perhaps, after all, it is the buzzing of that *b* in blooms

and bold, answering his brother *b* in ballads, that
b-witched me, and merely changing "could" to "dared"
is all that is wanted.

The sentiment of this sonnet pleases me.

TO MRS. ———

Elmwood, June 3, 1875.

. . . An author who was not pleased with the friendly warmth of a letter like yours must be more super-
human than I can pretend to be. I *am* pleased, and
I thank you very cordially for this proof that I have
been of some use in the world.

Your list is nearly complete, and I can make it so
as to the *names*, though I cannot furnish you with the
books. My first publication was a small volume of
poems ("A Year's Life"), printed in my twenty-first
year and long out of print. In 1844 I printed a prose
volume of "Conversations on Some of Our Old Poets."
They were mainly written three years before, and are
now also these many years out of print. I have lately
been urged to reprint them and possibly may, though
they are naturally somewhat immature. There is a
second series of "Biglow Papers" (and in my opinion
the best), prefaced by an essay which, I think, might
interest you. In the *North American Review* (some
time in 1872, I believe) I printed an essay on Dante
which contained the results, at least, of assiduous study.
In the April number of this year is an article on Spenser. These would be in the library of the Peabody
Institute probably. In the "Diamond" edition of my
poems there are a few verses added to the "Cathedral"

—perhaps some others, though I am not sure. I think
your list is otherwise complete. If not, I shall be
obliged to you if you will allow me to send you any
that may be lacking. In the *Atlantic Monthly* for
May, 1874, is an "Elegy on Agassiz" which, I suspect,
is among my best verse. In the *Atlantic* for August,
1870, is an introduction by me to some "Extracts from
the Journal of a Virginian travelling in New England."
Towards the end of it is a passage the sentiment of
which will perhaps please you. At any rate, it has
always been my own way of thinking on that point. I
was roundly abused in some of the newspapers at the
time, but I am happy in believing that the whole North
is now come round to where I then stood.

But pardon me, I am getting garrulous without the
excuse of senility. One is liable to these pitfalls when
rapt in the contemplation of that precious being, who,
in proportion as he interests us, is apt to be a bore to
the rest of mankind. Be so good as to let me know
what volumes you want, and they shall be sent to your
address. . . .

TO THE SAME

Elmwood, June 15, 1875.

. . . I meant that so important a package as that
which you acknowledged in such friendly terms should
have been heralded by a letter in answer to yours. I
meant to have torn out all the prints in the book
(which are simply disgusting—especially that of *Zekle
and Huldy*), but I forgot it. I divine in your note of
this morning a certain sensitiveness about its unan-

swered forerunner (as if you had said too much) which
quite justifies me in the pleasure I had when I read it.
Mrs. Lowell liked it as much as I did. I am quite sure
there can be no sweeter and kindlier feeling than having been something to somebody in this purely disem-
bodied way.   Only the Somebody must be of the right
kind. You must pardon me the unseemly confidence,
but I receive a great many letters from women (I suppose all poets do), and hardly ever one that I can answer. They are commonly like those of Mrs. Tilton,
some of which I have seen in the newspapers, a kind
of stuff that makes sensible women doubt the capacity
of their sex for any political association with men.   I
need not say that yours was of quite another com-
plexion, and such as an honest man could be heartily
pleased with.   So far from tickling my vanity, it added
to my self-distrust, and made me wonder how I had deserved so grateful a congratulation.   It did me real good
in quickening my feeling of responsibility to myself,
while it encouraged me to think that I had sometimes
cast my bread upon waters which did not steadily ebb
towards oblivion.

I fear the volume I sent you will try your eyes sadly, but it is the most complete edition of what I have
written in verse. I hope you will permit me to send
you also my two volumes of prose, to which a third
will be added next autumn. The article on Spenser
has been wholly rewritten since you heard it, and con-
tains only a passage or two here and there which were
in the lecture.

I should have answered your letter at once, but I am

really a very busy man, and (except in verse) a much slower writer than when I was younger. It is harder to weigh anchor than it used to be, and there is no Lapland witch to sell a fair wind to an old fellow of fifty-six. You shall let me count you for one, nevertheless, for I felt my sails strain at the yards in the friendly breath of your sympathy.

Expect another package from me ere long, but do not feel that I shall be forever bombarding you with my books. I doubt if I shall ever lecture in Baltimore (or anywhere else again)—for I like it not. I am sure I should have done it with more spirit before, had I known how sympathetic an auditor I had. . . .

TO THE SAME

Elmwood, July 6, 1875.

. . . My having been very busy must plead my pardon (for I assume it in advance) for not answering your last letter sooner. We, too, here in my birthplace, having found out that something happened here a hundred years ago, must have our centennial, and, since my friend and townsman Dr. Holmes couldn't be had, I felt bound to do the poetry for the day. We have still standing the elm under which Washington took command of the *American* (till then *provincial*) army, and under which also Whitefield had preached some thirty years before. I took advantage of the occasion to hold out a hand of kindly reconciliation to Virginia. I could do it with the profounder feeling, that no family lost more than mine by the civil war. Three neph-

ews (the hope of our race) were killed in one or other
of the Virginia battles, and three cousins on other of
those bloody fields. The poem will be printed in the
Atlantic for August, and will, I hope and believe, do
good.

So you are in Alexandria, a town of which I have
very pleasant memories, now fifty years old. I spent
some days in the old Carroll house there with the Car-
rolls, who are connections of mine by marriage. They
are all gone, but I hope the dear old house is still
standing. Pray go and see it and tell me if the river
behind it be as pretty, and the English walnuts in front
as fine as I remember. The house, I think, must be
large, for (unless it loom through the haze of memory)
it was larger than that in which I was born and still
live, and that is not a small one.

I suppose it must have been the extreme solitude in
which I grew up, and my consequent unconsciousness
of any public, that made me so frankly communica-
tive. Poets get their sorrows and passions out of themselves by carving the lava (grown cold) into pretty
forms. I should not be so indiscreet now, I suppose,
and yet a living verse can only be made of a living
experience—and that our own. One of my most personal poems, " After the Burial," has roused strange
echoes in men who assured me they were generally insensible to poetry. After all, the only stuff a solitary
man has to spin is himself.

I am sorry you should write in so desponding a tone
of yourself. Surely at your age life (imposture as it
often is) has many satisfactions left. Dame Life, to

be sure, keeps a gambling-table; but even if we have played for a great stake and lost, we must recollect that she is always ready to lend us what we need for another chance. Literature and work are the exhaustless *solamina vitae*, and if you find so much pleasure in what I have done (who am but third-rate compared with the masters) you have yet a great deal to enjoy.

Do not let your friendly enthusiasm (a very great pleasure to me personally) lead you to exaggerate my merits, or overlook my defects. I think more might have been made of me if I could have given my whole life to poetry, for it is an art as well as a gift, but you must try to see me as I am.

I have ordered my two books to be sent to your Alexandria address, and enclose two slips of paper with my good wishes on them that you may paste them into the volumes to remind you whence they came. I should have sent them sooner, but besides my Centennial task, I had to preside over our Commencement dinner, a service that seems simple enough, but which worries a shy man like myself to a degree that would make you laugh. . . .

TO JOHN W. FIELD

Elmwood, July 14, 1875.

. . . I am sitting now (with Fanny sewing beside me) on our new veranda, which we built last fall on the north side of the house, and find inexpugnably delightful. We are having a *green* summer this year, and to-day is rather like June than July, with a sea-breeze (you call it east wind, I believe, in Europe) winnowing the heat away, and trees and clouds as they only are at home where they are old friends. The catalpa is just coming into blossom under my eyes, and the chestnut hard by is hoary with blossoms, making it look all the younger, like powder on the head of a girl of eighteen. A quail is calling "Bob White" over in the field, butterflies are shimmering over Fanny's flowers, robins are singing with all their might, and there will come a humming-bird before long. I see the masts in the river and the spires in the town, and whatever noise of traffic comes to me now and then from the road but emphasizes the feeling of seclusion. What is your lake of Geneva to this? . . .

TO C. E. NORTON

Elmwood, Aug. 3, 1875.

. . . It is now thirty-seven years since I first knew him [Emerson], and he showed me some of his walks in Concord, especially, I remember, "the Cliff." And Edmund Quincy is sixty-eight! How we move on, without show of motion, like shadows of trees in the sun! But one's horizon widens, thank God! I often wonder over this unconscious broadening of the mind. We absorb experience at all our pores till by and by our whole substance is changed and renewed. But in order to be wise we must be able to enter again into the consciousness of these modes of being we have sloughed off.

> All that I was I am, and all the more
> For being other than I was before;
> And what I spent is still my best of store. . . .

TO MRS. ———

Elmwood, Aug. 5, 1875.

. . . Your letter gave me a great deal of pleasure, for surely there can be no purer satisfaction than that of feeling that you are making another person happier; and, though I may think that you exaggerate my absolute merits, yet I can gratefully accept your statement of them so far as regards yourself without abatement. It is something to be that to somebody which in the day of inexperience one dreamed of being to all. It is, I assure you, a great encouragement to me, and of the kind that suits my temper best, for it will be a spur in the flank of my endeavor to deserve such gratitude. I have always had a profound contempt for what is called Public Opinion (that is, the judgment of the incapable Many as compared with that of the discerning Few), and a rooted dislike of notoriety, which, in this age of newspapers, is our German - silver substitute for real plate, and "in all respects as good as" the true thing— except that it isn't the true thing. But I am not insensible to such hearty sympathy as yours, and at fifty-six, after a life honestly devoted to what I conceived the true aims of literature, I may confess without vanity that it is very sweet to encounter a reader like you. None of my critics, I am sure, can be more keenly aware than I of my manifold shortcomings, but I think I have done some things well, and I was pleased to find that you had read my essay on Dryden oftener than any other, for I believe it to be my best. This encouragement of yours has been a real help to me, for

II.—10

it has turned the scale of my decision not to be content with a critique of Wordsworth written twenty years ago (and which the hot weather had almost persuaded me to print with a little cobbling), but to rewrite it. So, if I make anything of it, I shall owe it to you in good measure, and shall feel so much the *less* in your debt—that does not strike you as inscrutable paradox, does it ?

Let me counsel you to read a little German every day, and you will be surprised to find how soon it grows easy to you. Insist on knowing the exact meaning of every sentence, and use your grammar for that only. In this way you will insensibly grow familiar with the grammatical construction. I think a great deal time is wasted in preliminary studies of grammar. Tumble into deep waters at once if you would learn to swim. German is the *open sesame* to a large culture, for it is the language of all others most pliable for the translation of other tongues, and everything has been rendered into it.

I am glad you have mountains to look out upon. My view is more limited, but is very dear to me, for it is what my eyes first looked on, and I trust will look on last. A group of tall pines planted by my father, and my lifelong friends, murmurs to [me] as I write with messages out of the past and mysterious premonitions of the future. My wife's flowers recall her sweetly to me in her absence from home, and the leaves of her morning-glories that shelter the veranda where I sit whisper of her. A horse-chestnut, of which I planted the seed more than fifty years ago, lifts its huge stack

of shade before me and loves me with all its leaves. I
should be as happy as a humming-bird were I not
printing another volume of essays. Everything I do
seems so poor to me when I see it in print. But courage! there is a kindly reader in Baltimore who will find
out some good in the book and thank me for it more
than I deserve.

> Not what we did, but what we meant to do,
>   Lay in your scales, just Fates, and so decide.
> Alas, even then how much remains to rue!
>   How little for our solace or our pride!
>
> They frown and answer: "Only what is done
>   We make account of; dreams may not be weighed,
> Nor with their down-shod feet the race is run,
>   And reached at last the laurel's sacred shade."

I read your essay on the weather with much interest.
Living in the country all my life, I am a good weather-
caster, and was pleased to find that I had discovered
by my own observation that upper current you speak
of. Thirty-four years ago, when you were a little girl, I
was writing,

> "Who heeds not how the lower gusts are working,
>   Knowing that one sure wind blows on above";

and had observed that its current was from north-west
to south-east, though I did not know why till you told
me. . . .

P. S. I give you our latest weather-news. A fine
thunder-storm is limbering up its guns in the south-
west. . . .

TO THE SAME

Elmwood, Sept. 21, 1875.

. . . That I did not sooner answer your letter, was simply because for the last six weeks I have been rather unwell. I am now better, and surely a man of fifty-six who had never taken a pill till now has no great reason to repine. . . .

You ask me if I am an Episcopalian. No, though I prefer the service of the Church of England, and attend it from time to time. But I am not much of a church-goer, because I so seldom find any preaching that does not make me impatient and do me more harm than good. I confess to a strong lurch towards Calvinism (in some of its doctrines) that strengthens as I grow older. Perhaps it may be some consolation to you that my mother was born and bred an Episcopalian. . . .

My essay on Wordsworth has been interrupted by my illness, which in some way confused my head so that I could not get on with it. I fear the essay when finished will show some marks of it. The mere physical exertion of writing makes me impatient. But after all, work of one kind or another is the only tonic for mind or character; . . . it makes me blush to think how dependent I am upon moods for the power to write with any hope of pleasing myself. I am just enough independent of literature as a profession to encourage this nicety (perhaps I should call it weakness) in me. Still I have the satisfaction of thinking that I have often worked hard when it was against the grain.

While I was most unwell, I could not find any reading that would seclude me from myself till one day I
bethought me of Calderon. I took down a volume of
his plays, and in half an hour was completely absorbed.
He is surely one of the most marvellous of poets. I
have recorded my debt to him in a poem, " The Nightingale in the Study." It is greater now, and I confess
that the power of his charm interested me enough to
make me think it might also interest you. . . .

TO C. E. NORTON

Elmwood, Sept. 23, 1875.

. . . For about a week I could read nothing but Calderon — a continual delight, like walking in a wood
where there is a general sameness in the scenery and
yet a constant vicissitude of light and shade, an endless
variety of growth. He is certainly the most *delightful*
of poets. Such fertility, such a gilding of the surfaces
of things with fancy, or infusion of them with the more
potent fires of imagination, such lightsomeness of humor! Even his tragedies somehow are not tragic to
me, though terrible enough sometimes, for everybody
has such a talent for being consoled, and that out of
hand. Life with him is too short and too uncertain for
sorrow to last longer than to the end of the scene, if
so long. As Ate makes her exit she hands her torch
to Hymen, who dances in brandishing it with an *Io !*
The passions (some of the most unchristian of 'em) are
made religious duties, which once fulfilled, you begin
life anew with a clear conscience. . . .

TO R. S. CHILTON

Elmwood, Oct. 16, 1875.

Dear Sir,—I *thought* I had answered your letter long ago as I ought, for I was much obliged to you for your kind remembrance of me and for the photograph.   But I was much worried during the spring and early summer by Centennials and things, and a heap of letters gathered ere I was aware under my bronze hen, till she looks as if [she had] been laying them ever since, and were now brooding on them with a fiendish hope of hatching out a clutch that shall hereafter pair and multiply.

I am glad you like my "Great Elm" poem.   Occasional verses are always risky, and Centennials most of all, as being expected to have in them the pith and marrow of a hundred years.   Then, too, in composing one is confronted with his audience, which he cannot help measuring by the dullest of his fellow-citizens, and this is far from inspiring.   However, I seem to have escaped falling flat and shaming my worshippers — which was more than I could hope.   The Concord poem was an improvisation written in the two days before the celebration, but the Cambridge one was composed amid all kinds of alien distractions.

Do you remember showing me, in Page's studio, more than thirty years ago, a pair of sleeve-buttons of Burns's?   I hope you have them still.   I have had a kind of poem about them buzzing in my head ever since.   It is better there than it would be if I could open the window and chase it out of doors.*

* One of these sleeve-buttons was afterwards given to Lowell; it is now in the Cabinet of the Library of Harvard University.

I suppose you are a gray old boy by this time. I am just beginning to grizzle with the first hoar-frost. I have two grandsons, children of my only daughter and surviving child, fine boys both of them. They make me younger, I think.

I enclose a photograph taken two years ago in Rome by an amateur. It is, I believe, a tolerable *dead* likeness, and may serve to recall me to your memory. I am printing a new volume of essays, my work on which was broken off by an illness, the first (except gout) I ever had. But I am now for a few days mending rapidly. It was *liver*, and upset me utterly.

With all kindly remembrance,

Cordially yours,

J. R. LOWELL.

TO MRS. ————

Elmwood, Nov. 20, 1875.

The thought of your so long unanswered letter has been giving my conscience an unpleasant twinge for some time, but I anodyned it with the assurance that you would be too kind to misinterpret my silence. The truth is that I have been fussing over the volume I am printing, and fussing, too, without much progress, for my wits are clogged by not being yet quite recovered from my late illness. But I hope to be rid of my task (after a fashion) in a few days now. The book will contain essays on Dante, Spenser, Wordsworth, and shorter ones on Milton (criticism of an edition, rather than of the poet) and Keats.

. . . I am often struck with the fact that people of a

sceptical turn, and who look upon all traditional faiths as broken reeds, are sure to lay hold of some private bulrush of credulity and fancy it an oak. For myself, I look upon a belief as none the worse but rather the better for being hereditary, prizing as I do whatever helps to give continuity to the being and doing of man, and an accumulated force to his character.

As for my coming to Baltimore, I fear it is out of the question, at least for the present. I have classes at the College three times a week and no long vacation till summer. At Christmas I always like to be by my own fireside, where a huge Yule-log always blazes. This year I shall be quite patriarchal, for my daughter with her husband and two boys will be with us. There is something wonderful in being a grandfather. It gives one a sense of almost tenderer paternity without the responsibilities that commonly wait upon it. . . .

TO R. W. GILDER

Elmwood, Dec. 15, 1875.

. . . As the sight of you four young lovers under my friend Norton's familiar pines transported me for a moment to a more innocent garden of Boccaccio, and prettily renewed for me my own youth and forward-looking days, so your little book has given me a pleasure the same in kind though more poignant in degree. I cannot praise it better than in saying that as I read I kept murmuring to myself, "It dallies with the innocence of love like the old age." Here and there I might shake my head (gray hairs, you know, have a trick of setting our heads ashake), but nearly all I liked and liked thoroughly. Your book is too subtle for the many, but the sense of lovers is finer and they will find it out. You will be the harmless Galeotto between many a dumb passion and itself.

But I know you are grumbling to yourself, "Why does he praise my verses and say nothing of *her* illustrations?" I could not help liking their grace and fancy. They seemed to me like flowers a lover had given his mistress and begged again, after she had worn them in her stomacher till they had caught some enchantment from their happy destiny. I thank you both for a great deal of pure pleasure that will last—as only pure pleasures do.

This is the first day I have had free of proof-sheets, or I should have written sooner. Cabbage-leaves and rose-leaves do not sort well together. Recall me, I pray you, to Mrs. Gilder's memory, and believe me

Very thankfully yours,
J. R. LOWELL.

TO MRS. ———

Elmwood, Dec. 25, 1875.

. . . I am reading and commenting " Don Quixote " to the students, and in order to do it intelligently have been making a careful study of it over again. I am not sorry, for it has been a long pleasure, and when one is obliged to read with a microscope, one sees many things that would otherwise escape him. It is, indeed, a wonderful book, as full of good sense and good feeling as of profound, and therefore imperishable, humor.

I had hoped before this to have sent you my new book, but it hung long on my hands and is not yet out. You are so partial (one of the many excellent qualities in your sex) that I dare say you may not find it so tedious as it has been to me. But if you should be bored by it, I shall like you none the less.

Your industry amazes me, who am rather an unwilling writer, though I am one of the last (I fear) of the great readers. If I were to tell how many hours a day I have studied, nobody would believe me except you. And the pitiful part of it is, that just when we are wise enough to profit by our accumulations our memory grows blurred, like the pencil entries in a note-book carried long in the pocket.

It is a gloomy Christmas day. Last night it snowed nobly for an hour or two and then turned to rain, and to-day is sullen with its disappointment. It is drizzling and freezing as it falls, and though the trees will look very pretty to-morrow if the sun shine, I never quite like it, because the trees always suffer, and I feel for them as my oldest friends.

I had expected my two grandsons to dinner, but the weather will not let them run the risk, so I am to have my old friend Mr. John Holmes (the best and most delightful of men), and a student whom I found to be without any chance at other than a dinner in Commons. . . .

TO THE SAME

Elmwood, Jan. 17, 1876.

. . . I sent you day before yesterday my new book,

and that copy was the first I sent to any one, for I thought your partiality would perhaps find more pleasure in it than the rest of the world. I took such a disgust at it while it was passing through the press that I have not ventured to look into it since it was published. Yet, though I could not (muddle-headed as I was all summer with illness) give it the order and proportion that I would, I think you will find something in it to like.

I go on in my usual routine, only varied by reading and commenting "Don Quixote" on Thursday evenings. An audience is apt to set me at cross-purposes with myself, but I am told that I give pleasure. . . .

TO JOEL BENTON

Elmwood, Jan. 19, 1876.*

Dear Sir,—I thank you for the manly way in which you put yourself at my side when I had fallen among

* This letter was printed, with a Note by Mr. Benton, in the *Century* magazine for November, 1891. The following is a portion of Mr. Benton's Note:

"On Mr. Lowell's return from Europe in 1875 he wrote two brief poems for the *Nation*, which were entitled respectively 'The World's Fair, 1876,' and 'Tempora Mutantur.' In these he described certain dangerous symptoms of the body politic. . . . The following lines are a fair sample of the tone and direction of the poems. Mr. Lowell, speaking for Brother Jonathan, recommends the exhibition of some of our political inventions of that day.

"'Show 'em your Civil Service, and explain
How all men's loss is everybody's gain;
Show your new patent to increase your rents
By paying quarters for collecting cents;
Show your short cut to cure financial ills
By making paper-collars current bills;
Show your new bleaching-process, cheap and brief,
To wit: a jury chosen by the thief;

thieves, still more for the pithy and well-considered
words with which you confirm and maintain my side of
the quarrel. At my time of life one is not apt to vex

Show your State legislatures; show your Rings;
And challenge Europe to produce such things
As high officials sitting half in sight
To share the plunder and to fix things right;
If that don't fetch her, why, you only need
To show your latest style in martyrs—Tweed:
She'll find it hard to hide her spiteful tears
At such advance in one poor hundred years.'

" In ' Tempora Mutantur' occur these lines:

"' A hundred years ago,
If men were knaves, why, people called them so,
And crime could see the prison-portal bend
Its brow severe at no long vista's end;
In those days for plain things plain words would serve;
Men had not learned to admire the graceful swerve
Wherewith the Æsthetic Nature's genial mood
Makes public duty slope to private good.

.   .   .   .   .   .

But now that " Statesmanship " is just a way
To dodge the primal curse and make it pay,
Since Office means a kind of patent drill
To force an entrance to the Nation's till,
And peculation something rather less
Risky than if you spelt it with an s;

.   .   .   .   .   .

With generous curve we draw the moral line:
Our swindlers are permitted to resign;
Their guilt is wrapped in deferential names,
And twenty sympathize for one that blames.

.   .   .   .   .   .

The public servant who has stolen or lied,
If called on, may resign with honest pride:
As unjust favor put him in, why doubt
Disfavor as unjust has turned him out?
Even if indicted, what is that but fudge
To him who counted-in the elective judge?
Whitewashed, he quits the politician's strife,
At ease in mind, with pockets filled for life.'

"These caustic lines awakened resentment. A large proportion of the press (and particularly that part of it which was of his

his soul at any criticism, but I confess that in this case I was more than annoyed, I was even saddened. For what was said was so childish and showed such shallowness, such levity, and such dulness of apprehension both in politics and morals on the part of those who claim to direct public opinion (as, alas! they too often do) as to confirm me in my gravest apprehensions. I believe "The World's Fair" gave the greatest offence. They had not even the wit to see that I put my sarcasm into the mouth of Brother Jonathan, thereby implying and meaning to imply that the common-sense of my countrymen was awakening to the facts, and that *therefore* things were perhaps not so desperate as they seemed.

I had just come home from a two years' stay in Europe, so it was discovered that I had been corrupted by association with foreign aristocracies! I need not say to you that the society I frequented in Europe was what it is at home—that of my wife, my studies, and the best nature and art within my reach. But I confess that I was embittered by my experience. Wherever I

own political faith) pursued him with no polite epithets, and with not a little persistence. It was charged that he was no true American ; that he was, in fact, a snob; that he had elbowed against dukes and lords so much and so long that he could not any longer tolerate Democracy. And for many weeks this and other equally puerile nonsense went on unrebuked.

"It occurred to me at last to say what was obvious, and record my sympathy with Mr. Lowell's position. That his character and motives were above all need of defence I knew, but such a shocking perversion of his ideas and intentions was altogether too flagrant to pass unnoticed. I therefore took up the cudgels for what seemed to me to be true ; and, under the title of 'Mr. Lowell's Recent Political Verse,' volunteered, in the *Christian Union* of December 15, 1875, a defence of his friendly chidings."

went I was put on the defensive. Whatever extracts
I saw from American papers told of some new fraud
or defalcation, public or private. It was sixteen years
since my last visit abroad, and I found a very striking
change in the feeling towards America and Americans.
An Englishman was everywhere treated with a certain
deference: Americans were at best tolerated. The example of America was everywhere urged in France as an
argument against republican forms of government. It
was fruitless to say that the people were still sound when
the Body Politic which draws its life from them showed
such blotches and sores. I came home, and instead of
wrath at such abominations, I found banter. I was profoundly shocked, for I had received my earliest impressions in a community the most virtuous, I believe, that
ever existed. . . . On my return I found that community struggling half hopelessly to prevent General Butler
from being put in its highest office against the will of all
its best citizens. I found Boutwell, one of its senators, a chief obstacle to Civil-Service reform (our main
hope). . . . I saw Banks returned by a larger majority
than any other member of the lower house. . . . In the
Commonwealth that built the first free school and the
first college, I heard culture openly derided. I suppose
I like to be liked as well as other men. Certainly I
would rather be left to my studies than meddle with
politics. But I had attained to some consideration, and
my duty was plain. I wrote what I did in the plainest
way, that he who ran might read, and that I hit the
mark I aimed at is proved by the attacks against which
you so generously defend me. These fellows have no

notion what love of country means. It is in my very
blood and bones. If I am not an American, who ever
was?

I am no pessimist, nor ever was, . . . but is not the
Beecher horror disheartening? Is not Delano discour-
aging? and Babcock atop of him? . . . What fills me
with doubt and dismay is the degradation of the moral
tone. Is it or is it not a result of Democracy? Is ours
a "government of the people by the people for the
people," or a Kakistocracy rather, for the benefit of
knaves at the cost of fools? Democracy is, after all,
nothing more than an experiment like another, and I
know only one way of judging it—by its results. Democracy in itself is no more sacred than monarchy. It
is Man who is sacred; it is his duties and opportunities,
not his rights, that nowadays need reinforcement. It
is honor, justice, culture, that make liberty invaluable,
else worse than worthless if it mean only freedom to be
base and brutal. As things have been going lately, it
would surprise no one if the officers who had Tweed in
charge should demand a reward for their connivance in
the evasion of that popular hero. I am old enough to
remember many things, and what I remember I medi-
tate upon. My opinions do not live from hand to
mouth. And so long as I live I will be no writer of
birthday odes to King Demos any more than I would
be to King Log, nor shall I think *our* cant any more
sacred than any other. Let us all work together (and
the task will need us all) to make Democracy possible.
It certainly is no invention to go of itself any more than
the perpetual motion.

Forgive me for this long letter of justification, which I am willing to write for your friendly eye, though I should scorn to make any public defence. Let the tenor of my life and writings defend me.

Cordially yours,

J. R. LOWELL.

TO EDWARD P. BLISS

Elmwood, April 4, 1876.

Dear Sir,—Though I don't think the function you wish me to perform quite in my line, I am willing to do *anything* which may be thought helpful in a movement of which I heartily approve. I am not so hopeful, I confess, as I was thirty years ago; yet, if there be any hope, it is in getting independent thinkers to be independent voters.

Very truly yours,

J. R. LOWELL.*

* Mr. Bliss has favored me with the following statement, explanatory of the preceding letter: "In the spring of 1876 some young men in Cambridge were not contented with the tendencies in the Republican party. We had a meeting in one of the rooms in Stoughton Hall, and planned to call a larger meeting, inviting about sixty citizens, at which we could better determine how to help right our politics. I was directed to invite Professor Lowell to preside at the proposed meeting. I received from him the foregoing letter.

"At this meeting Mr. Lowell advised with us very seriously, and the result was that we organized a committee of forty, eight from each ward, to see that we had fair caucuses. At that time the Boston Custom-House officials were used to managing all our caucuses, and just then they wanted to secure delegates favorable to Mr. Blaine's nomination. Mr. Lowell was elected president of the whole committee. The caucuses in all wards were so well looked after by these amateurs in politics that anti-Blaine delegates were chosen, to the surprise of the Custom-House men. At Jamaica Plains there was a similar committee. We were in the same district then. Members of their committee arranged with some of us that at the district convention we

TO LESLIE STEPHEN

Elmwood, April 10, 1876.

. . . Last night I appeared in a new capacity as chairman of a political meeting, where I fear I made an ass of myself. It was got up by young men who wish to rouse people to their duty in attending caucuses and getting them out of the hands of professionals. I haven't much hope (one has rounded that cape by the time he is fifty), but am willing to try anything. We have got to work back from a democracy to our original institution as a republic again. Our present system has resulted in our being governed by a secret and irresponsible club called the United States Senate for their own private benefit. Our Republican newspapers seem to find a strange consolation in the vile character of the witnesses against our more illustrious swindlers; but how are we to get over the fact that, however rotten and perjured these rascals may be, they were all in the confidential employment of the very men who try to discredit them? I think the row is likely to do good, however, in getting us better candidates in the next presidential election, and waking everybody up to the screaming necessity of reform in our Civil Service. It doesn't cheer me much to be told that it was just as bad in England under Sir Robert Walpole. In the first place, it wasn't, and, in the second, suppose it was? . . .

would try to send as delegates to Cincinnati the presidents of the two committees, who were the Rev. Dr. James F. Clarke and Professor J. R. Lowell. We were successful. Mr. Lowell was a new personage in active politics, and as delegate and afterwards presidential elector drew special attention."

II.—11

TO MRS. ———

Elmwood, April 19, 1876.

. . . But I did not tell you the worst. Horace confesses that he was stout, or at any rate implies it. Thomson says plumply that he was *fat*—an odious word. I suppose Coleridge would have admitted a certain amiable rotundity of presence. Byron wrestled with increasing flesh, as it had been well for him to do against growing fleshliness. But such is the weakness of our poor human nature that never one of them could bring himself to the shameful confession that he had lost his *waist*. There is the tender spot, and I claim a certain amount of admiration when I admit that *mine* has been growing more and more obscure (like many a passage in Browning) for several years. Now, a waist is as important in a poet's economy as in a woman's. But this is too sad a topic. You see I disenchant you by installments—and, how shall I say it? I am writing at this moment with spectacles (not *nippers*, mind you, but the steel-bowed deformity which pale young parsons love) across my prosaic nose. It is horrible, but it is true. I have, to be sure, the saving grace of being still a little touchy about them, and have never yet allowed any of the servants to see me in my debasement. *Nippers* have still a pretension of foppishness about them, and he who is foppish has not yet abandoned the last stronghold of youth, or, if he has, he at least marches out with the honors of war. I have laid down my arms. That steel bow is Romance's Caudine Forks. I used to have the eye of a hawk, and a few days ago

I mistook a flight of snow-birds for English sparrows! Have you still the courage to come? If you have, we shall be all the gladder to see you, and I will make you welcome to whatever I have contrived to save from the wreck of myself. Age makes Robinson Crusoes of the best of us, and makes us ingenious in contrivances and substitutes, but what cunning expedient will ever replace youth? In one respect only I have lost nothing. I think I am as great a fool as ever, and that is no small comfort. I believe, too, that I still feel the blind motions of spring in my veins with the same sense of *prickle* as trees do, for I suppose their sense of April must be very much like ours when a limb that has been asleep, as we call it, is fumbling after its suspended sensation again.

Are you a stout walker? If you are, I will show you my oaks while you are here. If you are not, I will still contrive to make you acquainted with them in some more ignominious way. They will forgive you, I dare say, for the sake of so old a friend as I. Besides, they are no great pedestrians themselves unless, like Shelley's Appenine, they walk abroad in the storm. We haven't much to show here. We are a flat country, you know, but not without our charm, and I love Nature, I confess, not to be always on her high horse and with her tragic mask on. Bostonians generally (I am not a Bostonian) seem to have two notions of hospitality—a dinner with people you never saw before nor ever wish to see again, and a drive in Mount Auburn cemetery, where you will see the worst man can do in the way of disfiguring nature. Your memory of the dinner is expected to reconcile you to the prospect of the graveyard. But I am getting treasonable.

Now to business. You must let me know in good season when you are coming, because I wish to make sure of some pleasant people for you to meet. Don't come till May, if you can help it, for our spring is backward and we don't do ourselves justice yet. But come at any rate. . . .

TO H. W. LONGFELLOW

Elmwood, May 3, 1876.

Dear Longfellow,—Will you dine with me on Saturday at six? I have a Baltimore friend coming, and depend on you.

I had such a pleasure yesterday that I should like to share it with you to whom I owed it. J. R. Osgood & Co. sent me a copy of your Household Edition to show me what it was, as they propose one of me. I had been reading over with dismay my own poems to weed out the misprints, and was awfully disheartened to find how bad they (the poems) were. Then I took up your book to see what the type was, and before I knew it I had been reading two hours and more. I never wondered at your popularity, nor thought it wicked in you; but if I *had* wondered, I should no longer, for you sang me out of all my worries. To be sure they came back when I opened my own book again—but that was no fault of yours.

If not Saturday, will you say Sunday? My friend is a Mrs. ——, and a very nice person indeed.

Yours always,

J. R. L.

TO LESLIE STEPHEN

Elmwood, May 15, 1876.

. . . *Have* I read your book?* I wish you had read it so carefully, for then I should not have a string of *errata* to send you for your next edition, the first of them peculiarly exasperating, because it spoils one of Browne's most imaginative passages, a passage I never think of without a thrill. It is on page 40, where "dreams" has usurped the place of "drums." . . . I may be partial, though I don't think I am, and even were I, towards whom have I a better privilege of partiality than towards you? To be sure, I could not help being constantly reminded of you as I read; but that surely is a chief merit of the book, proving it to be distinctively yours and nobody's else. I *was* especially interested in Jonathan Edwards, with whom (except in his physical notions of hell) I have a great sympathy —a case of *reversion*, I suppose, to some Puritan ancestor. If he had only conceived of damnation as a spiritual state, the very horror of which consists (to our deeper apprehension) in its being delightful to who is in it, I could go along with him altogether. What you say of his isolation is particularly good, and applies to American literature more or less even yet. We lack the stimulus whether of rivalry or sympathy. I liked your estimate of Browne very much. It is very subtle and appreciative, though I think you misapprehend the scope of the "Pseudodoxia" a little. Browne was Montaigne's truest disciple, and his deference to certain

* "Hours in a Library."

superstitions is greatly analogous to old Michel's pil-
grimage to Loreto. He always assumes the air of a
believer the more devoutly when he is about to hint
something especially unorthodox. Always sceptical, he
makes us feel the absurdities of the vulgar faith by setting forth some monstrous deduction that may be drawn
from them. Take the passage you quote from the "Re-
ligio," on pages 23–24, for example. In the "Pseudodoxia" Browne is always scattering (as it seems to me)
the seeds of scepticism, though the bags that contain
them are all carefully labelled "Herb of Grace." But
I may be wrong, for I speak from a long-agone general
impression, not having studied Browne much for a good
many years. I was glad of your kind word for good
old Crabbe, which was very just and discriminating. I
thank you also for your *Rettung* (as Lessing would
have called it) of Horace Walpole. The "Hazlitt," too,
though you rate him higher than I should, strikes me
as very good. In the whole book there is a union of
impartial good sense and sensibility of appreciation
that is very rare in criticism. And then there are
charity and modesty. I read it straight through at a
sitting and wished there had been more, and not because it was yours, but because I was interested. But
because it was yours, I am heartily glad it is so good.
I am impatient for your other book.* It is on a
capital subject and I am sure it will be ably handled.

I have published another volume, and I ought long

* "English Thought in the Eighteenth Century."

ago to have sent you a copy, but I took a disgust at
it so soon as I saw it in print.   I was really ill all the
time it was going through the press, so that I sometimes could not even read a proof for weeks, and had
to put in at random some things I would rather have
left for a posthumous edition of my works (if I ever
have one), when people read with kindlier eyes.   But I
will post you a copy soon.

Thank you for the plan.*   I shall be able to fancy
you now very well in your new house, for I remember
all that neighborhood well, and it is already associated
with you, since I used to pass it in my way to South-
well Gardens.   I am glad to think that little Laura will
be so near a good playground and something like the
country.   I fear you will not have a study I shall like
so well as that *Stylites* one on the top of your other
house, which I know so thoroughly.   It was the one
place in the wilderness of London where I felt thoroughly at home.   I was somehow an American everywhere else, but there I was a friend, and so far, you
know, it was a foretaste of heaven.

I didn't mean any reproach (but then you wouldn't
have thought I did) in what I said about Providence,
whatever it was.   I don't meddle with what my friends
believe or reject, any more than I ask whether they
are rich or poor.   I love *them*.   I sometimes think
they will smile (as Dante makes St. Gregory) when
they open their eyes in the other world.   And so
doubtless shall I, for I have no Murray or Baedeker

* Of Mr. Stephen's new house, for which Lowell had asked.

for those parts. I don't think a view of the universe from the stocks of any creed a very satisfactory one. But I continue to shut my eyes resolutely in certain speculative directions, and am willing to find solace in certain intimations that seem to me from a region higher than my reason. When they tell me that I can't *know* certain things, I am apt to wonder how *they* can be sure of that, and whether there may not be things which they *can't* know. I went through my reaction so early and so violently that I have been settling backward towards equilibrium ever since. As I can't be certain, I won't be positive, and wouldn't drop some chapters of the Old Testament, even, for all the science that ever undertook to tell me what it doesn't know. They go about to prove to me from a lot of nasty savages that conscience is a purely artificial product, as if that wasn't the very wonder of it. What odds whether it is the thing or the aptitude that is innate? What race of beasts ever got one up in all their leisurely æons?

Our spring is very cold and backward, though peaches, pears, and cherries are grudgingly blooming. I hope yours is more generous, for I think May sovereign for an inward wound. I can't recollect whether you know the Gurneys, who are now in London. If not, I must have given them a letter. You will like them in every way. They are delighted with dear Old England.

Always affectionately yours,

J. R. Lowell.

TO MISS NORTON

Elmwood, July 3, 1876.

. . . What can I tell you about Cincinnati? The journey impressed me, as a journey in America always does, with the wonderful richness and comfort of the country, and with the distinctive Americanism that is moulding into one type of feature and habits so many races that had widely diverged from the same original stock. Is the West to reproduce the primitive Aryan who wandered out of the East so long ago? One gets also an impression of size which enables one to sympathize with his countrymen (as I love to do) in the mere bigness of the country. These immense spaces, tremulous with the young grain, trophies of individual, or at any rate of unorganized courage and energy, of the people and not of dynasties, were to me inexpressibly impressive and even touching. The whole landscape had a neighborly air, such as I feel in no other country. The men who have done and are doing these things know how things *should be* done, and will find some way, I am sure, of bringing the country back to business principles. It was very interesting, also, to meet men from Kansas and Nevada and California, to see how manly and intelligent they were, and especially what large heads they had. They had not the manners of Vere de Vere, perhaps, but they had an independence and self-respect which are the prime element of fine bearing. I think I never (not even in Germany) sat at meat with so many men who used their knives as shovels, nor with so many who were so quiet and self-restrained in their demeanor. The Westerners, especially, may be Grangers, or what you will (it won't be the first case in history where self-interest has blinded men to the rights of others—nor the last), but you feel that they have the unmistakable makings of *men* in them.   They were less sensitive to the offences of Blaine than I could have wished, but I suspect that few of our Boston men who have had to do with Western railways have been more scrupulous.   I rather think they set the example of tempting legislators with the hope of questionable gains.

I am glad you liked Stephen's article as well as I did.   It seems to me, on the whole, the best thing I have read about Macaulay, doing more justice than the rest to the essential manliness and Britishism of his character.   Morley's paper seemed to me altogether too *a priori* and Teutonically abstruse.   He was so profound that he dug under his subject rather than into it, and I confess the universe is so brutally indifferent to *us*, that I am not greatly interested in the discussion of any particular man's relation to it.   That very small arc of which the eye of man (however tall) can grasp is enough for me. . . .

TO MRS. ———

Elmwood, July 4, 1876.

. . . You must be beginning to think me the most inconstant of men to have left your last letter so long without an answer.   But the explanation of it is simple enough, though women, I believe, are so wise as never to be satisfied with an explanation, because the need of

one can never be explained.   I meant to have written
to you from Cincinnati, whither I went in the hope of
helping to get Mr. Bristow nominated as the Republican candidate.   There, I thought, I should have plenty
of spare time, and plenty of new and amusing things to
tell you about.   But I had no leisure, the weather was
stewing hot, and I spent all the intervals of business in
trying to make myself clean with a very stingy supply
of water, for the blacks of their coal-smoke stick faster
than the most scriptural brother.   I was wholly de-
moralized by the unwonted color of my finger-nails, and
kept my fists carefully doubled to hide them lest I
should be mistaken for a partisan of ———, the dirtiness
of whose hands seemed rather an argument in his favor
with many.   I had little hope before I went of Mr.
Bristow's nomination, but desired it greatly because he
had shown himself a practical reformer, and because I
believed that a Kentucky candidate might at least give
the starting-point for a party at the South whose line
of division should be other than sectional, and by which
the natural sympathy between reasonable and honest
men at the North and the South should have a fair
chance to reassert itself.   We failed, but at least succeeded in preventing the nomination of a man whose
success in the Convention (he would have been beaten
disastrously at the polls) would have been a lesson to
American youth that selfish partisanship is a set-off for
vulgarity of character and obtuseness of moral sense.
I am proud to say that it was New England that defeated the New England candidate.

I hope you are as far away from the noises of this

boisterous anniversary as I. I was asked to write an ode for the celebration at Taunton, where Mr. C. F. Adams is to deliver the oration. But the Muse was unwilling, and I would not condescend to the mechanical compromise of a hymn with verses set stiffly as pins in a paper, but, unlike them, of a non-conducting material. It is no use setting traps for inspiration till the right bait shall have been discovered. With the thermometer at 90° in the shade, I am, on the whole, glad I wasn't inspired.

Since you were here I have changed my quarters, and moved out of the library into the room in front of it, where a long window gives me more breeze, and where I shall have the morning sun in winter, which I crave more as I grow older. When you come again, I hope you will like me as well in my new refuge as in the old. But perhaps by this time my silence has vexed you enough to make you reconsider your good opinion of me altogether?

I am writing to cannon music, for the noon salutes are just booming in every direction, and with something of the effect of a general engagement. Women, I think, are quiet when they are happiest, and can stitch their superfluous exhilaration into a seam, but the coarser fibre of men demands an immense amount of noise to make it vibrate and convince them they are happy. Or is it that uproar deadens reflection, and that in the confusion they escape arrest by that consciousness of the futility of things in general which is so saddening? However it be, I am glad the nearest guns are a mile away from me. I remember how, fifty years ago to-day, I, perched in a great ox-heart cherry-tree, long ago turned to mould, saw my father come home with the news of John Adams's death.   I wish I could feel, as I did then, that we were a chosen people, with a still valid claim to divine interpositions.   It is from an opposite quarter that most of our providences seem to come now.   But those peaceful fields that rimmed the railway all the way to Cincinnati, trophies of honest toil, and somehow looking more neighborly than in other lands, were a great consolation and encouragement to me.   Here was a great gain to the sum of human happiness, at least, however it be with the higher and nobler things that make a country truly inhabitable.   Will they come in time, or is Democracy doomed by its very nature to a dead level of commonplace?   At any rate, our experiment of inoculation with freedom is to run its course through all Christendom, with what result the wisest cannot predict.   Will it only insure safety from the more dangerous disease of originality? . . .

TO THOMAS HUGHES

Elmwood, July 12, 1876.

Dear old Friend,— . . . I have taken my first practical dip into politics this summer, having been sent by my neighbors first to the State Convention and then to the National at Cincinnati.   I am glad I went, for I learned a great deal that may be of service to me hereafter.   You are wrong about Hayes; he was neither unknown nor even unexpected as a probable nominee.

He was not adopted as a compromise in any true sense of the word, but as an unimpeachably honest man, and the only one on whom we could unite to defeat Blaine, who had all the party machinery at his disposal. The nomination of the latter would have been a national calamity—the most costly tub of whitewash yet heard of. For, really, a large part of the feeling in his favor was an honest (though mistaken) feeling of indignation at a partisan persecution, for such he had cunningly contrived to make the inquiry into his stock-jobbing proceedings appear. His nomination might have done good in one way—by leading to the formation of a new party based simply on reform. Such a party would have been certainly formed, and I should not have regretted it, for I very much doubt the possibility of purifying either of the old ones from within. There is very little to choose between them; though, so far as the South is concerned, I rather sympathize with the Democrats. The whole condition of things at the South is shameful, and I am ready for a movement now to emancipate the whites. No doubt the government is bound to protect the misintelligence of the blacks, but surely not at the expense of the intelligence of the men of our own blood. The South, on the whole, has behaved better than I expected, but our extremists expect them to like being told once a week that they have been *licked*. The war was fought through for nationality; for that and nothing more. That was both the ostensible and the real motive. Emancipation was a very welcome incident of the war, and nothing more.

Ever since '65 the Republican party has done its best (I mean its leaders, for selfish ends) to make our victory nugatory, so far as Reunion was concerned. The people I believe to be perfectly sound, and as honest (if not more so) as any other on the earth. But it takes a great while for the people to have its way. There is a good deal of blundering at first, a good deal of righteous wrath that misses its mark, but in the long run we shall win.

I think the intelligence of the country is decidedly on the Republican side, and cannot quite get over my distrust of the Democracy, which is mainly to blame for our political corruption.

In England you are misled by your free-trade notions in your judgment of the two parties here. (I don't mean you personally.) Free trade has nothing to hope from either of them, and perhaps the most ardent free-traders are Republicans, but we shall have no free trade till our debt is cancelled.

Our real weak point is in Congress, and your zealous enlargers of the suffrage had better think twice. I think we shall gradually get better men, but it will be a slow business. I myself have been asked to stand in my district, but do not see my way clear to so very great a sacrifice. I am hopeful of purification, but not sanguine.

Emerson is well, but visibly aging. He was not at our Commencement this year, the first time I have ever missed him there. He is as sweetly high-minded as ever, and when one meets him the Fall of Adam seems a false report. Afterwards we feel of our throats, and are startled by the tell-tale lump there. John Holmes is well, and delightful as usual. He is lame again just now, but it does not make him blue as formerly. I wish we could have you here again. We have a new veranda on the north side, which is a great success. (I enclose a print.) I had hoped for you during the Centennial year. We are taking it gravely, I am glad to see, and rather incline to be thoughtful than bumptious. I wish your queen (or empress) would have had the grace to write a letter. It would have done good, and we would rather have had one from her than from all your Wilhelms and Vittorio Emanueles together. . . .

Sept. 24, 1876.

P. S. You will see by the date of my other sheet that it was written more than two months ago. I wrote that I should enclose a print, and found that the magazine containing it had been given away. So that very day I ordered another of our periodical-dealer (as we call a newsman here) and he promised to get one at once, adding that he wished for a copy himself also, as it contained an article on Cambridge. At intervals ever since I have asked for it and never got it, but am always told by the merchant of news that he wants one himself. It tickles me as one of the last samples to be found of a certain Constantinopolitan way of doing business which used to be characteristic of the Cambridge of my boyhood.

Politics have not changed much since I wrote—only the worst element of the Republican party has got hold of the canvass, and everything possible is done to stir

up the old passions of the war. Of course I with all
sensible men hate this, but our protest is drowned in
the drums and trumpets of a presidential election. On
the whole, I shall vote for Hayes, and the best judges
think his election the likelier of the two. But there
will be a strong reaction from the violences of the contest now going on, and Congress will be more in opposition with the executive than ever. The same thing
will happen if Tilden comes in, for the Democratic party
is very hungry for place, and their professions of reform
will be severely tested. Now, as the good men of both
parties are honest reformers, I think we shall gradually
get an independent party, and then the country will
divide on rational issues, such as currency and tariff.
Faith in democratical forms of government will be
painfully strained in many minds if Butler should carry
eastern Massachusetts, as he probably will. I shall still
think them, however, as nearly ideal as some other ways
of doing clumsily what might be done well. It will go
hard with me to vote against Mr. Adams here at home,*
and perhaps, if things go on from bad to worse, I sha'n't.
But I cannot easily bring myself to trust the Democrats.
His nomination has had one odd (and good) effect here
in dividing the Irish vote. The Fenians regard him as
an enemy of Ireland, because he did his duty as ambassador, so the Irish Democratic orators are laboring
to convince their countrymen that a man can't have
two countries at once, though most of 'em see nothing

* Mr. Charles F. Adams, late U. S. Minister at the Court of
St. James, was the candidate of the Democratic party for governor.

wonderful in Sir Boyle Roche's bird. If I ever get the
print I will send it, for we are rather proud of our new
veranda, which longingly awaits you. . . .

TO MISS NORTON

Elmwood, Aug. 6, 1876.

. . . You should see me in my new study, with the
arches wide open into the library, as we shall call it. . . .

> Now can I taste the pleasures of retreat;
> Days loitering idly with snow-silent feet,
> Truants of Time, to-morrow like to-day,
> That come unbought, and claimless glide away
> By shelves that sun them in the indulgent Past,
> Where Ill hath ceased or turned to song at last.

Tell Charles that these verses are adapted from a poem
I told him I was writing. And, lest I never finish them,
I will copy a bit or two more:

> Oh, as this pensive moonlight blurs my pines
> (Here as I sit and meditate these lines)
> To gray-green dreams of what they are by day,
> So would some light, not reason's clear-edged ray,
> Trance me in moonshine, as before the blight
> Of years had brought the fatal gift of sight
> That sees things as they are, or will be soon,
> In the frank prose of undissembling noon!
>
> *　*　*　*　*　*
>
> Are we not changed? Is this the Senate now
> Where Clay once flashed, and Webster's cloudy brow
> Brooded those bolts of thought that blazing flew,
> And whose long echoes all the horizon knew?

I think that will do for once. Tell Charles, also, that

copying the first passage brought back to my memory the inscription on a dial which I fished for vainly the other night. It is *Pereunt et imputantur*. The *Horas non numero nisi serenas* is epicurean, but this other is *gnomic*, and therefore more suitable to a sundial. . . .

By the way, don't translate *pereunt* (in the dial epigram) by *perish*. Any fool might do that. It has the literal meaning which we have lost. " They go by and are charged to our account," as I ought to know if anybody, for I have thrown away hours enough to have made a handsome reputation out of. I am an ass, but then I know it, and *that* kind (a rare species), though pastured on east wind and thistles like the rest, do yet wear their ears with a difference. . . .

TO W. D. HOWELLS

Elmwood, Aug. 9, 1876.

Dear Howells,—You are very kind to my verses, but I can stand it, especially as what you say applies to a much younger fellow than I, twenty years younger, in fact, and who had not yet been tripped up by a professor's gown. . . .

I have been trifling with foolish epigrams lately. Here is one I made last night as I lay awake:

A DIALOGUE.

" Jones owns a silver mine."   " Pray, who is Jones?
Don't vex my ears with horrors like *Jones owns !*"
"Why, Jones is Senator, and so he strives
To make us buy his ingots all our lives

At a stiff premium on the market price:
A silver currency would be so nice!"
"What's Jones's plan?"   "A coinage, to be sure,
To rise and fall with Wall Street's temperature.
You wish to treat the crowd: Your dollar shrinks
Undreamed percentums while they mix the drinks."
Jones' mine's quicksilver, then?"   "Your wit won't pass;
"His coin's mercurial, but his mine is brass.
Jones owns"—"Again! Your iteration's worse
Than the slow torture of an echo-verse.
I'll tell you one thing Jones won't own: that is,
That the cat hid beneath the meal is his."

You see I am getting old. The compliment I paid
you to-day is no sign of it, however. I had all your
books catalogued with my library to-day. "Howells,"
said I to the young man who is doing the work for me,
"is going to last. He knows how to write." If you
notice the poetry from the *Harvard Advocate*, pat him
on the back. His name is Woodberry, and his "Violet
Crown" is a far cry beyond anything else in the volume. I hope the country air is doing lots of good to
Mrs. Howells and the weans. As for you, you are already, like dear old Jemmy Thomson, more fat than
bard beseems, though God knows you don't dwell in
the Castle of Indolence. . . .

TO C. E. NORTON

Elmwood, Monday Night, Aug. 21, 1876.

. . . I received a deputation this evening to persuade
me to reconsider my refusal to stand for Congress. They
tell me I am the only candidate with whom the Republicans can carry the district, that they have thoroughly

canvassed it and are sure that I should be elected without the need of any effort, that no one else could get the nomination against Claflin, but that I should have it by acclamation. I confess that I was profoundly touched by this testimony of my neighbors, but did not yield. They strove to make me see it as my duty, but I cannot. I will confess to you that I was never so surprised in my life, for I had not looked on my candidacy as serious. The members of this delegation were not even known to me by sight — except one, whom I remembered at our ward caucus. As Sumner said at our club, "This is *history*, and you had better listen to it!" (He was talking of himself.) I compare myself (*facendo questo gran rifiuto*) to Cæsar and Cromwell on a like occasion. . . .

TO MISS NORTON

Elmwood, Oct. 2, 1876.

. . . I have been again urged to stand for Congress (only yesterday), and again wisely declined. I beat Cæsar and Cromwell and the other historical examples, who only put aside the offered crown thrice, and this is my half-dozenth self-denial. The truth is, and I have frankly told 'em so, that I should not make half so good a member as they think. They think not, but I *know* it.

Term has begun, and I think I shall enjoy my classes. I begin in a more cheerful mood than usual, though rather in the dumps about politics, which have taken a turn all through the canvass much to my distaste, and now all this end of the State seems likely to be given over, by bargain and sale, into the hands of the regular old set of corruptionists. Even in this district they mean to force on us as candidate for Congress the man who presided at a reception of Blaine the other night. I preserve my equanimity, but am losing my temper. . . .

. . . I trust your native air will set you on your feet again. There is nothing like it, I think, in spite of the strong taint of Butlerism just now. But think how many times the world has been ruined and got over it so bravely. I am more alarmed at what they say of the sun's cooling. It takes the very rowels from the spur of noble minds. For what is a beggarly twenty million of years? I lose all interest in literature. Let us write for immediate applause—and done with it. . . .

TO MRS. ———

Elmwood, Oct. 9, 1876.

Dear Mrs. ———,—I haven't been forgetting you all this while, but all kinds of preoccupations of one kind and another (including politics) have not conduced to the untrammelled mood of mind which is the main condition of agreeable letter-writing. I am worried about the turn the canvass has been taking, and while too full of traditional and well-founded doubts of the Democratic party to be a willing helper in the success of its candidates, an equal distrust of the present managers of the Republican party hinders me from giving any cordial support to that. Whichever way I look I see cause of reasonable anxiety, and since, as you know, I do not value even my own opinions till they are rooted in experience and have weathered the blasts of argument, I am slow in making up my mind. About one thing I am settled, and that is that the reviving of old animosities for a temporary purpose (and that, too, a selfish one), the doing evil that a problematical good may come of it, is nothing short of wicked. The good hoped for is questionable and at best temporary, while the harm is of the most far-reaching consequence. We are deliberately trying to make an Ireland of the South, by perpetuating misgovernment there. Scotland, instead of being as now quite as loyal as any part of Britain, might easily have been made what Ireland is by the same treatment. I don't know whether the Mr. Lamar whose speech I have read be the friend of whom I have heard you speak, but if so, I congratulate you in having at least one friend who is both an able man and a wise one, if indeed the one quality do not necessarily imply the other.

I think I wrote to you about my change of quarters. I am in the front room now, with a bright October sun shining in on me as I write, and I dare say it was the sense of cheerfulness that reminded me of you, for we found you all sunshine while you were with us. When the sun gives out (as you awful scientific people tell us it will one of these days) I shall turn to you for a spare pinch of warmth now and then—if the catastrophe take place in my time. . . .

TO R. W. GILDER

Elmwood, Nov. 29, 1876.

. . . I have read the review of " Deirdré " * you were

* " Deirdré," a poem by the late Dr. R. D. Joyce.

good enough to send me, and think it kindly and discriminating. I read the poem in manuscript, and recommended it for publication on the ground of the freshness and force which gave it a sincere originality, in spite of an obvious external likeness to Morris. Of course I never spoke of it as I hear I have been represented as speaking. At my age one has no more extravagant opinions —or keeps them for his own amusement.

Thank you for the kind things you say of my ode. I value highly the sympathy of one who is qualified to judge and who works in the same spirit in which I try to work, though in a different line. . . .

TO LESLIE STEPHEN

Elmwood, Dec. 4, 1876.

. . . I have received your book* and hasten to thank you for it—not, however, before reading it with the attention it deserves. I thank you also for the Crabbe, for which I must be indebted to somebody in good shillings and pence, but no bill came with it. Will you kindly find out for me what I owe and to whom? Your book interested me profoundly and instructed me as much as it interested. . . . Yet I was conscious of you (and this was very pleasant) all the while I read. Some of your *obiter dicta* tickled me immensely by their wit and keenness. How the deuce you read all those books and escaped to tell us of 'em is a conundrum I shall carry unsolved to my grave. I am very much in the state of mind of the Bretons who revolted against the

* " English Thought in the Eighteenth Century."

Revolutionary Government and wrote upon their banners, " Give us back our God!" I suppose I am an intuitionalist, and there I mean to stick. I accept the challenge of common-sense and claim to have another faculty, as I should insist that a peony was red, though twenty color-blind men denied it. Your book has fortified me, and one thing in it constantly touched me, namely, that, whatever your belief, and whatever proof you ask before believing, you show much tenderness for whatever is high-minded and sincere, even where you think it mistaken. About most things, I am happy to think, we are agreed. . . .

I sat down to write this letter in entire peace of mind, but had hardly begun it when in came a reporter to "interview" me as one of the presidential electors of Massachusetts, and at intervals since three others have presented themselves. There was a rumor, it seems, that I was going to vote for Tilden. But, in my own judgment, I have no choice, and am bound in honor to vote for Hayes, as the people who chose me expected me to do. They did not choose me because they had confidence in my judgment, but because they thought they knew what that judgment would be. If I had told them that I should vote for Tilden, they would never have nominated me. It is a plain question of trust. The provoking part of it is that I tried to escape nomination all I could, and only did not decline because I thought it would be making too much fuss over a trifle. . . .

VIII

1877–1880

VISIT TO BALTIMORE.—APPOINTED MINISTER TO SPAIN.—LIFE
IN MADRID.—JOURNEY IN SOUTHERN FRANCE.—VISIT TO
ATHENS AND CONSTANTINOPLE.—ILLNESS OF MRS. LOWELL.
—TRANSFERRED TO LONDON.

LETTERS TO MRS. ———, J. B. THAYER, C. E. NORTON, F. J. CHILD,
MISS NORTON, MRS. E. BURNETT, MISS GRACE NORTON, THOMAS
HUGHES, H. W. LONGFELLOW, GEORGE PUTNAM, J. W. FIELD,
MRS. W. E. DARWIN, LESLIE STEPHEN, R. W. GILDER.

TO MRS. ———

Elmwood, Jan. 14, 1877.

Dear Mrs. ———,—This morning I poured some ink
for the first time into your pretty inkstand, and, as in
duty bound, hansel it by writing to you. It has been
standing on the shelf of my secretary, its mouth wide
open with astonishment at my ingratitude in not writing to thank you, ever since it came. It needn't have
been so jealous though, for I have written to nobody
else meanwhile, and it should remember that I can at
any moment shut it up tight, deny it ink, pen, and
paper, and thus cut it off from all its friends. " Mon-
ster!" I seem to hear it say, "you would not surely
deny me the sad consolation of sending my love to Mrs.
——— and telling her how homesick I am? There are

all kinds of fine things in me, as good as were ever in
any inkstand that ever lived, if you had but the wit to
fish them out.   If I had stayed with my dear mistress
I should ere this have found a vent for my genius in a
score of pleasant ways, but with you I fear lest I go to
my grave an *encrier incompris !* "   " Well, well, so long
as you don't make me uneasy with your reproaches, I
shall be sure to treat you kindly for the sake of your
old mistress, . . . who is always contriving pleasant ways
of making her friends grateful." . . .

I hope you maintain your tranquillity in this ferment of politics.   I do, for, as I made up my mind deliberately, so I do not change it to please the first man I
meet.   As I consider the question of good government
and prosperity in the Southern States the most pressing
one, I voted for Mr. Hayes on the strength of his letter.   I think it would be better for North and South if
he were President.   He would carry with him the better elements of the Republican party, and whatever its
shortcomings (of which none is more bitterly conscious
than I), the moral force of the North and West is with
them and not with the Democrats.   Above all, if Mr.
Hayes should show a wise sympathy with the real
wants and rights of the Southern whites (as I believe
he would), it would be felt at the South to be a proof
that the whole country was inclined to do them justice.   From Mr. Tilden and the Democrats it would be
received as a matter of course.   You see what I mean?
Of course I am not one of those who would have Mr.
Hayes " counted in."

I shall have the pleasure of seeing you now in a few

weeks. We have decided that, on the whole, it is best
that Mrs. Lowell should not come with me. We both
regret it, but it is wise. Wisdom always has a savor
of regret in it ever since Eve's time. We have been
having a noble winter. The old fellow has been showing a little feebleness for a year or two, and we
thought he had abdicated. But now he has grasped
his icicle again and governs as well as reigns. The
world looks like a lamb in its white fleece, but some of
us know better.

Mrs. Lowell sends her love, and I wish you and yours
many happy returns of the New Year. Unhappily it is
generally the Old Year that comes back again. However, we all *play* it is the New, and that is something.
Good-by.

Affectionately yours,

J. R. Lowell.

TO JAMES B. THAYER

Elmwood, Jan. 14, 1877.

Dear Sir,—I am heartily thankful to you for your
very encouraging note. I write verses now with as
much inward delight as ever, but print them with less
confidence. For poetry should be a continuous and
controlling mood, the mind should be steeped in poetical associations, and the diction nourished on the purest
store of the Attic bee, and from all these my necessary
professional studies are alien. I think the "Old Elm"
the best of the three,* mainly because it was composed

* Three Memorial Poems : "Ode read at the One Hundredth

after my college duties were over, though even in that
I was distracted by the intervention of the Commencement dinner.

But what I wished to say a word to you about (since
you are so generous in your judgment) is the measures
I have chosen in these as well as the " Commemoration
Ode." I am induced to this by reading in an article on
Cowley copied into the *Living Age* from the *Cornhill*
(and a very good article too, in the main) the following
passage, "As lately as our own day" (*my* ear would
require " *So* lately as," by the way) " Mr. Lowell's ' Commemoration Ode' is a specimen of the formless poem
of unequal lines and broken stanzas supposed to be in
the manner of Pindar, but truly the descendant of our
royalist poet's ' majestick numbers.' " Now, whatever
my other shortcomings (and they are plenty, as none
knows better than I), want of reflection is not one of
them. The poems were all intended for public recitation. That was the first thing to be considered. I suppose my ear (from long and painful practice on Φ. B. K.
poems) has more technical experience in this than almost any. The least tedious measure is the rhymed
heroic, but this, too, palls unless relieved by passages of
wit or even mere fun. A long series of uniform stanzas
(I am always speaking of public recitation) with regu-
larly recurring rhymes produces somnolence among the
men and a desperate resort to their fans on the part

Anniversary of the Fight at Concord Bridge, April 19, 1775";
"Under the Old Elm," poem read at Cambridge on the hundredth anniversary of Washington's taking command of the
American army, July 3, 1775; an "Ode for the Fourth of July,
1876."

of the women. No method has yet been invented by which the train of thought or feeling can be shunted off from the epical to the lyrical track. My ears have been jolted often enough over the sleepers on such occasions to know that. I know *something* (of course an American can't know much) about Pindar. But *his* odes had the advantage of being chanted. Now, my problem was to contrive a measure which should not be tedious by uniformity, which should vary with varying moods, in which the transitions (including those of the voice) should be managed without jar. I at first thought of mixed rhymed and blank verses of unequal measures, like those in the choruses of "Samson Agonistes," which are in the main masterly. Of course, Milton *deliberately* departed from that stricter form of the Greek Chorus to which it was bound quite as much (I suspect) by the law of its musical accompaniment as by any sense of symmetry. I wrote some stanzas of the "Commemoration Ode" on this theory at first, leaving some verses without a rhyme to match. But my ear was better pleased when the rhyme, coming at a longer interval, as a far-off echo rather than instant reverberation, produced the same effect almost, and yet was grateful by unexpectedly recalling an association and faint reminiscence of consonance. I think I have succeeded pretty well, and if you try reading aloud I believe you would agree with me. The sentiment of the "Concord Ode" demanded a larger proportion of lyrical movements, of course, than the others. Harmony, without sacrifice of melody, was what I had mainly in view.

The *Cornhill* writer adds that "Keats, Shelley, and Swinburne, on the other hand, have restored to the ode its harmony and shapeliness." He and I have different notions of harmony. He evidently means uniformity of recurrence. It isn't true of Shelley, some of whose odes certainly were written on the Cowley model. All of Wordsworth's are, except the "Power of Sound" and the "Immortality," which is irregular, but whose cadences were learned of Gray. (Our critic, by the way, calls the latter, whose name he spells with an *e*, a "follower of Cowley." Gray's odes are regular.) Coleridge's are also Cowleian in form, I am pretty sure. But all these were written for the closet—and mine for recitation. I chose my measures with my ears open. So I did in writing the poem on Rob Shaw. That *is* regular because meant only to be read, and because also I thought it should have in the form of its stanza something of the formality of an epitaph.

Pardon me all this. But I could not help wishing to leave in friendly hands a protest against being thought a lazy rhymer who wrote in *numeris* that seem, but are not, *lege solutis*, because it was easier. It isn't easier, if it be done well, that is, if it attain to a real and not a merely visual harmony of verse. The mind should be rhymed to, as well as the ear and eye. *Mere* uniformity gives the columns and wings and things of Herbert and Quarles. If I had had more time to mull over my staves they would have been better.

Gratefully yours,

J. R. LOWELL.

TO C. E. NORTON

Baltimore,* Feb. 18, 1877.

. . . It happened that Judge Brown spoke of a letter he had received recommending somebody for the Professorship of Philosophy here. This gave Child a chance to speak of —— (Judge Brown is one of the trustees of the Johns Hopkins), which he did as excellently well as he lectures on Chaucer and reads him, and that is saying a great deal. You lost, by the way, a very great pleasure in not hearing him read the Nonnes Prestes tale. I certainly never heard anything better. He wound into the meaning of it (as Dr. Johnson says of Burke) like a serpent, or perhaps I should come nearer to it if I said that he injected the veins of the poem with his own sympathetic humor till it seemed to live again. I could see his hearers take the fun before it came, their faces lighting with the reflection of his. I never saw anything better done. I wish I could inspire myself with his example, but I continue dejected and lumpish. . . .

Child goes on winning all ears and hearts. I am rejoiced to have this chance of seeing so much of him, for though I loved him before, I did not know *how* lovable he was till this intimacy. . . .

TO MISS NORTON

"Bahltimer," Feb. 22, 1877.

. . . We have just come back from celebrating our

* This visit to Baltimore was for the purpose of giving a course of lectures on Poetry at Johns Hopkins University.

Johns Hopkins Commemoration, and I came home
bringing my sheaf with me in the shape of a lovely
bouquet (I mean nosegay) sent me by a dear old Quaker
lady who remembered that it was my birthday. We
had first a very excellent address by *our* President Gil-
man, then one by Professor Gildersleeve on Classical
Studies, and by Professor Silvester on the Study of
Mathematics, both of them very good and just enough
spiced with the personality of the speaker to be taking. Then I, by special request, read a part of my
Cambridge Elm poem, and actually drew tears from
the eyes of bitter secessionists—comparable with those
iron ones that rattled down Pluto's cheek. I didn't
quite like to read the invocation to Virginia here—I
was willing enough three or four hundred miles north
—but I think it did good. Teakle Wallace (Charles
will tell you who he is), a prisoner of Fort Warren, came
up to thank me with dry eyes (which he and others
assured me had been flooded), and Judge Brown with
the testifying drops still on his lids.

Silvester paid a charming compliment to Child, and
so did Gildersleeve. The former said that he (C.) had
invented a new pleasure for them in his reading of
Chaucer, and G., that you almost saw the dimple of
Chaucer's own smile as his reading felt out the humor
of the verse. The house responded cordially. If I
had much vanity I should be awfully cross, but I am
happy to say that I have enjoyed dear Child's four
weeks' triumph (of which he alone is unconscious) to
the last laurel-leaf. He is *such* a delightful creature.
I never saw so much of him before, and should be

II.—13

glad I came here if it were for [nothing but] my nearer knowledge and enjoyment of *him*.

We are overwhelmed with kindness here. I feel very much as an elderly oyster might who was suddenly whisked away into a polka by an electric eel. How I shall ever do for a consistent hermit again Heaven only knows. I eat five meals a day, as on board a Cunarder on the mid-ocean, and on the whole bear it pretty well, especially now that there are only four lectures left. I shall see you I hope in a week from to-morrow. Going away from home, I find, does not tend to make us *under*value those we left behind. . . .

Your affectionate old friend,

J. R. L.

TO MRS. E. BURNETT

Elmwood, June 5, 1877.

. . . It must be kept close, but I have refused to go either to Vienna or Berlin. Indeed I have no desire to go abroad at all. But I had said that " I would have gone to Spain," supposing that place to have been already filled. But on Saturday I saw Mr. Evarts (by his request) at the Revere House, who told me that the President was much disappointed by my refusal. He (Mr. Evarts) thought it possible that an exchange might be made, in which case I shall have to go. It will be of some use to me in my studies, and I shall not stay very long at any rate. But it is hard to leave Elmwood while it is looking so lovely. The canker-worms have burned up all my elms and apple-trees, to be sure, but everything else is as fresh as Eden. I tried troughs and kerosene round the two elms near the house and they are not wholly consumed, but are bad enough. The crow blackbirds, after prospecting two years, have settled in the pines and make the view from the veranda all the livelier. It is a very birdy year for some reason or other. I can't explain it, but there is a great difference in the *volatility* (as Dr. Hosmer would have said) of the seasons. . . .

TO MISS GRACE NORTON

Elmwood, July 1, 1877.

. . . We have been having a very busy week as you know. The President's visit was really most successful, so far as the impression made by him went. He seemed to me simple and earnest, and I can't think that a man who has had five horses killed under him will be turned back by a little political discomfort. He has a better head than the photographs give him, and the expression of the eyes is more tender. I was on my guard against the influence which great opportunities almost always bring to bear on us in making us insensibly transfer to the man a part of the greatness that belongs to the place. . . . Mrs. Hayes also pleased me very much. She has really beautiful eyes, full of feeling and intelligence, and bore herself with a simple good-humor that was perfectly well-bred. A very good American kind of princess, I thought. Don't fancy I am taken off my feet by the enthusiasm of contagion. You know I am only too fastidious, and am too apt to be put at a disadvantage by the impartiality of my eyes. No, I am sure that both the President and his wife have in them that excellent new thing we call Americanism, which I suppose is that "dignity of human nature" which the philosophers of the last century were always seeking and never finding, and which, after all, consists, perhaps, in not thinking yourself either better or worse than your neighbors by reason of any artificial distinction. As I sat behind them at the concert the other night, I was profoundly touched by the feeling of this kingship without mantle and crown from the property-room of the old world. Their dignity was in their very neighborliness, instead of in their distance, as in Europe. . . .

You must remember that I am "H. E." now myself, and can show a letter with that superscription. I haven't yet discovered in what my particular kind of excellency consists, but when I do I will let you know. It is rather amusing, by the way, to see a certain added respect in the demeanor of my fellow-townsmen towards me, as if I had drawn a prize in the lottery and was somebody at last. Indeed, I don't believe I could persuade any except my old friends of the reluctance with which I go. I dare say I shall enjoy it after I get there, but at present it is altogether a bore to be honorabled at every turn. The world is a droll affair. And yet, between ourselves, dear Grace, I should be pleased if my father could see me in capitals on the Triennial Catalogue.* You remember Johnson's pathetic letter

* The triennial (now quinquennial) catalogue of the graduates of Harvard College; now, since Harvard has grown to a University, deprived alike of the dignity of its traditional Latin and

to Chesterfield. How often I think of it as I grow older ! . . .

TO THOMAS HUGHES

Elmwood, July 2, 1877.

. . . I should have written to you at once, when I finally made up my mind to go to Madrid, but that I heard of the death of Mrs. Senior. Just after this I lost one of my oldest and dearest friends in Jane Norton, and then went Edmund Quincy, an intimate of more than thirty years, at a moment's warning. I had always reckoned on their both surviving me (though Quincy was eleven years my elder), for they both came of long-lived races. Of Mrs. Senior I have a most delightful remembrance when we rowed together on the Thames, and she sang " Sally in our Alley " and " Wapping Old Stairs " in a voice that gave more than Italian sweetness to English words. I thought that her sympathy with the poor, and her habit of speaking with them, had helped to give this sweetness to her voice. If heaven were a place where it was all singing, as our Puritan forebears seem to have thought, the desire to hear that voice again would make one more eager to get there. I was in a very gloomy mood for a week or two, and didn't like to write. There is no consolation in such cases, for not only the heart refuses to be comforted, but the eyes also have a hunger which can never be stilled in this world. . . .

of those capitals in which the sons of hers who had attained to public official distinction such as that of Member of Congress, or Governor of a State, or Judge of a U. S. Court, were elevated above their fellow-students. To have one's name in capitals in the catalogue was a reward worth achieving.

TO MISS GRACE NORTON

Grosvenor Hotel, Park Street,
London, July 29, 1877.

. . . I have just come in from Hyde Park, whither I
go to smoke my cigar after breakfast. The day is as
fine as they can make 'em in London: the sun shines
and the air is meadowy. I sat and watched the sheep
crawl through the filmy distance, unreal as in a pastoral
of the last century, as if they might have walked out of
a London eclogue of Gay. Fancy saw them watched by
beribboned shepherdesses and swains. Now and then a
scarlet coat would cross my eye like a stain of blood on
the innocent green. The trees lifted their cumulous outlines like clouds, and all around was the ceaseless hum
of wheels that never sleep. . . . This scene in the Park
is one of which I never tire. I like it better than anything in London. If I look westward I am in the country. If I turn about, there is the never-ebbing stream
of coaches and walkers, the latter with more violent con-
trasts of costume and condition than are to be seen anywhere else, and with oddities of face and figure that
make Dickens seem no caricaturist. The landscape has
the quiet far-offness of Chaucer. The town is still the
town of Johnson's London. . . .

TO THE SAME

Hôtel de Lorraine, 7 Rue de Beaune,
Paris, Aug. 8, 1877.

. . . Here we are in the same little hotel in which
you left us five years ago, and I never walk out but I

meet with scenes and objects associated with you.   It is
the same Paris, and more than ever strikes me as the
handsomest city in the world.   I find nothing comparable to the view up and down the river, or to the liveli-
ness of its streets.   At night the river with its reflected
lights, its tiny *bateaux mouches* with their ferret eyes,
creeping stealthily along as if in search of prey, and the
dimly outlined masses of building that wall it in, gives
me endless pleasure.   I am as fond as ever of the perpetual torchlight procession of the avenue of the *Champs
Elysées* in the evening, and the *cafés chantants* are more
like the Arabian Nights than ever.   I am pleased, too,
as before with the amiable ways and caressing tones of
the French women—the little girl who waits on us at
breakfast treats us exactly as if we were two babies
of whom she had the charge—and with the universal
courtesy of the men.   I am struck with the fondness of
the French for pets, and their kindness to them.   Some
Frenchman (I forget who) has remarked this, and con-
trasted it with their savage cruelty towards their own
race.   I think, nevertheless, that it indicates a real gen-
tleness of disposition.   The little woman at the kiosque
where I buy my newspapers asked me at once (as does
everybody else) after John Holmes.   (She had a tame
sparrow he used to bring cake to.)   "Ah!" exclaimed
she, "*qu'il était bon!   Tout bon!   Ce n'est que les bons
qui aiment les animaux!   Et ce monsieur, comment il
les aimait!*" . . .

TO GEORGE PUTNAM

Hôtel de Paris, Madrid,
Thursday, Aug. 16, 1877.

. . . We are obliged to go about somewhat in the heat of the day house-hunting. We can't go in a cab like ordinary mortals, but must have coachman and footman in livery, with their coats folded over the coach-box in a cascade of brass buttons. The first day it rather amused me, but yesterday the whole thing revealed itself to me as a tremendous bore—but essential to the situation. *Tu l'as voulu, Georges Dandin!* There are moments when I feel that I have sold my soul to the D—l. I am writing post-haste now because this leathern inconveniency will be at the door in half an hour, and I must find work for it or— . . .

TO MRS. EDWARD BURNETT

Legacion de los Estados Unidos
    de America en España.   Aug. 24, 1877.

. . . We arrived here on Tuesday, the 14th, and on Friday, the 17th, I started with Mr. Adee (the late chargé-d'affaires here) for La Granja. This is a summer palace of the king, about fifty miles from Madrid, among the mountains. You go about half the distance (to Villalba) by rail, and there we found awaiting us the private travelling-carriage of the prime minister, which had been very courteously put at our disposal. Our journey was by night and over the mountains, the greatest height reached by the road being about that of Mt. Washington. Eight mules with red plumes and other

gorgeous trappings formed our team. A *guardia civil,*
with three - cornered hat, white cross - belts, and rifle,
mounted the rumble, and with a cracking of whips
quite as noisy as a skirmish of revolvers in Virginia
City, and much shouting, away we pelted. After crossing the pass and beginning to go down-hill the road was
very picturesque, through a great forest of heavy-nee-
dled pines whose boughs, lighted up by our lamps, were
like heavy heaps of smoke in a still air. We reached
La Granja at midnight, beating the *diligence* by more
than an hour. Our rooms at the only inn had been
engaged by telegraph, so we supped and to bed. The
next morning the second Introducer of Ambassadors
(the first was at the sea-shore) came to make arrangements for my official reception and Mr. Adee's (late
Chargé) audience of leave. The introducer was in a
great stew (for he had never tried his hand before), and
made us at least six visits, to repeat the same thing in
the course of the forenoon. At ten minutes before two
a couple of royal coaches arrived, the first for Mr. Adee
and the second (more gorgeous) for me. Mounted
guards, with three-cornered hats and jack-boots, looking
like the pictures of Dumas *père's* mousquetaires, rode on
each side in files. The introducer, blazing with gold
and orders, sat on my right, and we started at a foot-
pace for the palace, about a hundred yards away. The
troops and band saluted as we passed, and alighting, we
were escorted through long suites of rooms to the royal
presence. There I found the king, with as many of the
court dignitaries as were at La Granja, in a long semicircle, his majesty in the middle. I made one bow at

the door, a second midway, and a third on facing the
king. I made my speech in English, he answered me in
Spanish, then came forward and exchanged a few com-
pliments with me in French, and all was over. Then
I was taken to another wing of the palace to pay my
respects to the Princess of the Asturias, the king's sister. Next morning (Sunday, 19th) we breakfasted *en
famille* with Señor Silvela, Minister of State. At two
the Duke of Montpensier (just arrived) held a reception
in my honor. All the diplomats at La Granja sat in a
circle. At the end of the room farthest from the door
sat the duke and duchess, with an empty chair between
them to which I was conducted. After five minutes of
infantile conversation the duke rose and the thing was
over. At five some of the *grandes eaux* in the garden
were played for Uncle Sam. It was a pretty and picturesque sight. The princesses and their ladies walked in
front abreast, followed by the king, his household, and
foreign ministers. I was beckoned to the king's side, and
he talked with me all the way—even quoting one of my
own verses. He had been crammed, of course, beforehand. The waters were very pretty, and the garden, set
as it is in a ring of mountains, far finer than Versailles.
At eight o'clock dinner at the palace, where I sat on
the left of the Princess of Asturias, the Duke of Montpensier being on her right, and the king opposite. The
king, by the way, is smallish (he is not nineteen), but
has a great deal of *presence*, is very intelligent and good-
looking. So young a monarch in so difficult a position
interests me. The same night, at two o'clock, we started
for Madrid. . . .

TO H. W. LONGFELLOW

Madrid, Nov. 17, 1877.

Dear Longfellow,—I have just had a visit from Sñr. D. Manuel Tamayo y Baus, secretario perpetuo de la Real Academia Española, who came to tell me that they had just elected you a foreign member of their venerable body. When your name was proposed, he says, there was a contest as to who should second the nomination, "*porque tiene muchos apasionados aquí el Señor Long-fellow*," and at last the privilege was conceded to the Excmo. Sñr. D. Juan Valera, whose literary eminence is no doubt known to you. You may conceive how pleasant it was to hear all this, and likewise your name pronounced perfectly well by a Spaniard. Among all your laurels this leaf will not make much of a show, but I am sure you will value it for early association's sake, if for nothing more. I told the Sñr. Secretary that one of your latest poems had recorded your delightful memories of Spain.

It made me feel nearer home to talk about you, and I add that to the many debts of friendship I owe you. I wish I could walk along your front walk and drop into your study for a minute. However, I shall find you there when I come back, for you looked younger than ever when I bade you good-by. (I forgot to say that your *diploma* will be sent to me in a few days, and that I shall take care that you receive it in good time.)

I have had a good deal of *Heimweh* since I got here, and a fierce attack of gout, first in one foot and then in the other. I am all right again now, and the November weather here (out of doors) is beyond any I ever saw. It beats Italy. And such limpidity of sky! Within doors it is chilly enough, and one needs a fire on the shady side of the house.

I have made few save diplomatic and official acquaintances thus far—very pleasant—but I miss my old friendships. But I don't know how many times I have said to myself, "*Tu l'as voulu, Georges Dandin, tu l'as voulu!*"

Keep me freshly remembered in your household, to the whole of which I send my love. Eheu!

Good-by. God bless and keep you!

Your affectionate friend,

J. R. LOWELL.

TO GEORGE PUTNAM

Madrid, Dec. 23, 1877.

Dear Putnam,— . . . You talk jauntily of journeys to Granada and the like! You've no notion how much there is to do here. My secretary, who was eight years in the State Department, says it is the hardest-worked legation of all. I am getting used to it, though I shall never like it, I think, for I am too old to find the ceremonial parts even amusing. They bore me. Then I had seven weeks of gout before I had learned to take my work easily, and I worried myself abominably over it. 'Tis a vile thing to have a conscience! But fancy a shy man, without experience, suddenly plumped down among a lot of utter strangers, unable to speak their language (though knowing more of it than almost any of them), and with a secretary wholly ignorant both of Spanish and French. (An excellent fellow, by the way, whom I like very much, and whose knowledge of official routine has been a great help.) And I was to get an indemnity out of them! It was rather trying, and I feared seriously at one time while I was shut up would affect my brain— for what with gout and anxiety I sometimes got no sleep for three days together. However, the gout let go its hold of my right foot just long enough for me to hobble with a cane and finish my indemnity job, and then went over into my left and pulled me down again.

From the first, however, I insisted on transacting all my business with the Secretary of State in Spanish, and now I get along very well, going to an interview with him quite at my ease. The offices of the legation are a mile from my house, and I have been there every day during office hours except when I was jugged with the gout. I hope to see Granada in the spring.

Next month we shall have prodigious doings with the king's wedding—such as could not be seen anywhere else, I fancy, in these days—for they purposely keep up or restore old fashions here, and have still a touch of the East in them so far as a liking for pomp goes. I like the Spaniards very well so far as I know them, and have an instinctive sympathy with their want of aptitude for business. My duties bring me into not the most agreeable relation with them, for I am generally obliged to play the *dun*, and sometimes for claims in whose justice I have not the most entire confidence. Even with the best will in the world, Spain finds it very hard to raise money. Fancy how we should have felt if a lot of South Carolinians during our Civil War could have got themselves naturalized in Spain, and then (not without

suspicion of having given aid and comfort to the enemy)
should have brought in claims for damage to their es-
tates by the Union Army! I think they would have
had to wait awhile! . . .

TO THE SAME

Madrid, Jan. 28, 1878.

. . . We are just getting done with the festivals incident to the king's marriage, to the great relief of everybody concerned. The display, in certain respects, has
been such as could be seen nowhere out of Spain, but
the fatigue and row have been almost unendurable. I
had just had two more of those dreadful attacks in the
stomach to which I have been liable for the last few
years, one on Tuesday, and a second still worse on Saturday—so bad, indeed, that I really thought something
was going to happen that would drive the legation to
black wax. Ether was of no avail, but on Sunday my
feet began to swell and the stomach was relieved. I
was forced to keep my bed for ten days. I am now
all right again, except that I have to wear cloth shoes
and cannot do any walking. But I took such care that
I was able to show myself at the more important ceremonies. I never saw a crowd before, and one night, on
my way to a reception at the prime minister's, I was
nearly mobbed (that is, my carriage was), and so were
several other foreign ministers. We were obliged to go
round by a back street—the mob being furious, and I
don't blame them.

The most interesting part of the ceremonies, on the

whole, was the dances of peasants from the different provinces of Spain before the king yesterday morning. It took place in the *plaza de armas* before the palace, and afterwards they were all brought up and ranged in a row for our inspection. The costumes were marvellous, and we could never have otherwise had such a chance to see so many and so good. In the evening the king dined the diplomatic body, and afterwards held a grand reception. The uniforms (there are six special embassies here with very long tails) and diamonds were very brilliant. But to me, I confess, it is all vanity and vexation of spirit. I like America better every day. . . .

TO MISS GRACE NORTON

Madrid, March 7, 1878.

. . . I don't care where the notion of immortality came from. If it sprang out of a controlling necessity of our nature, some instinct of self-protection and preservation, like the color of some of Darwin's butterflies, at any rate it is there and as real as that, and I mean to hold it fast. Suppose we don't *know*, how much *do* we know after all? There are times when one doubts his own identity, even his own material entity, even the solidity of the very earth on which he walks. One night, the last time I was ill, I lost all consciousness of my flesh. I was dispersed through space in some inconceivable fashion, and mixed with the Milky Way. It was with great labor that I gathered myself again and brought myself within compatible limits, or so it seemed; and yet the very fact that I had a confused consciousness all the while of the Milky Way as something to be mingled with proved that *I* was there as much an individual as ever. . . .

TO JOHN W. FIELD

7 Cuesta de Sto. Domingo,
March 14, 1878.

. . . Thanks, too, for the *République Française.* The article amused me. Devotion to money quotha! The next minute these Johnny Crapauds will turn round and say, " Was there ever anything like us? See how we paid the German indemnity, and all out of our old stockings—the savings of years." The donkeys! You can raise more money for public purposes by subscription in a Boston week than in a French twelvemonth. *That's* not the weak point of democracy, whatever else may be. And in Gambetta's paper, too! What has been the strength of his Jewish ancestors and what is the strength of his Jewish cousins, I should like to know! That they could always supply you or me with an accommodation at heavy interest. Where would a Jew be among a society of primitive men without pockets, and therefore *a fortiori* without a hole in them? . . .

TO GEORGE PUTNAM

Madrid, March 16, 1878.

. . . What I meant by my not blaming the crowd that night was that the whole street from one end to t'other was so crammed with people that a carriage passing through really endangered life or limb. I intended no communistic sentiment, but, though I am one of those who go in chariots for the nonce, I confess that my sympathies are very much with those who don't. Communism seems to have migrated to your side of the water just now. But I confess I feel no great alarm; for if history has taught us any other lesson than that nobody ever profits by its teachings, it is that property is always too much for communism in the long run. Even despite the Silver Bill, I continue to think pretty well of my country, God be praised! . . .

TO H. W. LONGFELLOW

Madrid, March 16, 1878.

Dear Longfellow,—I meant to have sent the diploma by Field, but as it was locked up in our safe at the Legation (I don't live there), I forgot it. I sent it yesterday to Paris by Mr. Dabney, our consul at the Canaries, who will deliver it to Ernest, and he will soon find a safe hand by whom to send it home. I am charmed with your simple Old Cambridge notion of our despatch-bags. God knows we have despatches enough to write, but we have only one bag, which we use only when we have reason to send a special courier to London, and the last one we sent left it behind him, so that we are bagless as Judas when he hanged himself (Old Play). I couldn't send the diploma, accordingly, with our regular despatches without folding it, which would have disfigured it abominably; and meanwhile you are as much an academician as if you had it, though I hope still young enough to wish to hold it in your own hand. By the

II.—14

way, the *Académicos de Número* are entitled to wear a gorgeous decoration round the neck.   If it had been that I shouldn't wonder at your feeling a little anxious, for if I hadn't stolen it I should have wondered, like Clive, at my own moderation.

Thank you for the poem, which Mrs. Lowell and I enjoyed together, and is so characteristic " that every line doth almost read your name."   I should have known it everywhere, and liked it very much—all the more that it convinced me you were as young as ever and with no abatement of natural force.

The forsythia is already in bloom here, and the almond-trees were three weeks ago.   The leaves are peeping. And yet to-day it is really cold again, and I suppose there was a fall of snow on the Guadarramas last night, for it was tumultuous with wind.   It is a queer climate —the loveliest I ever saw—and yet it sticks you from behind corners, as we used to think Spaniards employed all their time in doing.   After all, Cambridge is best.

My love and best wishes on your latest birthday (I was going to write "last," and superstitiously refrained my pen).   I won't read the milestone, but I am sure it is on a road that leads to something better.   Two countrymen interrupt me, and I end with love from your

Affectionate

J. R. LOWELL.

TO F. J. CHILD

Madrid, Palm Sunday, April 14, 1878.

Dear Ciarli,*—I have noticed that Class and Phi Beta

* "Ciarli" was the attempt of an old Italian beggar at Professor Child's name.

poems almost always begin with an " as "—at any rate, they used to in my time, before a certain Boylston professor took 'em in hand.   E. g.,

> As the last splendors of expiring day
> Round Stoughton's chimneys cast a lingering ray,
> So——

And sometimes there was a whole flight of *as*-es leading up to the landing of a final *so*, where one could take breath and reflect on what he had gone through.   Now you will be sure that I didn't mean to begin my letter thus, but it was put into my head by the earthquake you have been making in Baltimore, the wave from which rolled all the way across the ocean and splashed audibly on these distant shores, and as all my associations are with dear Old Cambridge, why naturally I found myself murmuring,

> As, when the Earthquake stomps his angry foot,
> A thousand leagues the frightened billows scoot,
> So when my Ciarli, etc.

I was delighted to hear of it, though it was just what I expected, for didn't my little bark attendant sail more than a year ago?   It gave me a touch of homesickness too, for I look back on that month as one of the pleasantest of my life, and here I am not as who should say altogether and precisely happy.   Yet I hope to get something out of it that will tell by and by.   The ceremonial, of which there is plenty, of course is naught, and I make acquaintance so slowly that I hardly know anybody (except officially) even yet, but I have at last got hold of an intelligent bookseller, and am beginning

to get a few books about me. . . . Gayangos has some
exquisite old books, by the way—a Góngora, among
others, that would have tempted me to ruin had it been
for sale.   It is a manuscript on vellum, made as a present to the Conde-duque de Olivares when he was in the
flush of his *privanza.*   Each poem is dated on the mar-
gin, and in the index the copyist marks certain ones as
falsely attributed to Góngora, and says the poet told
him so himself.   It is exquisitely done, like that little
Greek book in Mr. Sibley's show-case—Anacreon, isn't
it ?

I have just succeeded in getting a copy of the series
printed for the *Bibliofilos Españoles,* which is very hard
to come at, and cost me $105 in paper.   It contains one
or two things worth having—but I bought mainly with
a view to the College Library one of these days.   I
have also bought the photolithographie of Cuesta's *edi-
tio princeps* of " Don Quixote " for the sake of Hartzenbusch's notes, which, by the way, show a singular dulness of perception, and *correct* Cervantes in a way that
makes me swear.   But they are worth having, as showing the emendations that have been made or proposed,
the *when* and *by whom.*   I have, too, the Burgos 1593 *Cró-
nica* of the Cid, a very fair copy, and Damas-Hinard's
edition of the *Poem.* . . .

I fear what you say of my being thrown away here
may turn out true.   There is a great deal to do, and of
a kind for which I cannot get up a very sincere interest
—claims and customs duties, and even, God save the
mark ! Brandreth's pills.   I try to do my duty, but feel
sorely the responsibility to people three thousand miles

away, who know not Joseph and probably think him un-practical. . . .

. . . We have seen Seville, Cordova, Granada, and Toledo, each excellent in itself and Toledo queer, even after Italy and Sicily. But the *shrinkage* is frightful. Toledo especially is full of ruin, and, what is worse, of indifference to ruin. Yet there is something oriental in my own nature which sympathizes with this " let her slide" temper of the *hidalgos*. They go through all the forms of business as they do of religion, without any reference to the thing itself, just as they offer you their house (dating their notes to you *de* SU *casa*) and every-thing in it. But they are very friendly, and willing to be helpful where they can. I love the jauds for a' that. They are unenterprising and unchangeable. The latest accounts of them are just like the earliest, and they have a firm faith in Dr. Mañana—he will cure everything, or, if he can't, it doesn't signify. In short, there is a flavor of Old Cambridge about 'em, as O. C. used to be when I was young and the world worth having. . . .

Good-by, dear old fellow.

Your affectionate

J. R. L.

TO C. E. NORTON

7 Cuesta de Sto. Domingo, 2°, izqª.
(second floor, left-hand door),
April 15, 1878.

. . . I write now because I am going away for two months and haven't time to write at all. Whither we shall go I hardly can tell. I have a furlough of sixty

days, and am going first into southern France to see
Toulouse and Carcassonne, which I never saw.   Then I
think we shall go to Genoa and Pisa, staying some little time, perhaps, in the *vituperio delle genti*.   Then we
may go on to Naples, take the steamer there, and be
carried round to Athens.   I am obliged to take my vacation now, to bring it within the year.   My heart is as
heavy as dough, so does the thought of travel always
depress me.   I don't know how I can come to grief—
but am sure I shall always.

I believe I have performed my functions here tolerably well, except those of society, and even those I have
not wholly neglected.   I have been out a great deal—
for *me*.   The hours here are frightfully late.   They go
to a reception *after* the opera, so that half-past 11 is
early.   At a dance they are more punctual, and I have
even known them to begin at 10—but they keep it up
till 2 or 3.   They seem childishly fond of dancing.   But
there is no such thing as conversation, nor any chance
for it.   As for scholarship, there is, I should say, very
little of it, in the accurate German sense.   I don't think
they value it any more than they do time, of which
they always have more on their hands than they know
what to do with, and therefore vastly less than they
want.

My own time has been very much broken up by my
not being well.   I think I told you that I have had
three fits of gout since I came, and I *worry* over my
duties. . . .

But I am learning something, I hope.   I get along
very well in Spanish now, and when I come back am

going to fasten an *abbé* to my skirts, so as to be forced
into talking. I have tried in vain to find out for you
whether there *are* any letters of Velasquez or not.
What they call their *archives* have never been sorted.
They don't know what they have. And then Siman-
cas is ever so far away, and Government won't consent
to have their documents brought to Madrid—nor even
to Valladolid. There are local jealousies in the way—
stronger even than ours. But next winter, when I am
more familiar with things and men, I hope to do something. There are no scientific booksellers—not one—
and I can't even procure what has been actually printed about Cervantes. I bought the other day the photo-
lithographic copy of the first edition of "Don Quixote,"
for the sake, mainly, of Hartzenbusch's notes. But they
are mostly worthless—of value mainly as collation. He
doesn't understand his author in the least, whose de-
lightfully haphazard style is too much for him. I shall,
however, bring home some books you will like to see. I
buy mainly with a view to the College Library, whither
they will go when I am in Mount Auburn, with so much
undone that I might have done. I hope my grandsons
will have some of the method I have always lacked.

. . . My little world is getting smaller and smaller,
and I am *not* reconciled. Still, I long for the Charles
and the meadows, and walk between Elmwood and
Shady Hill constantly. I feel much older in body and
mind—I can't quite say why or how, but I feel it. I
cling to what is left all the more closely. . . .

Always your loving

J. R. L.

TO MRS. E. BURNETT

Arles, April 27, 1878.

. . . Mamma has told you that we were to go off on a leave of absence, and we have now been on our travels eleven days. Thus far we have enjoyed it very much. Our itinerary has been: from Madrid to Tarbes, then Toulouse, then Carcassonne, then Nismes, then Avignon, and then hither. We have thus had a pretty good glimpse of the south of France, and very lovely it is. At Toulouse and Carcassonne I had never been before, and Toulouse, I confess, disappointed me, though there was an interesting old church (St. Sernin) and an old house worth seeing. But Carcassonne is wonderful, a fortified place of the twelfth and thirteenth centuries, as perfect as if it had been kept in a museum. As you look across the river at it from the *new* town (six hundred years old) it seems like an illumination out of some old copy of Froissart. I positively thought I was dreaming after looking at it for long enough to forget the modernness about me. Its general aspect is of the dates I have given, but parts are Roman, parts Visigothic, and parts Saracenic. The past is ensconced there as in a virgin fortress, and will hold out forever.

From Nismes we drove out about twelve miles to the Pont du Gard. It rained all the way out; but just as we got there it cleared, and all the thickets (in every one a nightingale) were rainbowed and diamonded by the sun. The *Pont* is a Roman aqueduct, which crosses the deep valley of a pretty river on three rows of arches,

one above another. It is really noble, and these gigantic bones of Rome always touch and impress me more
the farther away they are from the mother city.   Then
we had some bread and sausages and wine in a little ar-
bor, served by a merry old man, who, when I told him
I had been there twenty-six years before, challenged me
to come back as many hence; "but," said he, touching
his white whiskers, and with a sly glance at mine, "*les
blancs ne se refont jamais bruns.*"   Jacques (our servant) resented this, as in duty bound, and insisted that
monsieur wasn't in the least white yet, at which the
heartless old boy only laughed, and I joined him in
order to put a good face on the matter. I compli-
mented him on his daughter, who was making a pretty
nosegay for mamma. "*Ah,*" said he, "*je lui légue les
bouteilles vides et les bouchons, mais avec de la santé et la
bonne volonté on arrive.*" So we parted, agreeing to
meet in 1904! Before we were half way home (if I
may call a hotel so) it began to rain again. So you see
what luck we had.

From Avignon we drove twenty miles to Vaucluse
(which I had not visited before), and found it worthy
of all Petrarca had said of it. The *onde* are as *chiare*
and *fresche* as ever, and the fountain one of the most
marvellous I ever saw. You follow a ravine deeply hol-
lowed in the soft rock for about half a mile, and there,
at the foot of a huge precipice, is the basin, which feeds
a considerable stream. A clear, calm pool. You see no
bubbling of springs from below, no fissure in the rock,
and perceive no motion in the water except where it es-
capes towards the valley. It is lined with factories now,

and French visitors have daubed the rocks with their vulgar names in black paint in every direction. You can't find a fragment to sit on without feeling discomforted by a guilty sense of complicity in hiding half a dozen of these profanations from the angry glare of the sun. We might have lunched at any one of three cafés —one of which invites you with the advertisement painted on its front that here Petrarch wrote his 129th sonnet! It is the Café de Pétrarque et Laure. " Great Cæsar dead and turned to clay," etc. . . .

I don't care to say how soft my heart gets when I think of you all at home. I fancy I am growing old. . . .

TO THE SAME

Athens, May 17, 1878.

. . . Here we are in Athens, and just come in from a visit to the Acropolis, which has served to balance our first impressions, which were rather depressing. For to drive from the Piræus through a dreary country, in a cloud of dust, drawn by two wretched beasts that ought to have been in their graves long ago, and unable to stop the driver from lashing because we could speak no tongue he could understand, and then to enter a shabby little modern town, was by no means inspiriting. I was for turning about and going straight back again, but am getting wonted by degrees, and I dare say shall come to like it after a while. I was stupid enough to be amused last night at hearing the boys crying the newspapers in Greek—as if they could do it in anything else —and fancied I caught some cadences of the tragic chorus in the bray of a donkey, the only "Attic warbler" that I have heard "pour his throat."

. . . Our first sight of Greece was the shores of the Morea, and anything more sterile and dreary I never saw. I thought some parts of our New England coast dreary enough, but this is even grimmer. We had for fellow-passenger a pretty little land-bird, which found the land inviting in spite of all, and flew away when he thought we were near enough. I couldn't help thinking how much better off he would be than we, having a command of the language wherever he lighted. The first natives we saw were two gulls (an imperishable race), probably much less degenerate from their ancestors than the men who now inhabit the country.

The position of the Parthenon, by the way, is incomparable, and, as mamma said, the general sadness of the landscape was in harmony with its ruin. It is the very abomination of desolation, and yet there is nothing that is not noble in its decay. The view seaward is magnificent. I suppose the bird of Pallas haunts the temple still by nights, and hoots sadly for her lost mistress. There was a strange sensation in looking at the blocks which Pericles had probably watched as they were swung into their places, and in walking over the marble floor his sandals had touched. . . .

TO C. E. NORTON

Athens, May 21, 1878.

. . . On the day of my arrival I was profoundly depressed, everything looked so mean—the unpaved and unsidewalked streets, the Western coat and trousers, and what costumes there were so filthy. And yet I was in luck, for the town is full of Thessalian insurgents, so that I see more that is characteristic than I had a right to expect. They are dreadful ruffians to all appearance, and reminded me of Macaulay's Highlanders. In consequence of them I refused to go out to Marathon with Jebb, who is here, and who, after all, went and came safely. But for my official character I should have gone. I could not afford the time to be sequestered (as we call it in Spain), and the Minister of State thought it risky. The returning patriots are of a class who are quite indifferent whether they learn the time of day from a Moslem or Christian time-piece, and to whom money from whatever pocket is orthodox.

In the afternoon of the day of my arrival I walked up to the Acropolis, and tuned my nerves and mind to a manlier key. It is noble in position and sublime even in ruin. The impression was all I could wish — profound beyond expectation and without artificial stimulus. You know I prefer Gothic to Grecian architecture, and yet (I cannot explain it) the Parthenon was more effective in its place than a shattered cathedral would have been. But imagination plays such tricks with us—

Madrid, Aug. 2, 1878.

I was in the middle of a reflection, my dear Charles, when in came Santiago to tell me that the steamer for Constantinople would leave the Piræus in three hours. It was my only chance, and I decided for going—Athens only half seen. But then, you know, I have a theory

that peaches have only one good bite in 'em, and that a
second spoils *that*. I am glad we went. The view of
Constantinople as you draw nigh is incomparable, and
one sees at once what an imperial eye Constantine had.
Planted firmly in Europe, it holds Asia subject with its
eye. The climate is admirable—Eastern sun and Western rains. The harbor ample for all the navies of the
world—the Bear, if he planted himself here, would get
wings and turn aquiline. We went as far as the Black
Sea in the track of the *Argo* and saw the Symplegades,
very harmless - looking rocks, like certain women when
their claws are sheathed. The captain of the French
steamer we came back to Marseilles in, who had been
in all seas, told me that in winter the Black Sea was
the worst of all. Our four days at Constantinople were
nothing more nor less than so many Arabian Nights. I
couldn't have believed that so much was left. Santa
Sofia is very noble, *really* noble, and one sees in it the
germ, if not the pattern, of all Oriental architecture—
Cordova, Granada, Seville, nay, Venice and St. Mark's.
This struck me very much.

The Turks are the most dignified-looking race I have
ever seen—a noble bearing even in defeat and even in
rags. Their exceeding sobriety of life no doubt helps
this—for all their faces look pure—and perhaps their
fatalism. Do you remember I prophesied (against Godkin) that they would make a better fight than was expected? I think they did, and that with competent
leaders they would have beaten the Muscovite, who,
after all, to my thinking, is a giant very weak in the
knees.

I saw Layard, by the way, just as he was concluding the Cyprus business, as I found out afterwards. I thought he seemed in tempestuous spirits, and no wonder! I am inclined to like the Asia Minor arrangement (because I wish digging to be done there!), and I think England strong enough for the job. I think if Beaconsfield weren't a Jew, people would think him rather fine. But they can't get over an hereditary itch to pull some of his grinders.

My Eastern peep has been of service in enabling me to see how oriental Spain still is in many ways. Without the comparison, I couldn't be sure of it. . . . I am beginning to feel competent to make some observations on the Spaniards, but shall keep them till they are riper. These things have to stand in solution a long while till the introduction of some new element, we scarce know when or how, precipitates out of mere vagueness into distinct and hard crystals which can be scientifically studied and assigned. I fancy it is otherwise with history, which is not so much "philosophy teaching by example" as clarified experience. It only has to stand on the lees long enough. One apothegm I have already engraved in brass: "The Spaniard offers you his house, but never a meal in it." I like them and find much that is only too congenial in their genius for to-morrow. I am working now at Spanish as I used to work at Old French—that is, all the time and with all my might. I mean to know it better than they do themselves—which isn't saying much. . . .

TO MRS. EDWARD BURNETT

Madrid, July 26, 1878.

. . . I was very far from well and in miserable spirits before my journey. I have come back a new man, and have flung my *blue* spectacles into the paler Mediterranean. I really begin to find life at last tolerable here, nay, to enjoy it after a fashion. . . .

I am turned school-boy again, and have a master over me once more—a most agreeable man—Don Herminegildo Giner de los Rios, who comes to me every morning at nine o'clock for an hour. We talk Spanish together (he doesn't understand a word of English), and I work hard at translation and the like. I am now translating a story of Octave Feuillet into choice Castilian, and mean to know Spanish as well as I do English before I have done with it. This morning I wrote a note to one of the papers here, in which my teacher found only a single word to change. Wasn't that pretty well for a boy of my standing? It was about Miss Dana's recollections (or records rather) of the convent days of our poor little Queen Mercedes. Anything more tragic than the circumstances of her death it would be hard to imagine. She was actually receiving extreme unction while the guns were firing in honor of her eighteenth birthday, and four days later we saw her dragged to her dreary tomb at the Escorial, followed by the coach and its eight white horses in which she had driven in triumph from the church to the palace on the day of her wedding. The poor brutes tossed their snowy plumes as haughtily now as then.

Her death is really a great public loss. She was amiable, intelligent, and simple — not beautiful, but *good-looking* — and was already becoming popular. Her malady was not thought serious at first, and, I fear, was all along mistakenly treated. . . .

TO MISS GRACE NORTON

7 Cuesta de Sto. Domingo, Aug. 11, 1878.

. . . Madrid is the noisiest city I ever dwelt in. The street-cries are endless, and given with a will and with such distortions of face as must be seen to be believed. None are musical. One always stirs my fancy by its association with Aladdin—the *lamparero*. Shall I try my luck? I think not, for in his cry I have the material for rows of palaces, whereas if I bought a lamp I might rub in vain. The first sound in the morning is the tinkle of bells on the necks of the she-asses that come in to be milked at the customer's door for surety. I know not who the customers are, but there must be many if there be any truth in the vulgar belief that children take after their nurses. Then there is a succession of blind players on the guitar, on the pipe and tabor, and on what I suppose to be the *gaita*. They sometimes also sing, but commonly have with them a boy or girl who shrieks a *romance*. All the tunes are the same so far as I can make out—just as in a school of poetry. Then the town is full of parrots and caged quails. I don't suppose we are exceptional, but there are five parrots in this house and the next together, all birds of remarkable talents. One hangs in the court-yard of our house and sings, shouts, calls names, and swears all day long.   In this same *patio*, by the way, I have heard songs issuing from the servants' quarters in every floor and from the grooms in the court-yard at the same time.   The voices are seldom agreeable and the tunes always monotonous.   Indeed they seem to have but one.   I can't catch much of the words, but the other day I heard, " *Yo soy el capitan de la tropa*," and presently, " *Yo soy el duque de Osuna*," from which I surmised a Lord of Burleigh who was gradually revealing himself.   I was wrong in saying that all the street-cries are harsh.   There is a girl who passes every day crying radishes who really makes a bit of melody with her *Rábanos !*   It is seldom that one does not hear (night or day) a thrumming or a snatch of nasal song, and I am pretty well persuaded that it was the Spanish dominion which planted the seeds of the Neapolitan street-music.

At this season they sleep in the day a good deal, and at night are as lively as certain skipping insects, with which many of them are only too familiar.   Far from being a grave people, they seem to me a particularly cheerful one, and yet I am struck with the number of deeply-furrowed faces one meets, the mark of hereditary toil.   I turn half communist when I see them.   The porters especially stir an angry sympathy in me, sometimes old men (nay, often) tottering under incredible burthens, which they carry on their backs steadied by a cord passed round the forehead.   Every day I recall that passage in Dante where he stoops from sympathy, like an ox in the yoke.   The traditional figures of the *genre* painters one sees rarely now, and

II.—15

yet there is no lack of costume. One meets constantly men in the very costume of Velasquez's "Lanzas,"
which sometimes has a very odd effect on my fancy.
The reality makes a very different impression from the
attempted illusion of the stage, and has made me understand better why I don't care for such pictures as
many of Meissonier's and the like—clever as they are.
But here is theme for a dissertation. I suppose that
in some remote way the notion of *sincerity* has something to do with it, and here, I suspect, is to be found
the distinction between the *reality* of Dante and modern
realism. A great deal of what is called pre-Raphaelite
on canvas and in verse gives me the same uncomfortable feeling of *costume*. You will guess what I mean if
I am not very clear. To come back to statistics.

I never saw anything like the fruit in Madrid for
abundance and variety. The oranges, plums, melons,
apricots, and nectarines are the best I ever saw. I have
sometimes eaten finer melons of my own growing—but
my average was never so high. Then we have grapes,
pomegranates, pears (not nearly so fine as ours), apples
(ordinary), prickly pears, peaches (tolerable), medlars.
What surprises me is how long the season is. We are
never without something. Grapes begin in June and
last till December.

The city of Madrid at first disappointed me greatly
by its modern look. I had expected to find the "mise
en scène" of Calderon. But I gradually became reconciled, and now like it. Moreover, I begin to suspect
that I hadn't understood Calderon, and that his scenery
is applicable to the present city—at least in a measure.

The Prado with its continuations is fine, and the Buen
Retiro as agreeable a drive as I know—more agreeable,
I add on reflection, than anything of the kind I know
of in any other city. But then I am bewitched with
the Campiña. To me it is grander than the Campagna;
of course I do not count the associations. I mean as a
thing to look at and fall in love with. The Guadarramas are quite as good as or better than the Alban mountains, and their color is sometimes so ethereal that they
seem visionary rather than real. The Campiña, I admit,
is sombre—but its variety and shift of color, its vague
undulations! At night, especially, it is like the sea, and
even in the day sometimes. We are, you know, twenty-
five hundred feet above the sea, but beside that, Madrid
stands on hills more considerable than those of Rome
and commanding wider horizons. The climate thus far
has been incomparable. In our year here we have had,
I believe, only three days when it rained. All blue,
night and day, and such a blue! Nothing so limpid
have I ever conceived. I should hate such a climate
were I living in the country. I should sympathize too
keenly with my trees, should be always feeling the
drouth of their roots, and being wretched. But here it
makes no odds. The trees are watered daily, and there
are really beautiful gardens.

This is the course of my day: get up at 8, from 9
sometimes till 11 my Spanish professor, at 11 breakfast,
at 12 to the Legation, at 3 home again and a cup of
chocolate, then read the paper and write Spanish till a
quarter to 7, at 7 dinner, and at 8 drive in an open carriage in the Prado till 10, to bed at 12 to 1. In cooler

weather we drive in the afternoon. I am very well—
cheerful and no gout. . . .

Your affectionate
J. R. L.

TO MRS. EDWARD BURNETT

Madrid, Aug. 25, 1878.

. . . Things go on here much as usual. The death
of Queen Cristina (the king's grandmother) I feel mainly because it gives us two months more of full mourning, and I am already tired of my sables. It will,
besides, cost mamma a new dress. Such are the painful responsibilities of diplomacy! Our flag is floating
at half-mast and wreathed in crape, from the balcony;
and what a handsome flag it is, by the way! . . .

I see that some good people at home are in a very
desperate mood over tramps and defalcations and so-
cialism and what not. For my part, I have been assured so often in the course of my life that the bottom
of the world had at last dropt out for good and all, and
yet have survived to see it hold water very tolerably
mouthless, that I am not much scared. I, who saw the
Irish mobbed in Boston ten years before you were born,
for the very same reason that the Chinese are now
hounded by the Irish in California, think it a good sign
that Kearney can address his countrymen in Faneuil
Hall and talk as much nonsense to 'em as he likes. It
proves the good sense of our people (in that respect at
least) and the solidity of our social framework. I expect to find you all safe and well when I come home
next summer—for I mean to come on a visit, if not to

stay. I begin to feel as if I should like to remain here longer, now that I have served my apprenticeship and feel at home in my business. But I have resolved nothing as yet, and what I say you must keep to yourself.

I am having a slight touch of gout since the last few days—not enough to keep me in the house, but only to remind me that I have joints in my feet. I have had to put on my cloth shoes again, but am in other respects in excellent health and spirits—very unlike what I was last year. Then I had not the spirit to be interested in anything, and wished myself at home every five minutes. Now I begin to be amused with what I see in the streets—for example, with the boys playing bullfight under my window. One boy (the bull) covers his head with a long basket with which he plunges at the rest, who irritate him with colored handkerchiefs and rags. When this has gone on for some time one of them goes to the sidewalk for two sticks sharpened at one end, which represent the *banderillas*. If he succeed in sticking them both through the interstices of the basket so that they stand up firmly, the bull drops and is despatched, and a fresh boy dons the basket and the bullship. They make me think of Jem and Joe, and are *somebody's* grandsons, I suppose, at any rate. . . .

TO MRS. W. E. DARWIN

Sept. 1, 1878.

. . . I have just been doing something that reminds me of you all the time. I should be willing to give you a thousand guesses and you wouldn't divine what. . . .

However, I will answer my own conundrum for you. I am turned Spanish author! "Why should that remind you of *me*, pray? Is there anything Spanish about *me?*" No, I'm sure there's not, but my authorship is of a very humble kind, indeed. "Worse and worse! Is there anything so *very* humble about me, sir?" No, I didn't mean that, but—in short, I have been translating into Spanish a sketch of Mr. Darwin's life—no, not *your* Mr. Darwin, certainly, you foolish little person, but his father. Not that I like science any better than I ever did. I hate it as a savage does writing, because he fears it will hurt him somehow; but I have a great respect for Mr. Darwin, as almost the only perfectly disinterested lover of truth I ever encountered. I mean, of course, in his books, for I never had the pleasure of seeing him. So I volunteered my services as dragoman, and when the opuscule is printed (which will not be for some time yet), I shall ask permission to lay a copy at your feet, as we say here. . . .

TO GEORGE PUTNAM

Madrid, Sept. 9, 1878.

. . . Your tobacco came safely (except that the Spanish customs officer stole one package and filled the gap with brown paper. I mention it because their system of appointment is just like ours) and is a great blessing. I wish you would send me a hundred more packages by the same route. Don't suppose I am consuming all this enormous quantity of smoke like a new-fashioned furnace. I want it for quasi-

diplomatic service. I found that my friend the Minister of State (for foreign affairs), who has been everything I could wish in amiability towards me, smokes a
pipe in the secrecy of his *despacho* at home, and as I
was sure he must be blistering his tongue with Spanish
mundungus, I sent him a package of mine. He writes
to say that " *es el mejor que ho fumado en mi vida; no
tenia idea de cosa tan buena!*" So I sent him yesterday ten more, and have promised to keep his pipe full
for so long as I am here. By the way, he is going to
have me elected a corresponding member of the Spanish Academy (this is between ourselves), which will be
very agreeable, as I shall be able to attend the weekly
meetings and discuss the new edition of the Dictionary. I am to be proposed by the Prime Minister Cá-
novas del Castillo, the Minister of State; and Excmo.
Sñr. Nocedal, leader of the Ultramontanes — an odd
combination for me. . . .

TO MISS GRACE NORTON

Madrid, Oct. 2, 1878.

. . . Yesterday (I mean night before last) we went to
the Teatro Español, and saw a very clever comedy of
Alarcon. Of course, it had been *adapted*, as all the old
comedies have to be; but they are not capable of being
Rowed and Cibbered as Shakespeare is, for they have
not the complexity of coherence (if I may venture the
Johnsonism) that characterizes him. It was the *Seme-
jante á si mismo.* The hero, with that whimsical jealousy of an accepted lover of which Spanish play-

wrights are so fond, resolves to test his mistress. His cousin Don Diego has just arrived from Peru, a perfect stranger, and has not yet presented himself to his relatives. Don Juan persuades him to give *him* his letters of credence, pretends a voyage to Peru, takes solemn leave, and presently returns as Don Diego. He contrives to have news arrive of his other self's loss at sea, and makes love to Doña Ana. She very readily accepts and even returns his advances. He is thus in the comical position of being jealous of himself. In his anger he tells her who he is. She excuses herself by saying that it was not with the name of Juan or Diego that she was in love, but with the qualities she found in the bearer of both. At last, after a very pretty complication, in which everybody refuses to believe that he is Don Juan, all ends happily. I was very much interested—it was so pleasant to *see* what I had so often had to imagine in reading Spanish plays. The acting was good — especially that of the *gracioso*. The heroine was perfectly a portrait by Vandyke in the Museo, so that by an odd trick of imagination she seemed real, a person I had already known. . . .

TO C. E. NORTON

7 Cuesta de Santo Domingo,
Madrid, Nov. 10, 1878.

. . . We have had General Grant [here], and I gave him a dinner and reception. As he speaks nothing but English, he was as incommunicable as an iceberg, and, I think, is rather bored by peregrination. What he

likes best is to escape and wander about the streets
with his Achates Young.   After being here two days, I
think he knew Madrid better than I.   He seemed to
me very simple-minded, honest, and sensible—very easy
to be led by anybody he likes.   He is perfectly unconscious and natural, naïvely puzzled, I fancied, to find
himself a personage, and going through the ceremonies
to which he is condemned with a dogged imperturba-
bility that annotated for me his career as General.   He
seemed anxious to explain to me his quarrel with Sumner—or Sumner's with him.   "Sumner is the only man
I was ever anything but my real self to; the only man
I ever tried to conciliate by artificial means"—those
are his very words. . . . Grant has an excellent memory and narrates remarkably well. . . .

TO THOMAS HUGHES

Madrid, Nov. 17, 1878.

My dear Friend,—Now and then there is an advantage in being a dilatory correspondent; as, for example,
if a friend had written to me offering the splendid opportunity of enrolling myself among the shareholders
of the Emma Mine, I should have been as safe as are
the pyramids from cholera.   More punctual men would
have been bitten, but I should have found so many
reasons for not writing to-day nor to-morrow nor next
day, that by the time I dipt my pen in the ink I
should have been as likely to subscribe for shares in
that railway to the moon chartered by the legislature
of New Hampshire as in the enterprise of Messrs.

Schenk & Park. Again, if I were one of those admirable persons who always reply by return of post, I should now find myself entangled in a web of contradictory opinions and prophecies about the Eastern Question, and should long ago have had to deliver an opinion or die, on the vext question whether the Plenipos at Berlin had applied a plaster or a blister to their unhappy patient. As it is, I have only been called on to shake my head and leave my interlocutors to guess what new shape I had thus given to my ideas. Between ourselves, by the way, I am satisfied that Dizzy's policy has done a good deal to restore the prestige of England among the " rest of mankind "; and as I back the English race against the field, I am not sorry for it. I hope you won't have a war, but at all events a war between England and Russia would be a war between civilization and barbarism. Moreover, I like the Turks for about as good a reason as the man had for not liking Dr. Fell, but still I like them. And then I think a good deal of the prejudice against Beaconsfield is mediæval, of a piece with the enlightened public opinion which dictated the legend of Hugh of Lincoln. There are plenty of other modern versions of the story of Joseph —only people know not Joseph, that is, his pedigree.

Yes, I am beginning to feel handier in my new trade, but I had a hard row to hoe at first. All alone, without a human being I had ever seen before in my life, and with unaccustomed duties, feeling as if I were beset with snares on every hand, obliged to carry on the greater part of my business in a strange tongue—it was rather trying for a man with so sympathetic and sensi-

tive a temperament as mine, and I don't much wonder
the gout came upon me like an armed man. Three
attacks in five months! But now I begin to take things
more easily.

Still, I don't like the business much, and feel that I
am wasting my time. Nearly all I have to do neither
enlists my sympathies much nor makes any call on my
better faculties. I feel, however, as if I were learning
something, and I dare say shall find I have when I get
back to my own chimney-corner again. I like the Spaniards, with whom I find many natural sympathies in
my own nature, and who have had a vast deal of injustice done them by this commercial generation. They
are still Orientals to a degree one has to live among
them to believe. But I think they are getting on. The
difficulty is that they don't care about many things
that we are fools enough to care about, and the balance
in the ledger is not so entirely satisfactory to them as
a standard of morality as to some more advanced nations. They employ inferior races (as the Romans did)
to do their intellectual drudgery for them, their political
economy, scholarship, history, and the like. But they
are advancing even on these lines, and one of these days
—but I won't prophesy. Suffice it that they have
plenty of brains, if ever they should condescend so far
from their *hidalguia* as to turn them to advantage. At
present they prefer the brook to the mill-pond. They
get a good deal out of life at a cheap rate, and are not
far from wisdom, if the old Greek philosophers who
used to be held up to us as an example knew anything
about the matter. . . .

TO MISS GRACE NORTON

Madrid, Jan. 15, 1879.

Dear Grace,—I wrote some verses thirty odd years ago called " Without and Within," and they originally ended with the author's looking up at the stars through six feet of earth and feeling dreadfully bored, while a passer-by deciphers the headstone and envies the supposed sleeper beneath. I was persuaded to leave out this ending as too grim—but I often think of it. They have a fine name for this kind of feeling nowadays, and would fain make out pessimism to be a monstrous birth of our century. I suspect it has always been common enough, especially with naughty children who get tired of their playthings as soon as I do—the absurdity being that then we are not content with smashing the toy which turns out to be finite—but everything else into the bargain. . . .

I wonder if somebody else, if I myself when I was younger, couldn't find enough that was interesting to say about this New World, that has become new by dint of staying pretty much where it was when Columbus left it to find another—because this, I suppose, had grown tiresome. I shall have a good deal to tell by the chimney-corner if ever I get back to it, I have no doubt, but it takes a great while for things to settle and separate themselves in my memory. Shall I tell you of a reception at the palace? It is so comically like what one sees on the stage, and really *is* so much a mere piece of acting here, that it seems hardly worth while. Or shall I write of the weather? That,

after all, in spite of the fun that has been made of it
as a topic of conversation, is the only one of universal
and permanent interest, and you will be glad to know
that we have had a rainy winter, on the whole, but roses
have been in bloom all the while, and the daisies were
opening their eyes in the grass more than a week ago.
There are great patches of green on the brown gaber-
dine of the Campiña, and there is a sound of spring in
the voice of the sparrows. But the Guadarramas (the
tallest of them) are dreamy with snow, and don ever
and anon (don anon!) a kind of luminous mantilla of
cloud that is wonderfully fine. I explain this nebular
radiance by the vapors being comparatively low, so that
the sunshine is reflected through them from the snow
behind. I think I have told you that I like the Campiña better than the Campagna. It is serious, it is more
than that—it is even sad, but it is the sadness and in-
communicativeness of nature and not the melancholy
of ruin. It is vast and grows vaster the more you see
it, and one conceives the rotundity of the earth, as at sea.
It always looks to me like a land not yet taken possession
of by man, rather than one that he has worn out. . . .

TO GEORGE PUTNAM

Madrid, March 3, 1879.

. . . I have pretty much made up my mind to stay
on here for at least another year—perhaps for two, if
they don't Motleyize me. I have now learned my business, and after two years of a discomfort that has sometimes been almost intolerable I should like to get a
little pleasure and profit out of my exile. . . .

TO MISS GRACE NORTON

Madrid, March 4, 1879.

. . . Since I have been here I have been reading a good many travels in Spain, beginning with a Bohemian knight of the fifteenth century and ending with Théophile Gautier. It is very curious in how many particulars the earliest and latest agree, proving, I suspect, that the condition of the country is not due to the expulsion of Moors and Jews, or to the House of Austria, or the Bourbons, so much as to something in the character of the people.

Generally the balls I have to attend are a bore, but I was interested in one the other night at the Duke of Osuna's, who lives in a real palace with family portraits and relics. The duke represents ten grandeeships of the first class—which ought to give him the right to wear ten hats in the presence of the king. He sums up in himself Béjar, Olivares, Lerma, and other names we all know. He is ruined, but comfortably so, for he is allowed a hundred thousand dollars a year by his creditors. But he cannot live on it. He has ruined himself magnificently. While ambassador at St. Petersburg he sent all his clothes home to be washed in the Manzanares, and had a table of fourteen covers set every day in his palace here. He seems to have inherited his magnificent wastefulness, for Lord Auckland speaks of a ball given by his grandfather (I suppose) in 1788 that cost £8000. It is a wonder he inherited anything else.

Field is still with us, and we propose, as he no doubt

has told you, a little excursion together to the Balearic
Islands, but as the ministry resigned yesterday I suppose I shall have to stick in Madrid for the present.
Politics here are in one respect interesting and worth
study. They are so personal and so much moved by
springs of intrigue that they help one to a more vivid
understanding of those of the last century. I can
make no guess as to what is to take place. . . .

TO W. D. HOWELLS

Madrid, May 2, 1879.

Dear Howells,—When Aldrich passed through here
he brought me some excuse or other from you for not
having answered a letter of mine. Was it an abominable
sarcasm sent all the way over the ocean with its subtile
barb dipt in sweetened poison—the worst kind of all?
If not, the sensation is so novel that I ought not to en-
danger it by any clumsy interferences of mine. I am
as sure as I well can be of anything that no man ever
before accomplished the feat of owing me a letter. Believe me, my dear boy, it is your most exquisite literary
achievement. My own debts of this kind commonly
gather and gather till bankruptcy is the only possible
outlet — and without a dividend. Never a court in
Christendom would whitewash me. Now I am going
to astonish you by paying you a penny in the pound.

And yet I can't say that you had wholly neglected
me. I always fancy that an author's works are more
intimately addressed to his friends, have passages in
them written in sympathetic ink invisible to the vulgar,

but revealing themselves to the penetrating warmth of friendship. And your " Lady of the Aroostook " was to me a delightful instance of this cryptography. I read it as it came out in the *Atlantic*, and was always as impatient for more as the French ladies used to be for more Arabian Nights. It is delightful, and there was never a slyer bit of satire than your Englishman who loves the real American flavor, while his wife is abolishing herself as hard as she can in a second-hand Anglicism. I am quite in love with your heroine, and am grateful to you accordingly. . . .

I am painfully struck, by the way, with the amount of discussion going on just now, which somehow implies a certain consciousness of inferiority on our part as compared with our English cousins. (I confess, let me say in passing, that I am tired to death of ——'s laborious demonstration that we have a right to our mother-tongue ! If he would devote himself to hunting down American vulgarisms and corruptions—I observe that even the *Atlantic*, in some sort the child of my entrails, confuses *will* and *shall*—more power to his elbow !) I think we were less conscious when I was a youngster. Nowadays Europe, and especially England, seems a glass of which everybody is uncomfortably aware, an horizon which, instead of suggesting something beyond itself, cuts us all off with reflections of (perhaps I should say on) our unhappy selves. We are all the time wondering what is thought of us over there, instead of going quietly about our business.

However, my opinion is of no earthly consequence, for I feel every day more sensibly that I belong to a former age. A new generation has grown up that knows not Joseph, and I have nothing left to do but to rake together what embers are left of my fire and get what warmth out of them I may. I still take an interest, however, in what some of the young ones are doing, as a gambler who has emptied his pockets still watches the game, and especially in you who always do conscientious work. So I venture to tell you that I think your new book especially *wholesome* and admirable.

You can't imagine how far I am away from the world here—I mean the modern world. Spain is as primitive in some ways as the books of Moses and as oriental. Spaniards have, I believe, every possible fault—and yet I love the jades for a' that! They find themselves in the midst of a commercial age, poor devils! with as little knowledge of book-keeping as the Grand Turk. But there is something fine in this impenetrability of theirs, and the grand way they wrap themselves in their ragged *capa* of a past and find warmth in their pride. Their indifference to legitimate profit is a continual comfort, and they have no more enterprise than an Old Cambridge man.

Good-by. Write another story at once, and don't forget

　　　　　　　　Your affectionate old friend,

　　　　　　　　　　　　　　J. R. L.

　　　　　　TO C. E. NORTON

　　　　　　　　　Madrid, May 4, 1879.

. . . One thing I have remarked here, not without serious foreboding. I mean the analogy between the

　　II.—16

Spanish civil service with its inevitable results, and our own. Politics here is a scramble for office. Leaders, therefore, represent not a principle, but simply a chance. A government once in power cooks the elections to its fancy, and there is absolutely no way to a change except through a *pronunciamiento*. Are we not moving more or less rapidly in the same direction? As we have no standing army, we choose the more cowardly way of fraud rather than the bolder of brute force. But the root of the matter seems the same—the hopelessness of getting power and place against the patronage and myriad means of influence of the cabal in possession. I have great faith in the good sense of our people, but deterioration of national character is always so gradual and imperceptible, and we are receiving so strong a dose of alien and more impatient blood, that there is certainly room for doubt. It all depends on our force of digestion, but with the utter decay of the principle of authority the world has a new problem before it. Perhaps Judge Lynch is not so bad a fellow after all from some points of view. . . .

TO LESLIE STEPHEN

Madrid, June 8, 1879.

My dear Stephen,— . . . What you say of politics and the D—l reminds me of the Universalist who announced his conversion to Calvinism during our civil war, because " he was satisfied that Hell was a military necessity." But to me over here in Spain, which is pretty much what it was when Gil Blas saw it, *any* kind of administration looks ideal. "War-horses" and "Favorite Sons" are plentier here than in the best country in the world.

Over there, by the way, I see they are in a great taking over the new California Constitution. I am rather pleased with it myself, for it is going to show how really healthy our body politic is. It is the great advantage of our system that one State can try quack medicines while the others look on and await the result. No Dennis Kearney was ever yet contrived who could make himself master of the helm. . . .

TO MISS GRACE NORTON

Madrid, Corpus Christi, June 12, 1879.

. . . I am still reading old travels in Spain, and with profit as well as interest. And this, with Harry James's and Howells's stories, has made me very vividly conscious of a sad change. The old travellers tell what they see, and talk of men as impartially—of men and their ways I mean—as they would of animals of any other species. They are interested, and seem rather glad than otherwise to come across strange habits as a relief from the general monotony of existence. They record facts, and neither draw conclusions nor make comparisons. Nations seem to have had an individuality that satisfied themselves and other people. Now they have become self-conscious. There is a standard somewhere or other to which they all strive more or less eagerly to prove themselves conformable, and which every traveller seems to carry in his pocket. No nation

seems to be free from this weakness, or to have that
high style of manners that comes of perfect self-possession or from interest in loftier matters than whether
they eat with their knives—we Americans least of all.
I know, of course, that there is a standard of good manners, and that the comfort of life and the security of
civilization are in some measure dependent on its main-
tenance.   But this is not precisely what I mean.   (Here
I was interrupted by a visitor, and can't knit together
again the broken ends of my thread of thought.)   But
one thing seems clear to me, and that is that the Americans I remember fifty years ago had a consciousness of
standing firmer on their own feet and in their own shoes
than those of the newer generation.   We are vulgar
now precisely because we are afraid of being so.   The
English press is provincializing us again.   I don't object
to English criticism, but I do to English influence, for
England seems to me the incarnation of the Kingdom
of this World. . . .

TO THE SAME

Madrid, Aug. 16, 1879.

. . . Life does seem sometimes a hard thing to bear,
and all that makes it bearable is to occupy the mind
with the nobler moods of contemplation—not shutting
our eyes to what is mean and ugly, but striving to inter-
pret it rightly.   However we explain it, whether as im-
planted by God or the result of long and laborious evolution, there is something in the flesh that is superior
to the flesh, something that can in finer moments abol-
ish matter and pain, and it is to this we must cleave.   I

do not see how even the loss of mind tells against a belief in this superior thing—for is the mind really dying
in the same way as the body dies? or is it only that the
tools it works with are worn out or bent or broken? . . .

TO THE SAME

Madrid, Sept. 12, 1879.

. . . They talk a good deal about *fetiches* nowadays,
but I confess that I have sometimes lately been in a
state of mind when I could have vowed a gigantic candle to a saint.   And why not, if I was baby enough to
be quieted a moment by a toy?   I think the evolution-
ists will have to make a fetich of their protoplasm before
long.   Such a mush seems to me a poor substitute for
the Rock of Ages—by which I understand a certain set
of higher instincts which mankind have found solid under their feet in all weathers.   At any rate, I find a useful moral in the story of Bluebeard.   We have the key
put into our hands, but there is always one door it is
wisest not to unlock.   I suppose there are times when
the happiest of us ask ourselves whether life is worth
living, but did you ever happen to hear of a pessimist
sincere enough to cut his own throat? . . .

TO F. J. CHILD

Madrid, Dec. 30, 1879.

. . . I will try, when I can pull myself together again,
to see if I can get you any inedited folksongs.   But I
greatly doubt.   The Spaniards are singularly indifferent

to such things, if not contemptuous of them. There is almost no scholarship here in our sense of the word, and most of the criticism is in the good old *isime* style. So entire a self-satisfaction I never saw in any people.

. . . The *penitus divisos ab orbe Britannos* were nothing to them in point of seclusion from the rest of mankind. But I love the jades for a' that—perhaps on account of a' that. I shout with laughter over their newspapers sometimes. For example, the *Imparcial* (a very clever paper by the way) had an article not long ago on "Longevity in Europe," based on one by Max Waldstein in a Viennese review. Here is a bit of it: "Salimos los Españoles los menos aventajados en eso de vivir mucho tiempo; pero *como es necesario dudar siempre de la veracidad de los extrangeros en todo cuanto atañe á nuestro pais*, etc., etc. Isn't that delicious? Commonly they bluntly attribute this malice of facts to envy. They fancy themselves always in the age of Charles V., and the perfect gravity with which they always assume the airs of a Great Power is not without a kind of pathetic dignity. We all wink at the little shifts of a decayed gentleman, especially when he is Don Quixote, as this one certainly is. . . .

TO MRS. EDWARD BURNETT

Madrid, Jan. 22, 1880.

. . . Day before yesterday I was startled with a cipher telegram. My first thought was, "Row in Cuba—I shall have no end of bother." It turned out to be this: "President has nominated you to England. He regards

it as essential to the public service that you should accept and make your personal arrangements to repair to
London as early as may be.   Your friends whom I
have conferred with concur in this view."   You see that
is in very agreeable terms, and at least shows that Government is satisfied with my conduct here.   I was afraid
of its effects on mamma * at first; but she was pleased,
and began at once to contrive how I could accept,
which she wished me to do.   I answered: " Feel highly
honored by the President's confidence.   Could accept if
allowed two months' delay.   Impossible to move or
leave my wife sooner."

The papers already announce the appointment of my
successor here, but say nothing about me.   The doctor
says I could safely leave mamma now for a few weeks,
in which case I could go to London and present my letters of credence and come back here.   The rent of my
house is paid to March 1st, and I should feel easier now
the Fields are here.   It is certainly an honor to be pro-
moted to the chief post in our diplomatic service, and
I should like to serve (if only for a year) for the sake
of my grandchildren if nothing else.   By this time you
probably know more about it than I. . . .

TO MRS. W. E. DARWIN

Madrid, Jan. 26, 1880.

. . . You look at only one side of the matter (and it is
one great merit of your sex that they always do), and
don't consider, first, whether I can afford it—though that

* Mrs. Lowell was recovering from long, desperate illness.

is the least, for I have no profound faith in fuss and feathers, and it is they that cost most—but, second, you don't consider how I hate snobs and bores, and how many of our richer countrymen have to be thus labelled by the scientific inquirer. Madrid is a kind of Patmos in comparison with London, and yet even here I have been hunted down by Monsieur Jourdains, whose great object in life seemed to be to inform everybody that they travelled with *two* servants or with a courier, or that somehow or other they were not Americans exactly.

And the worst of it is that the Eastern States provide most of these vermin. Your Westerner, thank God! if he hasn't the manners of Vere de Vere, has at least that first quality of a gentleman, that he stands squarely on his own feet and is as unconscious as a prairie. You can fancy how many of our countrymen are speedily convinced that I am wholly unfit to represent the great republic—and all of 'em pass through London! But, after all, the Senate hasn't confirmed me yet. . . .

TO R. W. GILDER

Madrid, Jan. 26, 1880.

Thank you for your congratulations. I know not whether I deserve them or no. At any rate, I had no choice, for I was nominated without consultation. Otherwise I hardly should have accepted. As I had consented to come hither for my own pleasure, I felt bound to obey orders.

I shall probably go to London to present my credentials, and then come back hither to remove Mrs. Lowell, who is better, but not yet able to leave her bed.

However, the Senate have not acted on me yet, so I may not come after all. . . .

IX

1880–1885

IN LONDON. — VACATION TOUR TO GERMANY AND ITALY. — DEATH OF MRS. LOWELL.—DEPARTURE FROM ENGLAND.

LETTERS TO C. E. NORTON, H. W. LONGFELLOW, MRS. W. E. DARWIN, R. W. GILDER, JOHN W. FIELD, T. B. ALDRICH, W. D. HOWELLS, F. J. CHILD, J. B. THAYER, GEORGE PUTNAM, MRS. W. K. CLIFFORD, O. W. HOLMES, MISS GRACE NORTON.

TO C. E. NORTON

37 Lowndes St., S. W., Aug. 17, 1880.

... I find that you have been very lenient in your judgment on my poems and have used a far finer sieve than I should have chosen if I had done the sifting. They always make me sad, thinking how much better I might have done if in the early years I *had* improvised less, and if in the later other avocations and studies had not made my hand more clumsy through want of use, than it might have been had I kept more closely to verse and to the mood which that implies. But it is something that three such friends as you and George Curtis and Child should still retain a certain amount of interest in what I have written. I not only approve, but shall perhaps go further if I once begin. The question was simply one of leaving out *any*thing—for the terrible *manet litera scripta* was staring me in the face, and positively made me unwilling to reprint at all.   By the way, I spent Sunday with Mr. Leveson Gower (Lord Granville's brother and a charming host), and coming in from out of doors came upon John Bright reading aloud from the " Commemoration Ode."   It sounded better than I feared—but when I am asked to read I never can find anything that seems to me good enough. . . .

TO H. W. LONGFELLOW

37 Lowndes St., S. W., Oct. 3, 1880.

My dear Longfellow,—I have just been reading, with a feeling I will not mar by trying to express it, your "Ultima Thule."   You will understand the pang of pleasurable homesickness it gave me.   I cannot praise it better than by saying that it is like you from the first line to the last.   Never was your hand firmer.   If Gil Blas had been *your* secretary he never need have lost his place.   I haven't a Dante by me, and my memory is in a very dilapidated state, but you will remember the passage I am thinking of, where the old poet in Purgatory says to him, *Or sei tu colui*, and so on.   *Io mi son uno che quando Amor mi spira* is a part of it.   If I could only drop into your study as I used, I should call you " old fellow," as we do boys, without any reckoning of years in it, and tell you that you had misreckoned the height of the sun, and were not up with *Ultima Thule* by a good many degrees yet.   Do such fruits grow there?

But you have made me more homesick than ever, and I feel like the Irishman whose friend was carrying him for a wager up to the roof on a ladder—"Begorra, whin you were at the thurrud story I had hopes!" So I begin to think it wouldn't be so bad if Hancock were elected—for he would recall me. I like my present life as Touchstone did his in the forest. However, I dare say Garfield will have somebody he would like to send in my place.

I hope the Club still persists. I have never found such good society and don't expect it. I forwarded to you yesterday a box containing a drawing of the Minnehaha Fall by Lord Dufferin. It goes to the care of the State Department, which I thought would save trouble. I hope it will arrive safely. Good-by, hoist sail again without delay, and correct your geography. You are sure of a welcome in every port.

Affectionately yours,

J. R. L.

TO MRS. W. E. DARWIN

London, Oct. 10, 1880.

. . . As you intervened unofficially (or *benevolently*, as we diplomatists say) in the affair of the Workingmen's College, I have the honor to report that I have fulfilled your instructions by talking to the unfortunate youth who compose the Body—as the teachers do the Soul— of that excellent institution. That part of Dogberry's charge to the watch in which he inculcates the duty of "*comprehending* all vagrom men," seems to me a very fair expression of the painful position in which a quasi-compulsory audience is placed by itinerant lecturers. But some pity is also due to the unfortunate creature who is obliged to inflict his particular form of aphasia (isn't that the word?) upon them. As for me, who value my own wisdom less the older I grow, and who found it absolutely impossible to prepare anything, I shall not attempt to pathologize for you the pangs I underwent. When I saw directly under me a row of eight reporters, I was abashed by the feeling that I was decanting my emptiness into a huge ear-trumpet which communicated with the four winds of heaven, whose duty it would be to bear every idle word I uttered to the uttermost parts of the earth. If you had been there, you would have swallowed it all without a wry face, and would have told me afterwards that it was a " splendid success," with that sweet partiality which characterizes all your sex . . . and which is one of the few things that make life endurable to its victims. I did not quite break down—but I heard several ominous cracks under me as I hurried over the slender and shaky bridge which led from my exordium to my peroration. . . .

TO R. W. GILDER

Legation of the United States,
London, Sept. 4, 1881.

Dear Mr. Gilder, — Your telegram scared me, for, coming at an unusual hour, I thought it brought ill news from Washington.* My relief on finding it innocent has perhaps made me too good-natured towards

* Of President Garfield's condition.

the verses I send you, but I have waited sixty-two years for them, and am willing to wait as many more (not here) before they are printed. Do what you like with them. They mean only my hearty good-will towards you and my hope for your success in your new undertaking. . . .

Faithfully yours,

J. R. LOWELL.

If I could see the proofs, very likely I could better it—they sober one and bring one to his bearings. Perhaps the metaphysical (or whatever they are) stanzas—what I mean is *moralizing*—were better away. Perhaps too many compound epithets—but I had to give up " visionary " in order to save " legendary," which was essential. Perhaps a note, saying that so long as the author can remember a pair of these birds (give ornithological name—*muscicapa ?*) have built on a jutting brick in an archway leading to the house at Elmwood—or does everybody know what a *phœbe* is? I am so old that I am accustomed to people's being ignorant of whatever you please.

PHŒBE

Ere pales in heaven the morning star,
    A bird, the loneliest of its kind,
Hears Dawn's faint footfall from afar
    While all its mates are dumb and blind.

It is a wee sad-colored thing,
    As shy and secret as a maid,
That, ere in choir the robins ring,
    Pipes its own name like one afraid.

It seems pain-prompted to repeat
   The story of some ancient ill,
But *Phœbe! Phœbe!* sadly sweet
   Is all it says and then is still.

It calls and listens. Earth and sky,
   Hushed by the pathos of its fate,
Listen, breath held, but no reply
   Comes from its doom-divided mate.

Phœbe! it calls and calls again,
   And Ovid, could he but have heard,
Had hung a legendary pain
   About the memory of the bird;

A pain articulate so long
   In penance of some mouldered crime
Whose ghost still flies the Furies' thong
   Down the waste solitudes of Time;

Or waif from young Earth's wonder-hour
   When gods found mortal maidens fair,
And will malign was joined with power
   Love's kindly laws to overbear.

Phœbe! is all it has to say
   In plaintive cadence o'er and o'er,
Like children that have lost their way
   And know their names, but nothing more.

Is it a type, since nature's lyre
   Vibrates to every note in man,
Of that insatiable desire,
   Meant to be so, since life began?

Or a fledged satire, sent to rasp
   Their jaded sense, who, tired so soon
With shifting life's doll-dresses, grasp,
   Gray-bearded babies, at the moon?

I, in strange lands at gray of dawn
 Wakeful, have heard that fruitless plaint
Through Memory's chambers deep withdrawn
 Renew its iterations faint.

So nigh! yet from remotest years
 It seems to draw its magic, rife
With longings unappeased and tears
 Drawn from the very source of life.

TO THE SAME

Legation of the United States,
London, Sept. 5, 1881.

Dear Mr. Gilder,—I sent off the verses yesterday, and now write in great haste to say that in my judgment the stanza beginning "Or waif from young Earth's," etc., were better away. Also for "doom-divided" print "doom-dissevered." I have not had time to mull over the poem as I should like.

Faithfully yours,

J. R. LOWELL.

P. S. I may write in a day or two suppressing more, after I have had time to think.

TO THE SAME

Legation of the United States,
London, Sept. 6, 1881.

Dear Mr. Gilder,—I bother you like a boy with his first essay in verse. I wrote yesterday to ask the omission of a stanza—but last night, being sleepless, as old fellows like me are too often apt to be, I contrived to

make a stanza which had been tongue-tied say what I
wished.

Let it go thus,

> "Waif of the young World's wonder-hour
>   .   .   .   .
>   .   .   .   .
>   .   .   .   .   to overbear," (comma).

Then go on—

> " Like Progne, did it feel the stress
>   And coil of the prevailing words
> Close round its being and compress
>   Man's ampler nature to a bird's?"

This manages the transition, which was wanting.   Perhaps this might follow :

> " One only memory left of all
>   The motley crowd of vanished scenes,
> Hers—and vain impulse to recall
>   By repetition what it means."

Faithfully yours,

J. R. LOWELL.

TO THE SAME

Legation of the United States,
London, Sept. 8, 1881.

Dear Mr. Gilder,—This is positively the last!   I wish
to omit the stanza beginning " Or a winged satire," etc.
I have been convinced by a friend whom I have con-
sulted that it was a cuckoo's egg in my nest.   *Item.*
The verse that had bothered me most of all was this :

> "Listen, breath held, but no reply," etc.

I wished to have a distinct pause after " listen," in accordance with the sense. Somehow I could not get the right, and "breath held" was clearly the wrong one, awkward, and with the same vowel sound in both halves. Print—

> "Listen : no whisper of reply
>   Is heard of doom-dissevered mate."

No; that won't do either, with its assonance of "heard" and "dissev*ered*"—so, though I prefer "dissevered" for sense, I will go back to the original word "divided," which I suppose was instinctive.

This is positively my last dying speech and confession. You need fear nothing more from me. I fancy you ducking your head for fear of another rap every time the postman comes.

I hope you will like my little poem, and tell me so if you don't.

Kindest regards to Mrs. Gilder.

Faithfully yours,

J. R. Lowell.

TO THE SAME

Legation of the United States,
London, Sept. 12, 1881.

Dear Mr. Gilder,—With (I am sorry to say) not unheard-of selfishness I forgot, in writing about my own little affairs, a much more important one of Aubrey de Vere. He is going to send you a poem (founded on an Irish legend) which is sure to be good—though whether good enough I cannot say, for I like him so much and have liked him so long that I can't tell for the life of me why and how he falls short. I told him I feared the poem would be too long for you, etc., etc., but the dear old boy has a self-possession of hope which would be creditable at ten years. He is naturally anxious about his manuscript, and I beg you to be careful of it and return it to Mr. Norton at Cambridge if you shouldn't want it.

As I am writing, I add that if you think (as I am half inclined)

"No whisper of reply
Comes from its doom-dissevered mate"

better than the other reading, print it so.

Faithfully yours,

J. R. LOWELL.

We are sadly anxious to-day about the President.

TO MRS. LOWELL

Victoria Hotel, Dresden, Oct. 16, 1881.

. . . It is just twenty-five years since I was in Dresden, and there is something sad in coming back an old man to a place familiar to you when much younger. But I must take up my diary again. When I wrote yesterday [from Weimar] I was uncertain whether I should see Goethe's house (I mean the inside of it) or not. At any rate, I would see the garden-house he built when he first came to Weimar. So I took the drollest little bow-legged valet-de-place, who touched his hat and called me *Excellenz* whenever he could catch my eye. I had taken him with the express stipulation that he shouldn't open his mouth, and this was the compromise he made. Our walk led through the

Park and along the Ilm. The Park, except the paths, is left pretty much to nature. It is very charming. The garden-house turned out to be about twenty minutes' walk. . . . It was a very simple affair of stone, about twenty feet square, roughly built, but beautifully set on the edge of a meadow sloping to the river. It was odd to find that my associations with Weimar, which are so vivid that I seem to have seen the persons and can hardly persuade myself I did not know Frau von Stein, should be more than a century old. Goethe was building this house just as our Revolution began. When I got back I found a card from Baron v. Brincken, informing me that Herr v. Goethe would be glad to see me at half-past one. So I saw what I went to Weimar for after all. There was a small collection of antique gems, of drawings and engravings, and of very good majolica. There were also some bronzes, none of them remarkable. The *Studienzimmer* was what interested me most—the plain little table and desk, with the chair waiting its master. Out of it opened the sleeping-room with the bed in which he died — about as large as a Spanish *alcoba*, and showing how little good air has to do with long life. Everything was very dingy, and the study especially ill-lighted. I have an engraving of it somewhere, so that I have been wondering ever since if I had not seen it before.

I am going out presently to see the Sistine Madonna and a few other old friends again. *They* will not have changed or grown older. . . .

TO R. W. GILDER

☞ ☞ Hôtel Danieli,
☞ ☞ Venice, Oct. 24, 1881.

Dear Mr. Gilder,—If you put up a warning hand to point at your new address—then, *a fortiori, I* may, who am in Venice. It is raining: never mind, I am in Venice! Sirocco is doing his worst: I defy him, I am in Venice! I am horribly done at my hotel: but what could I expect? I am in Venice! But it is base in me to crow in this way over a young poet who perhaps would be more in keeping here than my gray hairs can hope to be. I find on looking back that I have crowed once oftener than the cock crowed at St. Peter; and as he (I mean the bird) was divinely inspired, he probably went to the precise limit that human nature could bear. Forgive me. I change my figure. I have seen a grave horse of thirty years, and a parson's, too, gallop and fling up his heels and roll and do all kinds of indecorous things on being turned into the pasture. I am that animal—or even lengthen my ears if you will and I am *that* animal—I am an escaped prisoner of the Bastile, I am a fugitive slave, more than all, I am an American public nigger out for a holiday! And I am come here to find a *bateau mouche* plying up and down the Grand Canal!

Thank you for the printed copy. Of course I am disgusted with it. Print somehow is like a staring plastercast compared with the soft and flowing outlines, the modest nudity of the manuscript clay. But it is a real pleasure to me that you like it.

"Robins *ring*" is right, and whenever you spend a
June night at Elmwood (as I hope you will so soon as
I am safe there once more) you will recognize its truth.
There are hundreds of 'em going at once, like the bells
here last night (Sunday), with a perfect indecency of
disregard for rhythm or each other. Mr. Burroughs, I
hear, has been criticising my knowledge of out-doors.
God bless his soul! I had been living in the country
thirty years (I fancy it must be) before he was born,
and if anybody ever lived in the open air it was I. So
be at peace. By the way, I took Progne merely because she was changed into a *little* bird. I should have
preferred a male, and was thinking of a fellow (trans-
formed, I think, by Medea), but can't remember his
name. While I am about it, I question *wee*. Is it
English? I had no dictionary at hand. But there is
one atrocity — "*mold*ered." Why do you give in to
these absurdities? Why abscond into this petty creek
from the great English main of orthography? 'Tis not
quite so bad as "I don't know *as*" for "I don't know
that," but grazes it and is of a piece with putting one's
knife in one's mouth.

As for your "remuneration" — it was most generous, and I had a kind of qualm as I impeticosed your
gratillity. I fear for authorship with these luxurious
rates.

Thank you for your good opinion of my ministerial
performances. I suppose I may be recalled, just as I
have learned to be easy in my seat. Such is the lot of
an American Minister—he fleeth away as a shadow and
hath no abiding *place*. Give my kindest regards to Mrs.

Gilder and the Boy.　As for writing a sonnet—in Venice?!　Ask me to saw wood.

Faithfully yours,

J. R. LOWELL.

P. S.　My flock of ☞'s on the other side remind me of my doves.　I have just fed them at my balcony. They came in scores, their wings whistling like shafts of Phoibos and so beautiful!　*Now* I have touched the quick; I see you wince with your "Union Square," marry come up!

TO MRS. LOWELL

Hôtel Bristol, Rome, Nov. 11, 1881.

. . . I came hither yesterday from Florence through beautiful weather . . . and a country which is to me always the most pathetic in the world.　I don't know why, but the desolation of Greece touches me less nearly.　I saw Cortona in the distance sunning its long wall on the slope of the hill, and close by the station were some roofs all gilt with lichen, on one of which a pair of white doves were philandering.　Then Orvieto on its crag . . . and queer, nameless little burghs that sought the hills for safety, and are now, consequently, *too* safe from the iron highway.　Then there came slopes smoky with olives, which somehow are quite another thing in Italy than in Spain, and the groves of oak I remembered so well and through which I loitered in a vettura so many years ago.

I am sitting in the shadow of the Barberini as I write, and am growing into a furious socialist at the sight of these upstart palaces that shut out the sun from Diogenes. . . .

Hôtel Bristol, Rome, Nov. 13, 1881.

. . . My windows here look out on one side towards the Barberini, and on the other towards the old Triton. . . . The weather is as fine as fine can be, and I do nothing with commendable assiduity — thawing myself out in the sun like a winter fly. William and John * and I idle about, telling over old stories and reviving old associations. . . .

I told you of the *vaporetto* on the Grand Canal (between ourselves, it was only sentimentally disagreeable, and, in point of fact, a great blessing to the poorer class), but I hesitate to tell you what I have seen here. — The only costumes left now are on the brazen-faced models, and one sees below—what? Those hateful boots with a high heel in the midst of the sole, on which they tottle about as on peg-tops. When I was first here every peasant woman one met wore sandals. I have always hated those eternal repetitions of women with a dirty towel on their heads which express the highest aspiration and conviction of modern art—but this is like the cloven hoof. . . .

Wordsworth speaks of a motion this way or that which is fateful—and I often think of it as I look at pictures and statues, and try to make out *what* it is that makes some eternally fascinating and leaves us cold before the rest. It is so little and it is everything—and the earth is full of the same beauty the Greeks and

* Mr. William W. Story and Mr. John W. Field.

Venetians saw. Why should they be the only ones
that ever saw it? . . .

TO R. W. GILDER

10 Lowndes Square, S. W., Jan. 9, 1882.

Dear Mr. Gilder,—I forgot all about the photograph
—my misfortunes in the way of engraved portraiture
(the only set-off to which is security against identifica-
tion by the police) having made me callous, if not indifferent. I don't know which you have got from Mrs.
Carter—for your description of it as "sitting in a chair"
doesn't help me much. Pray, what should the poor
thing be sitting in? Go on and do your worst—or
rather (vanity would say) your prettiest. The Storys
showed me an old photograph of myself in Rome the
other day, which I should not have believed taken from
me but for their assurance. How young it looked! and
what a wealth of curls! It must have been about thirty
years old—I mean the photograph. Was *I* ever thirty?
It seems impossible, though folks tell me I am no more
than that now. *Posthume! Posthume!*

I don't think much of any international copyright bill
which is drawn by publishers—always in the interest of
the manufacturers and not the makers of books. The
clause you mention was no doubt meant for a sop to
our protectionists. The British Government has already
expressed its indifference thereanent. But I don't see
how it can do you much harm.

I have just heard of the death of my old schoolmate
Dana*—a friend of more than fifty years. I am so glad

* Mr. Richard Henry Dana.

that I saw him in Florence and Rome lately—for we
never expect these things. He was a very able and
high-minded man, who (if Captain Ill had not so much
influence in politics) should have been one of the Senators from Massachusetts. But he would never condescend to the means of such advancement, and I dare
say is the happier for it now.

 With kindest regards to Mrs. Gilder and young Prince
Aureole,   Yours always,

                                    J. R. LOWELL.

                 TO JOHN W. FIELD

                          [London], Jan. 17, 1882.

 . . . I was greatly startled by the death of Dana, of
which we got news by telegraph before hearing that he
was ill. It is the first time Death has so distinctly
nudged me with his elbow, for, though four of my own
classmates have died this year, he, if a year or two older
than I, belonged more immediately to my own set, and
I had known him lifelong. I am very glad now that I
saw as much of him as I did in Florence and Rome.
He is a very great loss in every way—a loss to the
world no less than to his country and friends—and he
died prematurely, before building the monument for
which he had gathered the material. He never had the
public career he should have had, both for his own sake
and ours, and it was from a quality of character pushed
to excess. He was, as you say, a "high-minded man,"
but he was more than that. He was a *lofty*-minded
man, and could not meet his fellows on such terms
(nowise degrading) as is needful for success in a democ-

racy. He ought to have been Senator from Massachusetts, Minister to England—indeed, he might have been almost anything but for this weakness. I do not know that he would have been happier for it, but at least the syllogism of expectation would have been more complete.

What you tell me Mrs. Dana said after the burial was very touching. Take care of yourself, my dear John. The lesson for us is to *close up*, and I think we *are* drawn nearer by these things—though Death seems less solemn than he used, now that we have seen him so often look at the number on our own door, as he was on his way to knock at a neighbor's. "Who knows?" and "Do I *really* wish it may be?" are all that the nineteenth century has left us of the simple faith we began life with. . . .

TO T. B. ALDRICH

Legation of the United States,
London, May 8, 1882.

Dear Aldrich,—If I could, how gladly I would!* But I am piecemealed here with so many things to do that I cannot get a moment to brood over anything as it must be brooded over if it is to have wings. It is as if a sitting hen should have to mind the door-bell. I speak as of the days of Æsop, which I mention lest some critic should charge me with not knowing what a mixed metaphor was—or rather an incongruous conception.

---

* Mr. Aldrich, then editor of the *Atlantic Monthly*, had asked Lowell to write a paper upon Mr. Dana.

Now, you who are young and clever will at once divine what I mean you to divine from that last sentence—namely, that a man with his mind in so self-conscious a state as that can't write *any*thing to advantage, and I should wish to do my best for a man so intimately associated with what is dearest to me. No, you must wait till I come home to be boycotted in my birthplace by my Irish fellow-citizens (who are kind enough to teach me how to be American), who fought all our battles and got up all our draft riots. Then, in the intervals of firing through my loopholes of retreat, I may be able to do something for the *Atlantic*.

I am now in the midst of the highly important and engrossing business of arranging for the presentation at Court of some of our fair *citoyennes*. Whatever else you are, never be a Minister!

With kind regards to Mrs. Aldrich,

Faithfully yours,

J. R. Lowell.

TO W. D. HOWELLS

Ashridge, Berkhampstead, Dec. 21, 1882.

Dear Howells,—I was very glad to get your letter, though it put me under bonds to be wiser than I have ever had the skill to be. If I remember rightly, Panurge's doubts were increased by consulting the Oracle, but how did the Oracle feel? Did it ever occur to you that a certain share of our sympathy should go in that direction?

My best judgment is this, and like all good judgment it is to a considerable degree on both sides of the question. If you are able now, without overworking mind or body, to keep the wolf from the door and to lay by something for a rainy day—and I mean, of course, without being driven to work with your left hand because the better one is tired out—I should refuse the offer,* or should hesitate to accept it. If you are a systematic worker, independent of moods, and sure of your genius whenever you want it, there might be no risk in accepting. You would have the advantage of a fixed income to fall back on. Is this a greater advantage than the want of it would be as a spur to industry? Was not the occasion of Shakespeare's plays (I don't say the motive of 'em) that he *had* to write? And are any of us likely to be better inspired than he? Does not inspiration, in some limited sense at least, come with the exercise thereof, as the appetite with eating? Is not your hand better for keeping it in, as they say? A professorship takes a great deal of time, and, if you teach in any more direct way than by lectures, uses up an immense stock of nerves. Your inevitable temptation (in some sort your duty) will be to make yourself *learned*— which you haven't the least need to be as an author (if you only have me at your elbow to correct your English now and then, naughty boy!). If you can make your professorship a thing apart—but can you and be honest? I believe the present generation doesn't think I was made for a poet, but I think I could have gone nearer convincing 'em if I had not estranged the muse by donning a professor's gown. I speak of myself because

* Of a Professorship of Literature.

you wanted my experience. I am naturally indolent, and being worked pretty hard in the College, was willing to be content with the amount of work that was squeezed out of me by my position, and let what my nature might otherwise have forced me into go. As I said before, if you can reckon on your own temperament, accept. If you have a doubt, *don't*. I think you will divine what I am driving at.

I find everybody here reading your books, and you know very well how much pleasure that gives me. They wish to see you, and I hope when you come back you will stay and let 'em do it. I wish you could know my hostess, for instance—noble in all senses of the word. I am staying here for a few days with a large party in a house as big as a small town, and a beautiful country of hill and dale and gray birch woods. Enough to say that there was once a convent here. The monks always had an eye for country.

You will have to be very fine when you show yourself in England, to look like the portrait I have painted of you—but I am willing to take the venture.

Inexorable lunch has sounded, and I must say goodby. I should say, on the whole—it is safe to ask my advice, but not to follow it. But then people never do. . . . Love to all.

Affectionately yours,

J. R. L.

TO F. J. CHILD

10 Lowndes Square, S. W., Feb. 2, 1883.

Dear Ciarli,—Thank you over and over again for

your beautiful book,* the only fault I can find with
which is the "Esq." you have added to my name,
and which seems to hold me at arm's length from you,
as it were. But I won't be held there, do what you
will!

I have been reading it with delight and wonder.
The former you will understand better than anybody;
the latter, called forth by the enormous labor you have
spent on it, you will be modestly incredulous about.
You have really built an imperishable monument, and
I rejoice as heartily as the love I bear you gives me
the right in having lived to see its completion. I
did not know you were to begin printing so soon,
and I wish my name to appear on the list of sub-
scribers, as it ought. I hope it is not too late. I am
particularly gratified with the dedication, which will
delight Furnivall, and which he in all ways so truly
deserves.

I am getting old, and my beard has now more white
than brown in it, but I on the whole enjoy my life here,
and feel that in some ways I have been and am useful.
London I like beyond measure. The wonderful movement of life here acts as a constant stimulus—and I am
beginning to need one. The climate also suits me better than any I ever lived in. I have only to walk a
hundred yards from my door to see green grass and
hear the thrushes sing all winter long. These are a
constant delight, and I sometimes shudder to think of
the poor dead weeds and grasses I have seen shivering

* The first part of "The English and Scottish Popular Ballads."

in the cast-iron earth at home. But I shall come back to them to comfort them out of my own store of warmth with as hearty a sympathy as ever.

I need not tell you how glad I was of the revulsion in our politics. I think we shall keep all the ground we have won, and before long bring the country forward—or back—to better ways. If not, I see no hope. Spain shows us to what a civil service precisely like our own will bring a country that ought to be powerful and prosperous. It wasn't the Inquisition, nor the Expulsion of Jews or Moriscos, but simply the Boss System, that has landed Spain where she is.

Give my love to all who care for it, and be sure that I am always, as I have always been,

Most affectionately yours,

J. R. L.

TO C. E. NORTON

10 Lowndes Sq., S. W., April 22, 1883.

. . . If one wait for the right time to come before writing, the right time never comes. I have been sitting like Horace's *rusticus* waiting for the stream of daily occupations to run dry, to be convinced only of the *labitur et labetur.* So I will prorogue no longer, but write a line to send you my love and to thank you for the "Carlyle-Emerson Correspondence," which I have read with pathetic interest. You can well imagine how many fading frescos it brightened in the chambers of my memory. It pleased, but not surprised me in what an ampler ether and diviner air the mind and thought of Emerson dwelt, than those that were habitual to his

correspondent. . . . I suppose you have read by this
time Mrs. Carlyle's "Correspondence." A very painful book in more ways than one. There are disclosures
there that never should have been made, as if they had
been caught up from the babblings of discharged house-
maids. One blushes in reading, and feels like a person
caught listening at the keyhole. . . .

I linger on here, partly from *vis inertiæ* and partly
because I have been, and may again be, of some use.
A year ago it would have been easy for the wrong man
to have made trouble between the two countries. The
Irish howl against me at home, by the way, received its
signal from here.

I like London, and have learned to see as I never saw
before the advantage of a great capital. It establishes
one set of weights and measures, moral and intellectual,
for the whole country. It is, I think, a great drawback
for us that we have as many as we have States. The
flow of life in the streets, too—sublimer, it seems to me
often, than the tides of the sea—gives me a kind of stimulus that I find agreeable even if it prompt to nothing.
For I am growing old, dear Charles, and haven't the go
in me I once had. Then I have only to walk a hundred yards from my door to be in Hyde Park, where,
and in Kensington Gardens, I can tread on green turf
and hear the thrushes sing all winter. I often think of
what you said to me about the birds here. There *are*
a great many more and they sing more perennially than
ours. As for the climate, it suits me better than any I
ever lived in, and for the inward weather, I have never
seen civilization at so high a level in some respects as

II.—18

here.   In plain living and high thinking I fancy we have, or used to have, the advantage, and I have never seen society, on the whole, so good as I used to meet at our Saturday Club.

Always affectionately yours,

J. R. LOWELL.

TO THE SAME

London, Dec. 4, 1883.

. . . On Saturday I went down to Cambridge to see "The Birds." It was really delightful, and more instructive than a tragedy, because its wild fancy is harder to conceive in visible types. The birds seemed to have been left inadvertently behind by a dream—such an unreal reality had they to the waking sense, and such a feeling had one that one had seen them somewhere before in some Zoo of Dreamland. I was glad to find that I knew more Greek than I expected, though that was hardly more than Swift bids us in his supplement to the "Beatitudes." They are now thinking of giving the "Œdipus Rex."

I can see that the Democrats have come to the conclusion that it would be wise to have some principles about them in case of a sudden call, and this I think increases the probability of my being your neighbor again eighteen months hence. A worse thing might befall me.

I am not yet rector of St. Andrew's. There is a question of eligibility. You will know what I mean when I say that I am utterly indifferent except on the score of the quinquennial College Catalogue. By the way, please

say *à qui de droit* to note me as Member of Spanish
Academy and of Philosophical Society at Philadelphia.
I wish to justify Parson Wilbur's augury, now nearly
forty years old. . . .

TO JAMES B. THAYER

London, Dec. 24, 1883.

Dear Mr. Thayer,—Many thanks for your *Reitung*, as
Lessing would have called it, which is excellently done,
and just both to Emerson and his critic.   From what I
have heard it was much needed, for though, of course,
the personal *equation* is to be allowed for in all criticism, there seems to be a tendency in America (fatal to
sound judgment) to treat it as if it were the same as
personal *bias*.

As for Emerson's verse (though he has written some
as exquisite as any in the language) I suppose we must
give it up.   That he had a sense of the higher harmo-
nies of language no one that ever heard him lecture can
doubt.   The structure of his prose, as one listened to
it, was as nobly metrical as the King James version of
the Old Testament, and this made it all the more puzzling that he should have been absolutely insensitive to
the harmony of verse.   For it was there he failed—
single verses are musical enough.   I never shall forget
the good-humoredly puzzled smile with which he once
confessed to me his inability to apprehend the value of
accent in verse.

I liked particularly what you say about his mastery of
English.   No man in my judgment ever had a greater,

and I greatly doubt whether Matthew Arnold is quite capable (in the habit of addressing a jury as he always is) of estimating the style of one who conversed with none but the masters of his mother-tongue. Emerson's instinct for the best word was infallible. Wherever he found one he *froze* to it, as we say in our admirable vernacular. I have sometimes found that he had added to his cabinet the *one* good word in a book he had read. Sir T. Browne is the only man I know of worthy to be named with [him] in the imaginative felicities and audacities—the *O altitudos,* as he himself would have called them—of speech. I think that Matthew Arnold, like Renan (who has had an evil influence over him), is apt to think the *super*fine as good as the fine, or better even than that.

Look at the list of prophetic honors with which Parson Wilbur has decorated himself in the preface to the "Biglow Papers," and you will condole with me in being excluded by my official position from the rectorship of St. Andrew's. As a lawyer, you will be amused to know that it is my extra-territoriality (an awful word and fit to conjure with !) that makes me ineligible.   If I picked his saintship's pocket—fancy stealing from a Scottish saint !—I could snap my fingers at the local tribunals. So I shall never be able to read Univ. Sanct. Andr. Scot. Dom. Rect.* Couldn't they count me as they do Louis XVII., though I never reigned?

Faithfully yours,
J. R. LOWELL.

* In the Quinquennial Catalogue of Harvard University.

Alas for the Holmes House,* so dear and sacred in my memory !

TO C. E. NORTON

London, 31 Lowndes Square, Jan. 11, 1884.

. . . We have been having a very mild winter, with thrushes and robins in full song. I often think of what you said to me years ago about English singing-birds. I remember I went to the Waverley Oaks and made a list of those I heard there, which pretty well matched the catalogue in the "Squier of Low Degre." But you were right. In early summer every bush here is musical. It is partly older civilization (there are few song-birds in the woods) and partly climate. The thrushes twitch out earth-worms here all winter long, and constantly remind me of their cousins our robins. . . .

TO JOHN W. FIELD

[London], Jan. 19, 1884.

. . . I wonder, by the way, when we shall see an American politician able to appreciate and shrewd enough to act on Curran's saying about his countrymen, that "An Irishman is the worst fellow in the world to run away from." . . .

TO F. J. CHILD

10 Lowndes Square, 1884.

Dear Ciarli,— . . . When I got up this morning it

---

* One of the fine Old Cambridge houses, then lately pulled down.

was snowing, and I had been lying for some time watching the flakes fluttering up and down, like the ghosts of moths seeking vainly the flowers they used to pillage, and thinking of home, as I always do when it snows. Almost my earliest recollection is of a snow-storm and putting crumbs on the window-sill for the redbreasts that never came. Yesterday there was one singing cheerily in Kensington Gardens. A thrush, too, was piping now and then, and the grass was as green as May. I think the climate more than anything else keeps me here. It is the best I have ever seen—at any rate the best for me, and the vapory atmosphere is divine in its way—always luminous, and always giving the distance that makes things tolerable. But I have pangs sometimes. . . .

I have no news except that my official extra-territoriality will, perhaps, prevent my being rector at St. Andrews, because it puts me beyond the reach of the Scottish courts in case of malversation in office. How to rob a Scottish university suggests a serious problem. I was pleased with the election and the pleasant way it was spoken of here, though I did not want the place. Had I known what I know now, I should not have allowed myself to be put up. But I was in Paris, and had forgotten among the bookstalls that I was an Excellency. . . .

TO GEORGE PUTNAM

London, April 8, 1884.

. . . On Monday we go to Edinburgh, where they are to have a most emphatic tercentenary, and make doctors enough for the three centuries to come. This will be my fourth gown, so that I beat Dogberry by two. I shall be able to keep myself warm without Harvard.* . . .

TO C. E. NORTON

31 Lowndes Square, S.W.,
Easter Sunday, April 13, 1884.

Dear Charles,—How strange a vision rose before me in the two letters you enclosed! I thought of that little picture of Rossetti's that you have, where the two lovers, walking in the *selva oscura*, meet the ghosts of their old selves. And what a foreign yet familiar thing the ghost of one's old self is. It is memory with its sharp edges renewed, memory without any softening perspective. But one must learn to face these *revenants* from the past. How vividly my old study under the roof (where you first knew me) comes back, and the dreary year I dragged through there thirty years ago in solitary confinement, finding a strange consolation in repeating the service for the dead which I had learned by heart. I see the old scribblings on the wall which I had traced there as prisoners are wont. . . . I remember the ugly fancy I had sometimes that I was another person, and used to hesitate at the door when I came back from my late night walks, lest I should find the real owner of the room sitting in my chair before the fire. A well-nigh hermit life I had led till then, and my fate often seems to me a strange one—to be snatched

---

* Harvard conferred upon him the honorary degree of LL.D. at her Commencement in June of this year.

away and set down in the midst of Babylon the great
city, obliged to interest myself in what to me are the
mirages of life, and, above all, to make speeches (which
I loathe), and to be praised for them, which makes it
more bitter. But for my sense of humor, I couldn't
stand it. I feel that my life has been mainly wasted
—that I have thrown away more than most men ever
had; but I have never been able to shake off the indolence (I know not whether to call it intellectual or
physical) that I inherited from my father. . . .

TO MRS. W. K. CLIFFORD

31 Lowndes Square, S. W., Oct. 9, 1884.

Dear Mrs. Clifford,— . . . How delightful it is to have
woman friends—they are such impartial critics. No,
I am not a genius, and very far from thinking myself
one. I was half meant for one, but only half. A genius
has the gift of falling in love with the side-face of truth,
going mad for it, sacrificing all for it. But I must see
the full face, and then the two sides have such different
expressions that I begin to doubt which is the sincere
and cannot surrender myself.

I was very sorry that I could not tea with you yesterday, but I got home too late and fearfully tired. I
shall try to find you this afternoon.

Yes, your note was a *little* extravagant, but I could
not help liking it all the same. My address would have
been far better if I had been plain J. R. L. and not His
Excellency.

Faithfully yours,

J. R. LOWELL.

TO C. E. NORTON

31 Lowndes Square, S. W., Oct. 17, 1884.

... I send you a copy of my address at Birmingham. * It has made a kind of (mildish) sensation, greatly to my surprise. I couldn't conceive, as I told Du Maurier, that I had made so great a splash with so small a pebble. I hear that even the G. O. M. has read it with interest. It *wasn't* revised (as they say it was) by me. I did but insert some passages I spoke, but which were not in the notes given to the press.

The most interesting part of my visit to Birmingham was a call I made by appointment on Cardinal Newman. He was benignly courteous, and we excellencied and eminenced each other by turns. A more gracious senescence I never saw. There was no "monumental pomp," but a serene decay, like that of some ruined abbey in a woodland dell, consolingly forlorn. I was surprised to find his head and features smaller than I expected—modelled on lines of great vigor, but reduced and softened by a certain weakness, as if a powerfully masculine face had been painted in miniature

---

* On Democracy. Mr. Lowell was the guest, during his stay at Birmingham, of Mr. Wilson King. "Professor Mahaffy, of Dublin, was also my guest at the time," writes Mr. King, "and the two 'took to' each other at once, and I never heard so much good talk in four days before or since. Mahaffy went off in the morning, and when, somewhat later, I was driving Mr. Lowell to the station, he put his hand on my knee and said, 'I think, on the whole, that is the most delightful fellow I ever met, and I wish you'd tell him I said so.' Of course it was pleasant for me to have such testimony to the success of my party. When I told Mahaffy, his characteristic reply was, 'Poor Lowell, never to have met an Irishman before.'"

by Malbone. He was very kindly and sympathetic—
his benignity as well as his lineaments reminding me
of the old age of Emerson. He has not been able to
preach, he told me, for two years. . . .

TO THOMAS HUGHES

31 Lowndes Square, S. W., Oct. 20, 1884.

Dear Friend,—I send back your boy's letter, which
gave the old man real pleasure. It even encouraged
him to read one of the " Biglow Papers " aloud to his
naval attaché yesterday, who seemed interested by
the unwonted performance of his chief. He (the old
man) was rather surprised with a certain pithiness in
the poem, and with the quantity of meaning he used
to have in himself. As his habitual feeling is that
he has never done anything, it is not disagreeable
now and then to find somebody who thinks that he
has.

I am in the midst of Froude—two new volumes of
Carlyle. Very interesting I find them, and him more
problematic than ever, but fine on the whole. A kind
of sentimental Ajax furens. I don't think that sincerity
towards his hero justifies Froude in printing Carlyle's
diatribes (result of dyspepsia mainly)—about Gladstone,
for example. In a world where there is so much unavoidable pain, why add to the avoidable? Gladstone
won't mind, but his wife and daughters?

With love to your wife,

Affectionately yours,

J. R. LOWELL.

TO MRS. W. K. CLIFFORD

31 Lowndes Square, S. W., Nov. 9, 1884.

. . . I enjoyed my visit to the country. I was among friendly people who all bewailed the chance of my being recalled, and one charming person told me that " all the women of England would rise as one man, if I were." I had no notion how charming I was—had you?

As for whether I shall be or not—I mean recalled, not charming—you, as one of the women of England, must be anxious to know what the chances are. All I can say to comfort you is, that you know as much about it as I do. I fear the chances are against me. Well, I shall have enjoyed my five years in England, where everybody has been kind to me, and shall find people to be kind to me at home also. It has been my luck to find them everywhere.

I wish I had some news of the Great World to send you, but there never has been any since I can remember, except that it was going to be wise one of these fine days. But no day has yet been fine enough for its purpose, and fine days are so rare in London! Yes, I have one bit of secret intelligence. His Excellency and Mrs. Lowell are going to see the Lord Mayor's Show to-morrow for the first time! Don't you envy us? Real camels and real elephants, with men atop of them, and Queen Bess in all her glory! I mean to be ten years old for the nonce. Generally I am younger. . . .

TO THE SAME

Hurstbourne, Nov. 16, 1884.

. . . Everybody has gone to church, and I have just come in from walking up and down the avenues of meditation, by which orientalism I mean an avenue of autumnal trees, in one of which (an elm that has changed all its leaves into fairy gold) a thrush has been singing to me, like Overbury's fair and happy milkmaid, as if he never could be old. I have been thinking that the decay of nature is far more beautiful than that of man, that autumn is rather pensive than melancholy, that the fall of the leaf does not work such dilapidation on the forest as on us the fall of the hair, but gives its victims a new beauty. I have been thinking—to about as much purpose as the deer who were browsing or dozing all about me, and now I have come in to answer your letter.

I am quite willing you should prefer disagreeable men (there are enough of them!), provided you will tolerate me. For my part, I prefer agreeable women. I must keep copies of my letters if I would understand the answers to them. Could I have been such an ass as to ask if I was charming? It is out of the question. Even if I thought I was, I should be too clever to inquire too nicely about it, for I hold with my favorite Donne that

"Who knows his virtue's name and place hath none."

And yet I should infer from your letter that I had been stupid enough to ask something of the kind. Nothing

in my life has ever puzzled me so much as my popularity here in England—which I have done nothing and
been nothing to deserve. I was telling my wife a day
or two ago that I couldn't understand it. It must be
my luck, and ought to terrify me like the ring of Po-
lycrates.

No, the Lord Mayor's Show was pure circus and poor
circus at that. It was cheap, and the other adjective
that begins with n. 'Twas an attempt to make poetry
out of commonplace by contract. 'Twas antiquity as
conceived by Mr. Sanger. Why, I saw the bottoms of
a Norman knight's trousers where they had been hitched
up into a tell-tale welt round the ankle by his chain
armor! There was no pretence at illusion; nay, every
elephant, every camel, every chariot was laden with
disillusion. It was worth seeing for once, to learn how
dreary prose can contrive to be when it has full swing.

It is cold here. Twelve degrees of frost this morning. My fingers are numb and my thoughts crawl
slowly as winter flies. Are you making notes as I bade
you? I have no news about myself yet, though I have
heard the name of somebody who expects to be my
successor. A very agreeable man, by the way, so you
won't like him. That's some comfort.

Faithfully yours,

J. R. Lowell.

TO THE SAME

31 Lowndes Square, S. W., Nov. 26, 1884.

. . . I should have answered your letter before if I
had not had somebody staying with me who took up all

my spare time. "If he couldn't *find* time he should have *made* it!" I hear you exclaim, and if I had been at St. Ives I would, but here there is nothing to make it with. I am not sure that I could have done it any-where, for the material of the manufacture is *method*, and I have too often turned all my pockets inside out and never found that I had any about me. I am steal-ing the time I need for this note—I hope nobody else will miss it. 'Tis a strong argument against commu-nism that time is one of the few things we hold in common, and there is none that we worse misuse. . . .

TO C. E. NORTON

London, Dec., 1884.

. . . Politics are rather interesting here just now. You will like to hear this: the other day I said to Glad-stone that I was very glad he had included Ireland in the Franchise Bill—or rather had not excluded her. " I had rather the heart were torn out of my breast than that clause out of the bill," said he. A day or two ago I met Morley at dinner, who regretted that I had not heard Gladstone a few nights ago, when he turned on Sir Stafford Northcote (his whilom private secretary) and rent him. I said that from what I had heard of it, I thought it must have been a fine exhibition—some-thing lion-like in the leap of it—but that mockers said that the passion was simulated. Morley laughed and said that in the lobby afterwards he had said to (I for-get the name), " What an old lion it is !" " What an old fox !" smiled the other. I think Gladstone's late illness (and I have pretty good intelligence) partly moral and partly diplomatic, by the way. Egypt is beyond even his powers of explanation, and Pharaoh seems to harden his heart and won't let Gladstone's people go. What puzzles and sometimes bores me in Gladstone is that he takes as much interest in one thing as in another, and is as diffusively emphatic about it—in John Inglesant (which I couldn't read) as in Gordon. Gordon, by the way, sent me his regards from Khartoum —which pleased me like a friendly message from Judas Maccabeus. . . .

TO THE SAME

31 Lowndes Square, S. W., Dec. 8, 1884.

. . . I post with this a corrected copy of my Address. Of course you must read between the lines. I couldn't speak my mind freely whether for this latitude or that. I see our blots only too plainly, and have not forborne my commentary on them in time past. I fear you see them *large*—and perhaps I see them *small*, as some artists do the heads they paint. We have enormous and exceptional difficulties in our foreign and half-digested population. I do not find the tone much higher here— for example, in the private talk about the Corrupt Practices in Elections Act—though I admit that this is a less dangerous symptom here where the traditions are all aristocratic.

As for the small majority for Cleveland, I am more than satisfied with *any*, considering the obstacles. That we are saved from Blaine is enough for the nonce. There are four more years to work in before the next election. The great vice is in the system of conventions, as I learned at Cincinnati in '76. . . .

TO JOHN W. FIELD

London, Dec. 11, 1884.

. . . As for coming to live in Washington, my dear boy, that is all very well for people that have " struck ile." But I haven't, and never shall. Besides, I have but one home in America, and that is the house where I was born and where, if it shall please God, I hope to die. I shouldn't be happy anywhere else, and might as well stay here where we are nearer the world's navel. . . .

TO MRS. W. K. CLIFFORD

31 Lowndes Square, S. W., Dec. 14, 1884.

. . . You have now all the prose I have collected into volumes. I am really glad that you find something in them to like, for I have a worse opinion of myself than of most authors, knowing only too well how much I have wasted such gift as I had.

I do not know whether I was happier when I wrote the second volume of " Among my Books," as you suppose. I am never very happy when I am writing about books that I like. I had much rather like them and say nothing about it — for one should be secret about one's loves and not betray the confidence they have put in one. But I *had* to write because I had foolishly allowed myself to be made a professor, and you will understand better the defects of some of my essays when I tell you that they were patched together from my lectures, leaving out a great part of the illustrative matter, and compressing rather than dilating as one should do for a miscellaneous audience.

As for happiness, a man with a sense of humor (as I in some measure have) has always a clot of black blood in his veins, always circulating, always lodging in the most unforeseen and discomfiting places, and if it once get into the heart or brain, always fatal to all that illusion which is the substance of content. And then I have inherited a Puritan conscience that will not let me alone. Every now and then my good spirits carry me away and people find me amusing, but reaction always sets in the moment I am left to myself.

But enough of Me! I am not very interesting to myself, except as a puzzle sometimes, and I do not wish to propose myself to you as a conundrum.

I have been reading Taine's new volume. It is interesting as a collection of *pièces justificatives*, but not judicial, as it seems to me. 'Tis argument of counsel, and not the charge of a judge weighing both sides. The way in which authors, especially French, who have found the *moyen de parvenir*, look backward and downward on the class they have risen from is bitterly amusing. There are no such aristocrats. They kick down the ladder behind them, quite unconscious that the height they have climbed to is the pillory. The agreeable aristocrats are those who are born to it and therefore unconscious—and women, who all have it in their blood. . . .

II.—19

TO THE SAME

31 Lowndes Square, S. W., Dec. 15, 1884.

. . . What you say about correctness of style both pleases and amuses me. The great fault I am always taxing myself with is impatience of revision. I am too prone to extemporize. A note on p. 76 of the "Essay on Dryden" will show that we are of one mind on this point. You will be glad to hear that a man once devoted an entire volume to the exposure of my *solecisms,* or whatever he chose to call them. I never read it— lest it should spoil my style by making it conscious. A *Scotsman,* too, gave me a dressing, I am told—but I don't mind their theories about English (which is always a foreign tongue to them), and, besides, he liked me all the same. By the way, a Scotsman had the ill-manners one day to compliment me on my English. "Why, I shouldn't know you weren't an Englishman. Where did you get it?" I couldn't resist, and answered with a couple of verses from a Scottish ballad—

"I got it in my mither's wame,
Whaur ye'll get never the like !"

He will never compliment me again, I fear. . . .

TO THE SAME

31 Lowndes Square, S. W., Christmas Day, 1884.

. . . I dare say you will have seen by the papers (for you seem to read them) what I have been about. But they won't have told you that I made a very stupid speech at Peterhouse Monday night. I couldn't help it.

I was dazed by the consciousness that there were to be eighteen speeches, and that everybody but I had his speech neatly written out in his pocket. I really had something pretty to say—I mean I might have had—but after hearing six or seven my mind was a blur. They droned away over their flowers of rhetoric as bees do over a tuft of lime-blossoms when they know that they have the whole day before 'em, and that the longest of the year. Why, we didn't rise from table till half-past one! Sir Frederick Bramwell made the best speech. He was called on to answer for Applied Science. "At this time of night," said he, " the only illustration of the toast I can think of would be the application of the domestic safety match to the bedroom candle." Whereupon I wrote on my *menu* and handed over to him,

> " Oh, brief Sir Frederick, might the others catch
> Your happy science and supply your match !"

I give it you as the best evidence of the comatose state to which I was reduced. But I enjoyed my visit at Peterhouse Lodge, where I was the guest of the master, Dr. Porter, an old friend of Leslie Stephen. . . .

TO O. W. HOLMES

31 Lowndes Square, S. W., Dec. 28, 1884.

Dear Wendell,—I was about to write thanking you for your " Emerson," when your letter was brought to me. I found the Emerson very interesting. You, more than anybody else, have the literary traditions of New

England in your blood and brain. It was this special flavor that pleased my palate as I read. I felt as
when I walk along one of our country lanes in early autumn—stone walls on either hand, a somewhat thrifty
landscape, and yet fringed all along with hardhack and
golden-rod. I recognize our surly limitations, but feel
also the edging of poetry—northern, not tropical, but
sincere and good of its kind. Nay, with you I may
trust a homelier image. You know that odor of sweet
herbs in the New England garret and its pungency of
association, and will know what I mean when I say that
I found much of it in your book. You have never written better than in some of the genially critical parts.
There are admirable things in the chapter about Emerson's poetry, many that made me slap my thigh with
emphatic enjoyment. You say the book tired you, but
I see no sign of it, and your wind is firm to the end.
I thank you for helping me to a conclusion (or a distinction) I was fumbling for. If Emerson show no sen-
suous passion in his verse, at least there is spiritual and
intellectual passion enough and to spare—a paler flame,
but quite as intense in its way. I go back, you see, to
my hardhack and golden-rod again. I talked with him
once about his versification, by the way, and he humorously confessed that he couldn't see the difference between a good verse and a bad one—so in that line you
cite from his " Adirondacks."

The first number of your new portfolio whets my appetite. Let me make one historical correction. When
I accepted the editorship of the *Atlantic*, I made it a
condition precedent that you were the first contributor

to be engaged.   Said I not well?   Underwood will remember this.

It was very good of you to take all that trouble about
me and my poor affairs with Mr. Cleveland and Boyle
O'Reilly.   As for the former, I shall be satisfied with
whatever he thinks fit to do in my case, for I have a
high respect for his character, and should certainly have
voted for him had I been at home.   As minister I have
always refused to have any politics, considering myself
to represent the country and no special party in it.   As
for Mr. O'Reilly, it is *he* that misunderstands the rights
of naturalized citizens, not I ; and he wouldn't have misunderstood them had they been those of naturalized
Germans, nor would Bismarck have been as patient as
Granville.   I made no distinction between naturalized
and native, and should have treated you as I did the
" suspects "—had there been as good ground.   There is
a manifest distinction, however, between a native American who goes abroad and a naturalized citizen who
goes back to the country of his birth, and we acknowledge it in our treaties—notably with Germany—making
two years' residence in the native country a forfeiture
of the acquired citizenship.   Some of my Irishmen had
been living in their old homes seventeen years, engaged in trade or editing nationalist papers or members of the poor-law guardians (like MacSweeney), and
neither paying taxes in America nor doing any other
duty as Americans.   I was guided by two things—the
recognized principles of international law, and the conduct of Lord Lyons when Seward was arresting and im-
prisoning British subjects.   We kept one man in jail

seven months without trial or legal process of any kind, and, but for the considerateness and moderation of Lyons, might have had war with England. I think I saved a misunderstanding here. . . . When I had at last procured the conditional (really unconditional) release of all the suspects, they refused to be liberated. When I spoke of this to Justin McCarthy (then the head of the Irish Parliamentary party, Parnell being in Kilmainham), he answered cheerfully, "Certainly: *they are there to make trouble*."

But enough of these personal matters. I shall come home with the satisfaction of having done my duty and of having been useful to the true interests of both countries—of the three if you count Ireland. The fun of the thing is that here I was considered a radical in my opinions about Ireland. I have always advised them to make Davitt or Parnell Irish Secretary.

Good-by and a happy New Year!

Affectionately yours,

J. R. LOWELL.

TO MISS GRACE NORTON

31 Lowndes Square, S. W., Jan. 15, 1885.

. . . Do you remember that in a month I shall be sixty-six? Luckily I am not reminded of it often, our decays are so full of *prévenances* and come to us shod in felt. Don't you know how we sometimes become instinctively aware that we have lost or forgotten something, we don't know what? So it is with the thefts of old age. We grow conscious of them only after all is over. . . .

A German band is noisy before my window as I write,

and it is a rainy day and there is a blue tinge in the atmosphere that mezzotints the bare trees of the square,
seeming to wrap their nerves against the east wind. . . .

TO GEORGE PUTNAM

Legation of the United States,
London, March 2, 1885.

. . . I am more than ever at a loss what to do with
myself. We had always taken it for granted together
that she would outlive me, and that would have been
best. But I cannot live alone in the old home. It
would be too dreary. Whatever I decide, I shall come
home for a visit. . . .

TO MRS. W. K. CLIFFORD

10 Lowndes Square, S. W., March 19, 1885.

Dear Mrs. Clifford,—In trying to piece together the
broken threads of my life again, the brightest naturally
catch the eye first. I write only to say that I do not
forget. . . .

I am getting on as one does—gradually getting my
wits together. . . .

I have at last found something I can read—Calderon.
He has stood me in stead before.

By and by I will write again.

Faithfully yours,

J. R. LOWELL.

TO C. E. NORTON

31 Lowndes Square, S. W., April 16, 1885.

. . . I sail for home on the 10th June (earlier if I

can), and will tell you all I have to say. My future is misty to me. What you write falls in with my own inward presentiment. . . . I should be happy nowhere but at Elmwood. There I cannot live now. . . .

TO W. D. HOWELLS

31 Lowndes Square, S. W., April 17, 1885.

Dear Howells,—I return your grasp of the hand with another as sincere, but in silence. What is there to be said?

If all go well I shall see you again in June—one of the greatest favors I have to thank President Cleveland for.

With kindest regards to Mrs. Howells,

Affectionately yours,

J. R. LOWELL.

TO R. W. GILDER

Deerfoot Farm, Southborough, Mass.,
June 14, 1885.

. . . I was to have gone to Washington last week (carrying my head, as Bertran de Born did, like a lantern) to take a look at my decapitators, but the illness of Mr. Bayard prevented me.

I am now waiting fresh orders here, where I ramble over the hills, hearing familiar birds and plucking familiar flowers. I find that my life hooks together across the eight years' gap as if nothing had happened so far as the outward world is concerned. Inwardly there is a breach, as you can imagine.

I should like to run down for a day to Marion, and will if I can. . . .

X

1885–1889

RETURN TO AMERICA.—LIFE IN SOUTHBOROUGH AND BOS-
TON.—SUMMER VISITS TO ENGLAND.

LETTERS TO W. D. HOWELLS, C. E. NORTON, R. W. GILDER,
J. W. FIELD, R. S. CHILTON, MISS GRACE NORTON, THE
MISSES LAWRENCE, MRS. LESLIE STEPHEN, MRS. EDWARD
BURNETT, G. H. PALMER, T. B. ALDRICH, THOMAS HUGHES,
MISS E. G. NORTON, LESLIE STEPHEN, MISS SEDGWICK, F. H.
UNDERWOOD, MRS. J. T. FIELDS, MR. AND MRS. S. WEIR
MITCHELL, MRS. W. K. CLIFFORD, MRS. W. E. DARWIN.

TO W. D. HOWELLS

Southborough, Mass., July 1, 1885.

Dear Howells,—Many thanks for your welcome
home—if home I may call it now. I had been count-
ing on seeing yours among other dear faces, and you
are as inaccessible as if I were still where the epigraph
on my paper puts me.*

I have been reading your "Silas Lapham" with great
interest and admiration. I have generally found romance more interesting and often more true than reality—but I am as weak as Falstaff and can't help liking
whatever you do, whatever it may be. This is more
your fault than mine, however, for it is sure to be
good. . . .

* The paper bears his old London address.

TO C. E. NORTON

Deerfoot Farm, Southborough, July 22, 1885.

. . . I am already in love with Southborough, which is a charmingly unadulterated New England village, and with as lovely landscapes as I ever saw. I entrench myself in a flannel shirt, and wander over the hills and in the lonely pastures, rejoicing in the immitigable sunshine. 'Tis an odd shift in the peep-hole of my panorama from London to this Chartreuse. For the present I like it, and find it wholesome. I fancy myself happy sometimes—I am not sure—but then I never was for long.

I shall appear in Ashfield in time for your rustic feast —though the notion of a speech embitters my future. . . .

TO THE SAME

Deerfoot Farm, Aug. 13, 1885.

. . . I got back yesterday morning from Washington, where I spent four days very pleasantly with Bayard, whom I liked before, but now like thoroughly. He is a gentleman all through, and as courageous as a tender heart will let him be. I mean that he has the sensitiveness as well as the high spirit of a refined organization, and that it would be better for him, perhaps for the country, if he could be brutal on occasion. His commerce has much of the same charm that Dufferin has beyond any man I ever knew, whose very teeth are engaging, though in Dufferin one sometimes fancies that one sees the ear-tip of highly perfected art. Cleveland I liked, but saw only for half an hour. I told him that

I came to him like St. Denis, with the head he had
cut off under my arm, at which piece of humor he
laughed heartily—and I think, on the whole, was not
sorry that he should be represented in England by
somebody else.

I took my grandson James with [me], and we went
to Mount Vernon together, whither I was taken by my
father fifty-nine years ago. I remembered everything
as if from yesterday, and went straight to the key of the
Bastile and to the honey-locusts in the garden. Washington must have found it hard to die and give up the
view from his veranda. It combines grandeur and pla-
cidity, as he did himself. I was struck in travelling with
Jem to find how much less the boys of this generation
know about American history than I did when I was
seven years his junior. . . .

TO THE SAME

Deerfoot Farm, Sept. 11, 1885.

. . . I got home safely, bearing constantly in mind
our modern version of the Spartan mother's parting
words to her son—"with your portmanteau, or on it"
—for as I had a special check and a very complicated
ticket, I felt myself walking in a series of pitfalls and
ambushes, where every baggage-smasher was a secret
foe. I waited three hours at Fitchburg, and wiled
away my time by eating a very durable substitute for
what is elsewhere called a beefsteak and in visiting the
principal objects of interest, including the Cathedral
and picture galleries. I saw also several sign-boards
which promised well for the future of Fitchburgian art.

My hills here in Southborough I found lower than I left them, but they are growing daily, and will be as tall as ever in a few days. I find I was right in falling so deeply in love with the " June grass." We have it here, as I thought, but it hasn't the same fine effects of color. I can't account for it, but the fact is so. Nature has these partialities, and makes no scruple of showing them. But we do very well, all the same. I climbed one of my hills yesterday afternoon, and took a sip of Wachusett, who was well content that Monadnock was out of the way. How lucky our mountains (many of them) are in their names, though they must find it hard to live up to them sometimes! The Anglo-Saxon sponsor would Nicodemus 'em to nothing in no time.

I found a bushel of cold letters awaiting me here, and I have spent most of my time with my hands across, gazing in despair at the outside of them. I am thinking seriously of getting a good forger from the state's-prison to do my autographs, but I suppose the unconvicted followers of the same calling would raise the cry of Convict Labor. Ashfield would be perfect but that it has a post-office. That fly would corrupt a pot of ointment as large as the cup of her horizon. . . .

TO R. W. GILDER

Southborough, Nov. 9, 1885.

. . . As for writing, if *peut* and *veut* were the same thing (and how easily they might be—only they won't —when *p* so often changes to *b* and that to *v*) I would swamp all the magazines, and forty *Centuries* should behold my exploits as they beheld the soldiers of the only sublime Charlatan on record. But—to take another illustration from Egypt—Horus didn't have to pick up his own *disjecta membra*, and I am trying to piece myself together again with no help save my own. When I am not answering letters, I strive for a little peace with my pipe and the small flock of books I have driven up hither from Elmwood—a flock which has the advantage of pasturing me instead of my doing it for them. It isn't Arcady exactly, but nobody knows how to find that nowadays except your friend Mr. Bunner, whose volume,* by the way, I read with so much pleasure. It has some real stuff in it—and woven, too, with no creak of machinery. But if it isn't Arcady ("to resume," as the "Compleat Letter-writer" would say), it pleases me for its analogy with my favorite hero Don Quixote. Like him I began with my tilt at windmills, and like him I seek repose from discomfiture in another phase of my monomania. Aren't the enchanters as active as ever? Haven't they resuscitated Sambo in a shape as *descomunal* as ever, after we had dismounted him once and for all?

And then there is the *Atlantic*. They (O. W. H. and the rest) all say that I owe a duty (and the first) to my own child, or, rather, the adopted foundling I taught to go alone. And I meanwhile have a sneaking disgust at the whole of it, as knowing that my value is due less to myself than to the abominable notoriety I have unhappily achieved in these latter years. . . .

* "Airs from Arcady."

TO JOHN W. FIELD

Boston, Dec. 13, 1885.

. . . Where did you get that extract from a letter of mine?* and to whom was it written? It antedates my abolitionism by two years. I thought it began in 1840. But when I read the passage you quote, I remembered having written on my Class poem (in which I made fun of the Abolitionists, 1838),

"Behold the baby arrows of that wit
  Wherewith I dared assail the woundless Truth!
Love hath refilled the quiver, and with it
  The man shall win atonement for the youth.". . .

TO R. S. CHILTON

68 Beacon Street, Boston, Dec. 17, 1885.

. . . No, I am not living at Elmwood, alas! and never look forward to living there again. I have let it, it being for me uninhabitable. I hope to die there, however.

I received your volume, and ought to have thanked you for it long ago. It revived so many pleasant old associations! I was naturally very much pleased with the poem with which you have honored me, but thought the entire tone and manner of the book an honor to you. . . .

TO MISS GRACE NORTON

Deerfoot, Christmas Day, 1885.

. . . The "Scepsis," too, completes my Glanvill, for the "Sadducismus" has stood on my shelves this many

* An extract from a letter to Dr. Loring, dated Nov. 15, 1838; see vol. i. p. 35.

a year, and will feel warmer with his brother beside him.
I shall read the "Scepsis" as soon as I have time, and
I am sure it will interest me as the other did, for I, too,
am a sceptic, with a superstitious imagination. . . .

TO THE MISSES LAWRENCE

Deerfoot Farm, Southborough, Mass.,
Jan. 4, 1886.

. . . I am living quietly here with my son-in-law, my
daughter, and five very creditable grandchildren, in a
pretty country village, all hill and dale, and every hill
a heap of boulders piled up by glaciers Heaven knows
how long ago. I like my grandchildren, and this is in
their favor, for I have none of that natural fondness for
children which some people have, who also, I have observed, like puppies in the same indiscriminate way. I
like my solitude, too, when I am allowed to have it all
to myself, for a solitude *à deux* is possible only with a
woman.

You must have had a pleasant continental trip, but I
can't understand your not liking Weimar. I liked it
immensely—a kind of puppet-theatre of the world, with
its little Schloss and little Park and little Army and lit-
tle Play-house and little Court and little men and wom-
en. And as for the little stream that runs through the
Park or along its edge, I fell in love with it, and so
would you had you seen the horse-chestnuts lying in
its bed, and more brilliant than balas rubies. And then
there was the grand duke — a man of genius (on perpetual furlough), and one can get on very well where
one has a man of genius to friend. And Frau v. Stein

—one can get on very well where there is one charming woman.   But I am glad you said what you did, because it confirms me in something I was going to say
about Hawthorne—that men of genius can manage anywhere, because they make the best part of their own
material. . . .

But you have Ireland still, and worse than ever.   'Tis
the clot of blood in England's veins, always discomforting, and liable always to lodge in the brain.   But then
we all have our difficulties—that's what we are put here
for, and they put here with us to test our doughtiness.
I often recall Hamlet's groan about the out-of-joint
world and the cruel spite—nevertheless.   But one can
be philosophical three thousand miles away!

What you say of Weimar convinces me of how London has thrown its dust in your eyes.   But I like it too,
and am glad even of a bit of gossip thence now and
then. . . .

You will divine, by what I say about gossip, that I
am growing old.   I used to be as stern about it as
Wordsworth.   You remember his "I am not one,"
etc.?   'Tis senescence or London, I know not which—
perhaps a mixture of both. . . .

TO R. W. GILDER

Deerfoot Farm, Southborough, Jan. 16, 1886.

Dear Mr. Gilder,—I return the portfolio with the
verses* you ask for therein.   It was an effort of hon-

* Autograph from "Commemoration Ode," for reproduction,
to precede the "Life of Lincoln."

esty on my part to send you back the former, for I felt
like "proud Dacres" when

> "He came aboard
> To deliver up his sword,
> He was loath to give it up—it looked so neat
> and handy, oh!"

(Pronounce the sw in "sword" as in "swore," and
"loath" "lawth," or you lose the local tone of the
period.) I have always thought this passage delightful—a wonderful bit of sympathetic divination by the
thrifty Yankee poet. Ah me, how the times change
and we with them! I have often seen rustics, buoyant
with Medford rum, dance the double shuffle on the
piazza of a country inn to the tune of Hull's victory,
and I saw that hero himself when his sword-belt would
have lapt over round a young elephant. As I looked
down on him, seated just under my perch in the gallery
of Funnle Hall (they call it *fan-you-well* now), he looked
like a huge terrestrial globe flanked with epaulets. I
think it was when General Jackson had a reception
there. But I am getting garrulous.

The passage about Lincoln was not in the ode as
originally recited, but added immediately after. More
than eighteen months before, however, I had written
about Lincoln in the *North American Review*—an article which pleased him. I *did* divine him earlier than
most men of the Brahmin caste. The ode itself was an
improvisation. Two days before the Commemoration
I had told my friend Child that it was impossible—that
I was dull as a door-mat. But the next day something
gave me a jog and the whole thing came out of me

II.—20

with a rush.   I sat up all night writing it out clear, and
took it on the morning of the day to Child.   " I have
something, but don't yet know what it is, or whether
it will do.   Look at it and tell me."   He went a little
way apart with it under an elm-tree in the College yard.
He read a passage here and there, brought it back to
me, and said, " Do ?   I should think so !   Don't you be
scared."   And I wasn't, but virtue enough had gone
out of me to make me weak for a fortnight after.   I
was amazed at the praises I got.   Trevelyan told me
afterwards that he never could have carried through
the abolition of purchase in the British Army but for
the reinforcement he got from that poem.   " I advise
you to listen to this," Sumner used to say when he
was talking about himself (as he commonly was) ; " *this*
is historical !"   So, having snubbed myself, I go on to
say that I send the portfolio by express. . . .

TO W. D. HOWELLS

68 Beacon St., Boston, Feb. 2, 1886.

Dear Howells,—I told you that I liked the plan of
the new story when you gave me a sketch of it.*   I like
the story itself so thoroughly that I must please myself
by telling you so.   So far, 'tis the best yet.   It made
me forget eighteen hours in a sleeping-car and the loss
of my only wearable-in-Boston hat.

But I won't let you say (when you reprint) as you
do on page 5, 1st col., " bring us *in* closer relations," for
that isn't what you mean.   You don't mean "bring-in

* "The Minister's Charge."

to us," but "bring us *into*"! That's what you mean.
I am going to get up a society for the Prevention of
Cruelty to Prepositions—I am getting so cross. Animals have certain natural means of defence. They can
bite and prepositions can't. The skunk—but I forbear
—you know what he can do in the newspapers. So be-
ware, my dear boy! The society will be immitigable. It
will spare neither age nor sex, and will be happiest when
dancing a war-dance on the broken ties of friendship.

On second thought, however (the hat having meanwhile come back), I still remain as always

Affectionately yours,

J. R. L.

Barring this bit of fruitless brutality, the story is
simply delightful.

TO THE SAME

Deerfoot Farm, Feb. 14, 1886.

My dear Valentine,—Come to 68 Beacon Street, Tuesday afternoon or late on Wednesday, for I don't wish
to miss you.

I ought to have said, but forgot it, that you will find
plenty of authority for *in* as you used it in our older
writers. I remember it in Latimer (he was burned alive
for that among other heresies, however) and elsewhere.
But that sprang from a false analogy with the Latin,
where the same preposition served both ends according
to the case it governed. I believe some grammars still
give no *cases*, but we have at best only one distinctive
case-ending that I can think of—the genitive.

Affectionately yours,   J. R. Lowell.

TO MRS. LESLIE STEPHEN

Boston, March 21, 1886.

. . . It is really too bad that I have been silent so long. But if you only knew how hard they work me with letters and speeches and things; and they have invented a new mode of torture—readings from one's poems, by Dr. Holmes and me, for the benefit of charities of one kind or another. We bow our necks to the yoke like patient oxen, and leaning away from each other as oxen will, strive to retrace our ancient furrows, which somehow will not gleam along the edge as when the turf was first broken. Admire, prithee, the aptness of my image, after first turning up in your Dixery the etymology of *verse*.

I am in Boston, and it is a rainy, dull day, such as we Americans, when we are in London, swear we never have at home. But we brought this wet with us also from the Old Home, and have improved upon it of course.

It rained all day yesterday, too, and when it rains here 'tis after the reckless fashion of our people, as if we would spend all at once. None of your effete-monarchy drizzles such as you have in London, penurious as the last drops from a washerwoman's wringing. . . .

TO C. E. NORTON

Deerfoot Farm, March 30, 1886.

. . . I send back the Dante, which you must have feared as irretrievably lost as Petrarch's copy of the " De Gloria.". . .

What I have for my book* makes only 140 pages, and they say it must be bigger. I had forgotten the Wordsworth address. Did I send you one? If so, send it to 68 Beacon Street, and let me use it to print from. I have another in London which I will give you.

I hate all the Addresses, now they are cold as Saul on Mount Gilboa. *Mi raccapricciono*—they give me the goose-flesh. As usual, I haven't left myself time to correct my proofs. What a pleasant life I shall have of it when I have all Eternity on deposit! Then the printers will say, "If you can with convenience return proofs before end of next century, you would oblige; but there is no hurry." 'Tis an invincible argument for immortality that we never have time enough here—except for doing *other things*. . . .

TO JOHN W. FIELD

Deerfoot Farm, March 30, 1886.

. . . I may be back before you leave Ashfield next summer, and if so, shall next see you there—as good a place as I know of this side heaven. Were I as good as you are, I should hope to meet you there also. If not, pitch me down a square of turf to stand upon when my birthday comes round. . . .

TO MRS. EDWARD BURNETT

40 Clarges Street, Piccadilly, W.,
May 3, 1886.

. . . I find myself very warmly welcomed back, and

* " Democracy, and Other Addresses."

shall soon be trotting round in the old vicious circle
of dinners and receptions. I have had to make one
speech at the dinner of the Royal Academy, and have
refused to make five others. The editor of the *Contemporary Review* has just gone out, having vainly endeav-
ored (at the instigation of John Morley) to persuade me
that I should be doing a public service by giving my
views on Mr. Gladstone's Home Rule project in that
periodical. But I prefer to keep clear of hot potatoes
—and Irish ones are apt to be particularly hot. Pretty
nearly Everybody who is Anybody here is furious—there
is no other word for it—and denounces the G. O. M. as
a kind of baser Judas Iscariot, all the more contempti-
ble because he will be cheated of his thirty pieces. The
Irish themselves are beginning to feel the responsibility
of governing Ireland, and Mr. —— has said that they
should "want an alien act to enable them to deal with
those d—d Irish-American scoundrels." (This is confidential.) The "situation" is a very grave one, and
everybody who isn't excited is depressed.

I have been to see Irving's "Faust" (a wonderful
spectacle, but a very disagreeable play) and Madame
Sara Bernhardt, who has gone off a little, but is still
diabolically effective in certain rather unpleasant ways.
I used to forget who and what Rachel was, but can't
divorce Sara from her . . . self. Whom the Devil
hath joined together can't be put asunder. I am to see
her again, nevertheless, to-morrow night. Both times I
have gone by invitation of people who had places to
spare. So you see I am emulating John Gilpin.

It has been very cold ever since I have been here—

but generally bright, which makes a great difference, and oh, how goldenly green the grass in the Parks is! The horse-chestnuts are getting ready their blossoms, and the thrushes need strait-waistcoats every one of them.

I don't know whether I am glad I came or not. My lodgings are good, but I haven't got wonted yet and can't do anything. Yes, I can preside at a dinner of the Dilettanti Society, as I did last night. But all dinners are alike, except one I have just lost with Froude to meet Matt Arnold and Morley. Unfortunately I had promised myself for the Sunday at Hurstbourne. . . .

TO R. W. GILDER

Care of Baring Brothers,
London [May ? 1886].

. . . I wish to do an act of charity to a dear old friend of mine here, and experience has taught me that it is more frugal to be vicariously beneficent. This won't give me a very high place in heaven perhaps, but I am modest, and with the pious Hebrew should be content with a portership in the House of the Lord— not only because it would keep me nearer earth, but because in that office I could slam the door in the faces of bores, critics, and booksellers. I have chosen you for my vicar.

The case is this. Miss Mary Boyle is a delightful old lady. How old she is may be inferred, without breach of the *bienséances* from the fact that Silvio Pellico wrote verses to her nearly sixty years ago. It is no fault of hers that they are not very good, still less that she should think them so. She is not only herself old, but

comes of an old family, so that she has a double share
of the infirmities of age. She is a descendant of that
Earl of Orrery who anticipated the dreary results of
modern science by substituting balls of cork on the ends
of wires for the lamps of heaven. (He was made Earl
of Cork afterwards in recognition of this service.) She
is also, I believe, a descendant of that Honorable Robert
Boyle whom Bentley roasted in his own bull of Phalaris.
Let not these facts prejudice you against her. She has
the blood of one martyr at least in her veins.

She has fifteen notes and letters of Landor (to her),
and is willing to part with copies for publication. Here
is no case of *dux femina facti,* for I suggested it. Some
of the letters are very interesting, and all are characteristic. They have never been printed. Would they be
worth £50 to you? or £40? I put the more generous
sum first in deference to my own hopes and your character. If, when you get them, you think you have been
cheated, I will make good the odds between my estimate and yours. When I get home (I come in September) I will write a short preface to them for nothing if
you wish. They are not *important* letters, but they are
Landor's. She is poor and nearly blind—as good as
gold, but without the broker's art of changing herself
into it. What say you?*

With all kindest regards to Mrs. Gilder,

Faithfully yours,

J. R. LOWELL.

* The letters were printed in the *Century,* with a pleasant introduction by Lowell, consisting mainly of his reminiscences of a
visit to Landor. This may now be found in the volume of his
"Latest Prose Essays."

If my wild demand bewilders,
    Think, 'tis only fifty pound!
Had I said as many Gilders,
    Where could such a sum be found?

TO MRS. EDWARD BURNETT

40 Clarges Street, Piccadilly, W.,
June 7, 1886.

. . . My life here amuses without satisfying me, and sometimes I am half sorry that I came.   The political situation, however, continues to be interesting, and opinion about the fate of Mr. Gladstone's bill varies from hour to hour.   I for a good while thought the second reading would be carried by a small majority, but believe now that it will be defeated.   I hear that Mr. Gladstone said to the Duke of Argyll, " I hoped in my old age to save my country, but this is a bitter, humiliating disappointment."   The fate of second reading depends somewhat on the fear of a dissolution of Parliament, but the general opinion now is that Government, if defeated, will dissolve.   I asked Mr. Chamberlain day before yesterday if he thought the G. O. M. was angry enough to dissolve, and he said *yes*.   I met Gladstone a few days ago, and he looked gay as a boy on his way home from school.   From what I hear I am inclined to think that what is called Irish public opinion in favor of Home Rule is nearly as factitious as that of our American meetings and resolutions. . . .

TO THE SAME

40 Clarges Street, Piccadilly, W.,
June 19, 1886.

. . . From Osterley I went to Holmbury (Leveson-
Gower's), where I spent a couple of days very pleasantly with Mr. and Mrs. Gladstone and other guests.
Mr. Gladstone was in boyish spirits. He told me,
among other things, that " in the whole course of his
political experience he had never seen anything like
the general enthusiasm of the country for Home Rule
in Ireland." I asked slyly " if it was not possible that
a part, at least, of this enthusiasm might be for the
Prime Minister?" " Oh no, no, not a bit of it!" he answered with eager emphasis. And I am inclined to
think he persuaded himself for the moment. This is
one secret of his power as a speaker—that he is capable of improvising convictions. He left us to go down
to Scotland, and I couldn't help remembering that I
first met him at a dinner at Lord Ripon's, in March,
'80, when he was on the eve of starting for Midlothian
on his first Scottish campaign. He was very confident,
and the result justified him. Perhaps it will again,
though the general opinion (as one hears it) is the other
way. But I still think the people strongly with him.

. . . On the 29th I go down to the Vice-Chancellor's
at Baliol to wear my gown at Commemoration and
help Dr. Holmes on with his. He is enjoying himself
immensely, and takes as keen an interest in everything
as he would have done at twenty. I almost envy him
this freshness of genius. Everybody is charmed with
him, as it is natural they should be. . . .

TO THE SAME

40 Clarges Street, Piccadilly, W.,
July 7, 1886.

. . . The elections are raging still, and I find myself quoted on both sides. I made an epigram (extempore) one day on the G. O. M., and repeated it to Lord Acton.

His greatness not so much in Genius lies
As in adroitness, when occasions rise,
Lifelong convictions to extemporize.

This morning I find the last lines quoted by Auberon Herbert in a letter to the *Times*, but luckily without my name. It is a warning. Mr. Gladstone hasn't been as lucky with the constituencies as I expected. Mr. Goschen, however, has been defeated at Edinburgh (for which I am sorry), and this seems to console the ministerialists for many other losses. I still remain convinced that Home Rule in some shape will carry it one of these days. . . .

TO C. E. NORTON

40 Clarges Street, Piccadilly, W.,
July 25, 1886.

. . . What you say of Carlyle is sympathetic (as it should be) and not dyspathetic. Of course every man that has any dimensions at all must have more than one side to him, and if he have dyspepsia one of those sides will have corners, and sharp ones, that find a sort of ease in the ribs of other folks. But, after all, Carlyle was a man of genius, and it is sheer waste of time to be

looking one's gift-horse in the mouth and examining his
hoofs, if he have wings and can lift us away from this
lower region of turmoil at will.   The rest is rubbish.
Biographies (except Plutarch's) seldom do a man any
good, and the less in proportion to the cleverness of the
biographer, for your very clever one is sure to mix a
good deal of auto- with his bio-graphy.   The beauty
and truth of impressions depend on the substance in
which they are made.   The main ingredient a biographer should contribute is sympathy (which includes insight).   Truth is not enough, for in biography, as in
law, the greater the truth sometimes the greater the
libel.   Happy those authors who are nothing more than
airy tongues that syllable our names when they have a
message for us!   Most Lives are more properly Deaths,
or at least might have for their title, like Chapman's
D'Ambois, "The Life *and* Death of So-and-so."

I am living a futile life here, but am as fond of London as Charles Lamb.   The rattle of a hansom shakes
new life into my old bones, and I ruin myself in them.
I love such evanescent and unimportunate glimpses of
the world as I catch from my flying perch.   I envy the
birds no longer, and learn better to converse with them.
Our views of life are the same.

As for politics—I saw Gladstone the other day, and
he was as buoyant (*boy*ant) as when I stayed with him
at Holmbury, just before he started for Scotland.   I
think the Fates are with him, and that the Tories will
have to take up Home Rule where he left it.   The
great difficulty is in making up an able Cabinet.   I suppose that ineptitudes will be neutralized with coronets

(or signalized by them, as we mark shoals with buoys), and room made for younger and abler men. Lord Randolph Churchill is taken seriously now, and will have a front seat. He ought to build a temple to the goddess Push.

I spent two days in the country lately (at the George Lewises) with Burne-Jones, and found him delightful. As Mrs. Lewis says, "If he were not a great artist, there would be enough left of him to make a great man of." His series of Perseus (did you see any of them?) is to my thinking the greatest achievement in art of our time or of any time. It has mannerisms which I don't like, but it is noble in conception and execution. Above all, it has the crowning gift of making an old story as new as if nobody had ever told it before. I feel as if I had heard the waves rustle under the bows of the *Argo*.

I suppose you are at Ashfield, and that the hills are as dear as ever, and Monadnock as like a purpose unfulfilled. Is the June grass golden on the upper slopes? Do the cloud-shadows still linger and hate to leave their soft beds in the woods and grass? Above all, are you and yours well and remember me? And G. W. C.? Sometimes I hear faintly the notes of S——'s violin singing "Scheiden, ach, scheiden!" and think of many things. . . .

TO MRS. EDWARD BURNETT

40 Clarges Street, Piccadilly, W.,
Aug. 6, 1886.

. . . There isn't a corner of England that has not its special charm, and the freaks of the atmosphere interest me more than any novel I ever read.

My last visit to the country was three days with the Darwins at Basset, which has more pleasant than sad associations for me. It was there that mamma began first to mend. I thought of you constantly. My bedroom window looked out towards the New Forest where the pony came from. We drove to the ruins of an old castle (*temp*. Hen. II.), standing (or falling) in a park whose turf was like soft moss. If trees would only grow with us as they do here, where their leaves are washed and their roots drink every day! . . .

TO C. E. NORTON

Deerfoot Farm, Southborough, Mass.,
Oct. 21, 1886.

. . . I am in despair about my address.* I have written a page only and made some notes. The bayonets must prick me more sharply from behind to set me going. Why did the Lord make us with ten fingers and toes that we might count up to fifties and hundreds and so make ourselves capable of this superstition of anniversaries? Had he curtailed our left foot, for instance, of one toe, we should never have missed it except as a gout-trap, and could never have divided any multiple of nine so as to suit our stupid love of symmetry. The Japanese might have done it, but nobody else. There would have been no Cornelius, and Napoleon would have lost his pyramidal allusion, but I see no other harm it would have done.

* For the two hundred and fiftieth anniversary of the foundation of Harvard University, delivered Nov. 8, 1886.

I have no books up here, and have to trust to my memory, which I could leave, with Lord Bacon, to after-generations without impoverishing my heirs.

The only thing that has made me feel as if I had any life in [me] of late was the music I heard at Shady Hill. . . .

TO THE SAME

Deerfoot Farm, Southborough, Mass.,
Oct. 26, 1886.

. . . The address drags like an ox-sled caught away from home by a January thaw. It *will* not take hold of me, do what I may. I have written a fair share of it, but I can't conquer our mutual alienation. My pitcher has gone once too often to the well. If I could scoop up a few drops with a shard of it, I were happy. But the well itself is dry!

What a scurvy trick —— has played me! If he had reported what I really said, instead of his version of it, I should not feel so bitterly. Well, this also shall pass away, and so shall we, thank God, one of these days. . . .

. . . Happy Mirabeau, to whom Dumont supplied the substance of his speeches, leaving to him only the *fioriture!* . . .

TO W. D. HOWELLS

Deerfoot Farm, Southborough, Mass.,
Nov. 11, 1886.

. . . I was very sorry not to be able to be with you to-day. I would have come if I could, but I had most imperative proof-sheets which I could correct only here, so I postponed pleasure to duty. " Be virtuous and you will be happy," says Whistler, " only you won't have a good time."

I am happy in your well-earned fame, my dear boy, and have just been reading your last chapters with the feeling Gray had about Crébillon *fils*.   Good-night.

To-morrow to fresh proofs and bothers new!

Affectionately yours,

J. R. LOWELL.

TO C. E. NORTON

Deerfoot Farm, Southborough, Mass.,
Nov. 22, 1886.

. . . I have been reading the book* with the greatest interest.   It not only makes Carlyle more agreeable to me, but confirms an opinion I formed several years ago in reading many of these early letters (lent to me by Mr. Ireland), that I know no man of letters so thoroughly *of a piece* as Carlyle.   The man who died sixty-four years later is all there in the earliest of his writing that we have (potentially there, in character wholly there).   And it is a fine character to my thinking, essentially manly and helpful to the core. . . .

TO G. H. PALMER

Deerfoot Farm, Southborough, Mass.,
Nov. 30, 1886.

. . . I wasn't thinking so much of the studies as of the method of teaching (by recitation and in divisions)

* Carlyle's " Early Letters."

when I wrote what gravels you.* I dare say also, as
you suggest, that I was thinking more of what the College was than of what it is. There is a certain impru-
dence in letting one's self live to be sixty-eight for which
one always has to pay. Had I been in Cambridge instead of Southborough, I dare say I should have written
differently. I am sure I should had I heard that excellent essay of yours, of which I afterwards listened to a
part with sincere admiration and profit.

You will observe that I have inserted a qualifying
sentence, in which the influence of that essay may be
traced.

Nothing could have been further from my thought
than to give aid and comfort to the enemies of what I
heartily approve in the main. *Nescit vox missa reverti*,
but I shall be in Cambridge this week, and will talk
over the matter with Norton. If I *can* frame such a
note as you wish, I gladly will. . . .

TO R. W. GILDER

Deerfoot Farm, Southborough, Mass.,
Dec. 2, 1886.

. . . I am one of those men who depend greatly on
the kind offices of the *genius loci*, and am a good while
in winning the confidence of a new one. I am just getting on speaking terms with the shy little fellow who
has charge of the hills and pastures and woodpaths
here, but am not yet in a position to ask him for a let-

* A sentence in the Harvard Address in which justice was
hardly done to the advance lately made in the University in the
methods of instruction, of discipline, and of investigation.

II.—21

ter of introduction to his cousin in Boston, whom I don't know. I don't believe I can write anything there. But we shall see. At any rate, I have been mulling over Landor, and shall be able to do a page or two of personal reminiscence and (pemmican) criticism wound up [by] an epigram of my own. The letters are less trivial than I feared, and one (about his dog Pomero) really touching. . . .

TO T. B. ALDRICH
Dec. 17, 1886.

. . . I have copied it all and I am tired, and it seems uninspired or ill-inspired, I hardly know which. But I send another that you may not be comfortless. It is shorter, and I advise you to take, as I should, the smaller pill of the two. I fear the long one ("Credidimus Jovem Regnare") will overrun your six pages, perhaps I hope it. Cut out what you please. There are two or three bright spots. If these be left, all will be well. Don't be tempted by a paginal vacuum to wrong your editorial conscience. Be frank; I am old and can stand it. My advice is—cage the cuckoo! 'Tis of the last century rather, but no harm in that. . . . If I hadn't lost a couplet I made last night while lying awake, there would have been one good verse in the longer poem. Always keep pencil and paper, as bird-lime, at the head of your bed. 'Tis worth more than "a twenty Bookës clothed in black and red "—unless, indeed, they are your own books. What shall I call it? Will "A Grumble " do?* . . .

* The little poem was finally named " Fact or Fancy?" Both poems appeared in the *Atlantic Monthly*.

TO C. E. NORTON

Deerfoot Farm, Southborough, Mass.,
Dec. 24, 1886.

. . . I *can't* do what they wish me to do in New
York. The consciousness that I had it to do would be
so constantly foraging on my equanimity and therefore
laying waste my time, that not a vine or a wheat-stalk
would be left me. If I could only so far conquer my
shyness as to be able to stand up and let myself run, I
would go with pleasure. How I envied the rector of
St. Olave's when the Pepys Memorial was unveiled! He
simply flowed in the *labitur et labetur* fashion as freely
as if he had been a Roman conduit. I knew my Pepys.
I went without notes, but with my head full of delightful things to say about him, and when I got up there
was a kind of *er-r-r-oo* in my brain—the noise of all my
fine things flying away from me like a flock of blackbirds when one comes suddenly on them over noiseless
ploughed land. I forgot even to say (though the only
one there who knew) that St. Olaf was the first viking
ever honored with that promotion—unless St. Magnus
was—and that therefore he would be sure to take good
care of the soul of a naval secretary which stood sadly
in need of such official intervention. I wonder at my
own audacity when I remember how I used to get up as
President of the Phi Beta or the Alumni and trust to
the spur of the moment. Yet I am alive to tell you so!
No; I must be left in such peace as I can contrive for
myself. Why, my dear boy, I am going on to seventy.
Nobody suspects it, least of all I.

I have got my Landor letters off my hands at last
—my "brief preface" resulting in twelve quarto pages
of manuscript as close-written as this! I can't tell what
it is till I see it in print. . . .

Now I shall buckle myself to my introduction to the
" Progress of the World." It rather attracts me through
my sense of humor. It will be pure creation made out
of nothing, not even nebula or star-dust. . . .

TO MISS LAWRENCE

Deerfoot Farm, Southborough, Mass.,
Christmas Day, 1886.

. . . Clever people are apt to be lucky, and when they
are clever and nice too, as they sometimes are, they are
sure to hit right. So I wasn't a bit surprised that your
kind letter, with its Christmas greetings, should arrive
this very morning, as if it had ridden post itself, and
could therefore adjust its speed to the occasion.

. . . I like to be serious all by myself, and to play
when I throw my working jacket off. Everybody
should write on my title-pages, *ridentem dicere verum
quid vetat ?* I have had reasons (if any man) for taking
life in earnest, but it pleased the Lord to fit me with an
"Æolian Attachment," which *will* strike in at the invitation of any breeze that takes it into its head to blow,
and I don't think it respectful to balk him.

I hadn't forgotten my promise—so far from it that I
had a twinge now and then. But I found there were
some misprints, and was content to wait for a new edition. As I commonly hate my own books, I don't easily
conceive of anybody else hungering after them. If my

friends only like *me*, forty thousand what's-his-names may fly away with what I write. Then, too, I live in Grub Street—so called because nobody is allowed to turn butterfly there—and its inhabitants may *call* their time their own if they will, but it is somebody else's all the same. But I send a copy by the same post with the errata corrected in my own neat hand, which will add to its value whenever it goes to the book-stall! . . .

Yes, your scandals are bad enough and sad enough; but I saw a good deal of people who are called of "a certain class" while I was in England, and they seemed to me as clean as New-Englanders, and that is saying a good deal. Take such as the Cowpers, the Greys, the Stanhopes, the Lytteltons, the Ashleys, to name no more, and where will you find purer or better?

. . . I write to you instead of going to church—but I sent my oblation to the offertory. I am a conservative (warranted to wash), and keep on the safe side— with God as against Evolution—but I do hate going to church. If Dr. Donne or Jeremy Taylor, or even Dr. South, were the preacher, perhaps—but I don't know. . . .

TO WALKER FEARN

Deerfoot Farm, Southborough, Mass.
Christmas Day, 1886.

Dear Mr. Fearn,—I am much obliged by your very friendly remembrance of me, and glad to be assured by yourself (I had heard it from others before) of the interest you take in the American School of Classical Studies at Athens. In order to hold and manage any funds that might come to our address, we have had ourselves incorporated under the Massachusetts law, and I am president of the Corporation. . . .

Yes, I have been at Athens—*et ego* in Arcadia—and shall never outwear the impression I brought away. Pardon what looks like a pun when I say that as I stood gazing up at the Acropolis, many new sensations were born in me by a very natural parthenogenesis. Perhaps what comes back to me oftenest when I think of Greece is the outline of the mountains, inexplicably graceful as if modelled by Pheidias, and the color of the sea. I am glad to hear that you are happy there. It is good to be so anywhere, but in Athens must be best of all!

I am glad also that you liked my address. It was first printed in a supplement to the *Atlantic Monthly*, and I shall ask my publishers to send you the copies for which you ask through the Department of State. It was a very interesting occasion and went off well. The President, I am glad to say, was received with great warmth and was deeply gratified—as indeed he more than once told me with a great deal of feeling. With all his firmness he has a very tender and sympathetic nature, or I am much mistaken. I think he has made some sad mistakes, but he is gaining ground with general public opinion, and I know how difficult his position is.

You speak of the pleasant people you see. This is one great advantage of Athens, that, being a little harder to get at than Rome, fewer of the wrong kind of people get there. You must find much to interest you also in your other posts, especially of late. You

are the very Cerberus of ambassadors—three rolled
into one !

I was pleased to hear of your appointment, and
should have written to say so had I known just where
you were. It is not too late to say so now.

Faithfully yours,

J. R. LOWELL.

TO C. E. NORTON

Deerfoot Farm, Southborough, Mass.,
Jan. 1, 1887.

. . . I am "awfully" afraid (as my grandchildren *will*
say—no d——g will stay this neophrastic flood) that
I have lost my Emerson letters. At any rate, I have
mislaid 'em. They are no longer in the little trunk
where I kept them, and I have no doubt that I took
them out, meaning to give them to you. I have one
hope and only one—that they may be in a desk I use
at my sister's. I am sorry, for I valued his verses
written for a dinner given me on my fortieth birthday,
in 1859. I read them over when I made away with
them last year. There will hardly be any other copy,
for he gave me the original manuscript, evidently written in haste. I remember he praised my healthy temperament (I'm glad he didn't know it so well as I),
calling me "well-born Lowell," and, what interested
me more, prophesied that, if the time ever came for
it, I should "lighten" or "thunder," I forget which,
perhaps both, for one is easy after you have accomplished t'other. I hope I shall find them yet, for I am
sometimes luckier than I deserve in that way. . . .

Have the clouds been playing the confectioner with you and are your trees all sugar-candied as ours are? I suppose not, for we are five hundred feet nearer heaven than you — a great start, if I should be put under ground here. I look out of window and see the woods grown grayer than I of a sudden, and find a sort of comfort in it. They have such a knack of renewing their youth in the spring, confound 'em! My sap feels the spur of the young year too, but won't do anything for my hair as it does for theirs. I know a tree or two that I would swap with if I had my life to begin over again. Then one might be made into a violin, perhaps, or into a coffin for somebody one hated, for trees have their likes and dislikes; they've often told me so. . . .

TO MISS GRACE NORTON

Deerfoot Farm, Southborough, Mass.,
Jan. 3, 1887.

. . . I don't get on with the world at all since I half promised to write an introduction to the "World's Progress," a megatherium of a book in two volumes quarto. I hear their heavy footfall behind me wherever I go, and am sure they will trample me into the mud at last. . . .

Oh, if you could see *my* moon—for all mine she must be now if, as I have no doubt, I am the last person up in all this village! I am having the luxury of a private view, and hasn't she found a new plaything in this plated snow, across which she has drawn a long moonglade as over the sea! She is evidently wondering why these multitudinous hill-waves of ours show no emotion, and thinks that either the ocean's heart has ceased to beat or grown as insensible as Endymion's. And every jutting bowlder is a Kohinoor almost big enough for the shirt front of a New York alderman on his way to Sing Sing. How I wish you could see it, with your poor suburban planet vainly trying to get an effect of light and shade out of the enormous flank of Memorial Hall. And all the while the cold is so still that I am sure it means mischief. . . .

TO THOMAS HUGHES

Deerfoot Farm, Southborough, Mass.,
Jan. 10, 1887.

Dear Tom Brown,—Your friendship is very dear to me, and accordingly I was very glad to get so pleasant a reminder of it, and to be assured that you were happy in your new home, as you, if ever any man, deserve to be. I look forward now to no removal except to the narrow house that contrives to hold us all, and hope to be comfortable there, though it do not command such a prospect as yours. I have seen it, you remember, and thought, as the American young woman of the period (born out of Boston) would say, that it was "just lovely!" If I had, or could have, a perch, I think I could be content there. You are beyond reach of the noise and smoke of Babylon, but within reach of its Hanging Gardens, for may I not call so those of the Temple where you breed your Judges! *Felix nimium, tua si bona noris*, as so few of us do, though you seem to be wiser.

My new book will be coming to you by and by. It would have come to you sooner, but that some vile misprints were discovered in the first edition which held my hand. So don't think the fifth thousand on the title-page (P. S. It isn't, I find on undoing the package) implies neglect, but only the second edition of twenty-five hundred copies. Rejoice with me that I am getting popular in my old age, and hope to pay my this year's trip to the dear old Home without defrauding my grandchildren. I get twenty-five cents, I think it is, on copies sold during the first eight months after publication, and then it goes into my general copyrights, for which I am paid £400 a year. Not much after nearly fifty years of authorship, but enough to keep me from the almshouse.

I am sorry you have no grandchildren, for I enjoy mine more and more. I have made up my mind to take them as they are, and not fash my beard too much when they say *will* for *shall* (the infection of which is now universal and past cure) or " I don't know as." They talk as naturally through their noses as friars sing through 'em. 'Tis an innovation in our family, and I hope they'll get over it—but 'twill be too late for me. I am thinking of making the eldest (my namesake) take my name in full and receive what heirlooms I have to leave, on condition that a jury of Britons pronounce him not guilty of this offence.

I am to be very busy this winter; indeed I fear I have undertaken more than I can do well, for I can't always write when I would, though I set myself never so doggedly about it. And Johnson himself, how little he'd have left us but for Boswell! However, I am going to talk on politics to the people of Chicago on my next birthday, and to give six lectures before the Lowell Institute in March. The latter will give me three or four hundred pounds, which will be a lift. If ever you have grandchildren you will grow miserly and approve of entails. Depend upon it 'twas grandfathers invented 'em. My own died seventeen years before I was invented, or perhaps I should be driving in my coach at this moment. On the whole I think I am better employed in writing to you. . . .

P. S. I have not thanked you for your kindness to young B——. He is carried away just now by the Something Brothers, a kind of Anglican monks (without monasteries) who wear cords round their waists, but resemble St. Francis in no other particular that I can discover. If these hempen girdles were worn in readiness for extemporal application to the gullets of many of our public functionaries, I would join the order myself. We need some strong doses of the herb Pantagruelion.

Pray, who is "F. T." who has been writing about me in so friendly a way in the *Cornhill?* He is a little out now and then, but strikes me as in the main judicious. He is wrong about the second part of the "Biglow Papers." I think had he read these first, he would have seen they had more permanent qualities than their predecessors, less fun and more humor perhaps. And pray what natural scenery would he have me describe but my own? If you know him, tell him I think two European birds beat any of ours, the nightingale and

the blackbird. The lark beats any of them also by
sentiment and association, though not vocally. I suppose I should have been a more poetical poet if I had
not been a professor. A poet should feed on nothing
but poetry, as they used to say a drone could be turned
into a queen-bee by a diet of bee-bread. However, my
poems have mostly written themselves and I cannot
account for them. But nothing is so uncomfortable as
an analysis of one's own qualities.

Give my love to England in general. I am as proud
of my two doctor's gowns as Dogberry of his two
cloaks, or M. Jourdain of his two lackeys. . . .

TO C. E. NORTON

Deerfoot, Jan. 26, 1887.

. . . What do you suppose I was doing at between
two and three last night? I couldn't sleep and so—
I took up Seneca's " Medea." I hadn't read it for
forty-eight years, and all I remembered of it was *Medea
superest*. I had forgotten that the *venient annis*, etc.,
was from there. I suppose his Latin is not very good,
but now and then there is a cadence that sticks in one's
ear, and a kind of Dr. Young sublimity, as where Medea
by her incantations draws down the serpent of Ophi-
ucus to earth. The passion is that of a stoic, and
leaves one stoical. He is turgid enough in all conscience, and when he swells gets turbid too, and brings
along with him whatever he comes across, trees and
bridges and cattle and herdsmen and Orpheus's head
and mud, lots of it. And yet I take a certain pleasure

in watching him go it — only one feels that it is all
let on, as Kauterskill Fall used to be. Lucan came
fairly by his style (a sort of Roman Cowley he), and I
am glad I took up the book, since I bethought me for
the first time that Lucan was the true protogenist of
the *concettisti*. . . .

TO R. W. GILDER

Deerfoot Farm, Feb. 9, 1887.

. . . I have often wondered if men lying supine " up
back of the meeting-house " (as we say here) may not
sometimes wile away the time by reading their own ep-
itaphs—no doubt with some surprise in most cases, and
perhaps (if in Latin) with some difficulty, though probably with a leaning towards favorable interpretation
where there was any doubt. To a certain extent I realized my own fancy in reading your proofs. In a literary life of now almost fifty years this is the first time
I was ever admitted to the confidence of anything written about myself. I should have refused it now if I
thought of it in time. But I had forgotten your promise to send me the proofs. However, as the Lowell of
twenty-four years ago is grown a comparative stranger
and an object of scientific curiosity to me, I won't send
back your proofs unread through an over-scrupulosity.

I have made a translation such as it is of the Italian
verses. I can't remember now whose they are. Not
Petrarch's, I think; perhaps Leopardi's, whom I used to
read in those days.

What you say about Bryant interests me very much.

Never being a great reader of newspapers, and never seeing the *Evening Post* (which I thought Godwin's mainly), I knew nothing about the matter. I am all the gladder I wrote my poem for Bryant's birthday—a kind of palinode to what I said of him in the " Fable for Critics," which has something of youth's infallibility in it, or at any rate of youth's irresponsibility. Besides, I wrote it (slapdash, in less than a week, I think) with no notion of publication. That was the doing of my friend C. F. Briggs (with whom I grew acquainted through Page), and to whom I sent it as fast as it was written; if I remember, I gave him the copyright. It turned out a better gift than I expected, for it was the first (perhaps the only) popular thing of mine. Under my own name I was tainted with Abolitionism, to which I swore fealty in 1839. The " Fable " (luckily for Briggs) was anonymous. So were all the first series of " Biglow Papers " as they originally appeared, and I had great fun out of it. I have often wished that I could have had a literary *nom de guerre* and kept my own to myself. I shouldn't have cared a doit what happened to *him*.

But I am writing an autobiography — I must pull up. . . .

TO C. E. NORTON

Deerfoot Farm, April 8, 1887.

. . . I am trying to get rested by reading Dickens, and am over " David Copperfield " now. I had never read it, I find, though Mr. Micawber has become so proverbial that, finding his name in it, I thought I had. Dickens says in his preface that David Copperfield was his "favorite child," and I don't wonder, for it is amazingly well done so far as I have got.

We have got back the birds again, but in this weather they seem as unseasonable as autumn blossoms on the trees. I hope it is warmer in your parts. The only bird that has my entire sympathy is a woodpecker which has been tapping at an elm opposite my window all the morning, as much as to ask, "Is Spring at home?" He has made up his mind that she isn't even expected, and has flown away. Still, there is a certain cheer in the bluebirds. They bid me not despair every day. . . .

TO THOMAS HUGHES

Deerfoot Farm, April 16, 1887.

My dear Friend,—I have just received your " Life of Fraser," * and have read enough of it to see that I shall find it very interesting. He was just the manly kind of fellow to awaken all your sympathy, and accordingly I was not surprised to see (before I got the book) that opinion was unanimous as to how admirably you had written his biography. Notwithstanding his Scottish name, he was a peculiarly English type of man, a type which I trust will long continue to be characteristic of the dear Old Home.

I naturally follow your politics with] great interest. You and I don't agree about the Irish question, I think, but we are sure to be of one mind about the Coercion Bill. It amuses me to see the Grand Old Man using the same arguments against this bill that I vainly urged

* Bishop of Manchester.

against "his" bill five years ago. You know that I am "principled agin" indulging in prophecy, but I made one at that time which has been curiously verified. I used to ask, "Suppose the Irish nation should strike, what are you going to do about it?" They have struck, and I am still at a loss. I am glad to see that their tone over here is much more moderate than it was. "Studiously moderate," you will say. But I think they begin to see the difficulties more clearly than they did. Meanwhile the coercion policy is crowding the emigrant ships to this country, and we have already as many as we can digest at present. We are really interested in your Irish question in more ways than one. It is really we who have been paying the rents over there, for we have to pay higher wages for domestic service to meet the drain.

But I did not mean to write a letter when I began, still less a political letter, but only to say that I sail by the *Pavonia* on the 21st, and mean to stop over and smoke a pipe with you before going up to London. So expect me about the 2d May, and get some fine weather and plenty of thrushes and blackbirds ready for me. We have been having a "saltatory" winter, all ups and downs. Old Hiems has behaved like the guest of the Satyr in the fable—blowing hot and cold—till we are glad to turn him out of doors. But the birds are come at last, though our landscape is as sallow as ever. Hardly a blade of green to keep the poor dears in heart. But the wild geese have been flying northward, and of course "they" know. At any rate, the tame ones are supposed to, or else what faith could one have in a government of majorities?

I shall be glad to clasp your honest hand again, which has done so much good work for all good things. Meanwhile, with love to Mrs. Hughes, I am always

Affectionately yours,

J. R. LOWELL.

TO MRS. EDWARD BURNETT

2 Radnor Place, Hyde Park, W.,
May 22, 1887.

. . . Nothing can be more bewildering than the sudden change in my habits and surroundings. Were it merely from the dumbness of Southborough to the clatter and chatter of London, it would be queer enough; from the rising and falling murmur of the mill to this roar of the human torrent. But I can hardly help laughing sometimes when I think how a single step from my hermitage takes me into Babylon. Meanwhile it amuses and interests me. My own vitality seems to reinforce itself as if by some unconscious transfusion of the blood from these ever-throbbing arteries of life into my own. Upon my word, I think I am beginning in my old age to find a more impressive and poignant solitude in the Great City than in the country. I get all the country I want in the Park, which is within five minutes of me, and the song of the thrush is more pathetic there, like a quotation of poetry in a dreary page of prose.

Last evening as I drove to dinner through the Edgware Road I seemed to get a glimpse of Fairyland in the Saturday-night fair which stretches along one side of the way and runs over into the by-streets. A dingy

II.—22

fairyland truly, and yet so remote from all my ordinary associations as to become poetic.

At dinner, by the way, I was glad to meet John Morley for the first time since my return. He welcomed me most cordially, but looks older and a little worn with the constant friction of politics. But the cheerful fanaticism of his face is always exhilarating to me, though I feel that it would have the same placidly convinced expression if my head were rolling at his feet at the exigence of some principle. He knows where he stands on the Home Rule question better than Gladstone, for his opinions are more the result of conviction than of sentiment.

My thrushes are singing under every discouragement, for everybody (with the usual shortness of memory and joy in generalization) agrees that "there never was such weather!" It has been and is indeed very cold, but the palace of English summer is always built of ice, and I continue to think the London climate the best in the world. At any rate it suits me. . . .

TO C. E. NORTON

2 Radnor Place, Hyde Park, W.,
May 26, 1887.

. . . I do like London, and it gives a fillip to my blood, now growing more sluggish than it used to be. I love to stand in the middle of the Park and forget myself in that dull roar of ever-circulating life which bears a burden to the song of the thrush I am listening to. It is far more impressive than Niagara, which has nothing else to do and can't help itself. In this vast torrent all the drops are men. There! I have unconsciously written a pentameter and it is time to stop.

I have seen Gladstone several times, and he is light-hearted as a boy—as lightheaded, too, I might almost say. I am amazed at the slowness of people here in seeing that the ice they have been floating on is about to break up—nay, will at the first rough water. The Irish question is only incidental to the larger question of their whole system of landholding, and the longer they delay settling *that* the more inevitable is it that this should stir itself. It is a misfortune and not a crime to be entangled in an anachronism, but if one won't do what he can to break loose one must share its fate without complaint or hope of compensation. You will be glad to hear that Morley has made himself re-spected both in Parliament and out of it, though on what is now the unpopular side. I think it will be the winning one in the end, for the stars in their courses are fighting against Sisera, and Sisera refuses to lift his eyes to them. It is a curious touch of nature that there should be such bitterness against Chamberlain—as if a self-made man had no right to opinions of his own, as the sons of dukes have as a matter of course. I met him last night at old Lady Stanley's (of Alderley), and he didn't show any sign of disheartenment. She is one of my favorites. She reminds me of the people I used to see when I was young—so frankly themselves. But this was before our individuality had been trampled out of us by the Irish mob. . . .

TO MRS. EDWARD BURNETT

2 Radnor Place, Hyde Park, W.,
June 12, 1887.

. . . I was very glad to get your letters day before yesterday, one of them including that of Joe. It was a statistical letter (as those of boys are apt to be), and told me just what I wanted to know—the blossoming of the apple and pear trees and the greenness of the lawn. He forgot to say how my friend the brook was, but as you speak of a three days' rain, I have no doubt he is in good health and spirits, rolling his amber over the dam with a full heart. Many a night have I listened to him crooning his poems to himself and the embowering elm-trees. Joe's letter I was glad to find carefully written. I am sorry that he is to lose his European trip, but dare say the Beverley shore will do quite as much for his health. After all, the kind of world one carries about in one's self is the important thing, and the world outside takes all its grace, color, and value from that.

. . . I am glad you have been reading Howell's letters. The book is not so good as Charles Lamb fancied it. His favorites were always a lover's "inexpressive Shes," endowed with every charm out of himself. If it was my copy of the letters you have been reading, you will find some interesting proposals for a reform of spelling (by Howell) on a leaf at the end. . . .

TO MRS. LESLIE STEPHEN

Whitby, Aug. 16, 1887.

. . . Your letter lost a couple of days by going to

seek me at Radnor Place. I have been here for a week, and find Whitby as delightful as ever. The Abbey stares at me with the empty sockets of its eyes, and tries, I think, to get a little friendly expression into them. St. Hilda seems to welcome me back, but I am not sure that Cædmon would be glad to see a brother poet. Goethe, you know, talks of the roaring loom of Time, and I suppose he weaves us all in somehow or other, whether we like it or no. Of you, no doubt, he will make a lovely white rose. I sha'n't cut much of a figure, I am afraid, but shall be content to be the dull ground on which you are woven.

I do little else than take longish walks by the sea or over the moors, which do me good and make my eyes *feel* a little better at any rate. But I feel that I am come to the period when decay begins to set in, and when I am tired of looking at the ruins of the Abbey I sit among my own and pensively contemplate them. I hope a flower or two will root in a crevice here and there for you to make a nosegay of when you chance that way. . . .

TO MISS SEDGWICK

2 Radnor Place, Hyde Park, W.,
Aug. 18, 1887.

Dear Dora,—Many thanks for so kindly remembering me. But how clever women are in flattering us with their pretended jealousies! No, there may be another Dora, but the first will always have that pre-eminence of priority that belongs to the first snowdrop and the first bluebird. You are Dora I., D. G.

In spite of the epigraph of my paper I am really at Whitby, whither I have been every summer but '85 for the last six years. This will tell you how much I like it. A very primitive place it is, and the manners and ways of its people much like those of New England. "Sir" and "ma'am" are only half-hardy exotics here. The great difference is that everybody here will take a shilling, failing that, a sixpence, and, in desperate circumstances, even a penny, as a kind of *tabula in naufragio*, God save the mark! The people with whom I lodge, but for accent, might be of Ashfield. 'Tis a wonderfully picturesque place, with the bleaching bones of its Abbey standing aloof on the bluff and dominating the country for leagues. Once, they say, the monks were lords as far as they could see. The skeleton of the Abbey still lords it over the landscape, which was certainly one of the richest possessions they had, for there never was finer. Sea and moor, hill and dale; sea dotted with purple sails and white (fancy mixes a little in the purple, perhaps), moors flushed with heather in blossom, and fields yellow with corn, and the dark heaps of trees in every valley blabbing the secret of the stream that fain would hide to escape being the drudge of man. I know not why, wind has replaced water for grinding, and the huge water-wheels, green with moss and motionless, give one a sense of repose after toil that, to a lazy man like me, is full of comfort. Not that I am so lazy neither, for I think a good deal— only my thoughts never seem worth writing down till I meet with them afterwards written down by somebody more judiciously frugal than I. Do you know I was

thinking this morning that Montaigne was the only
original man of modern times, or at any rate the only
man with wit enough to see things over again in his
own way, and to think it as good a way as any other,
never mind how old?

I wish you could see the "yards"—steep flights of
stone steps hurrying down from the West Cliff and the
East, between which the river (whose name I can never
remember) crawls into the sea, and where I meet little
girls with trays bearing the family pies to the baker, and
groups of rosy children making all manner of playthings
of a bone or a rag. And I wish you could see the pier,
with its throng of long-booted fishermen, looking the
worthy descendants of the Northmen who first rowed
their ships into the shelter of the cliffs and named the
place. And I wish you could breathe the ample air of
the moors—I mean with me.

Your little gift, dear Dora, has been very useful. I
carry it in my pocket, not without fear of wearing away
the birds and flowers, and so changing its summer to
autumn, as my own has changed. I use it almost every
day. I dare say you are in Ashfield now. Greet the
hills for me, especially Peter's, and the June grass that
I still see making them so beautiful in velvet. Give
my love to all wherever you are, and tell Sally that I
shall write to her soon. I take my letters in order, and
yours came before hers; and oh, if I am tardy, remember how many I have to write and that my life is event-
less.

Affectionately yours,

J. R. LOWELL.

TO C. E. NORTON

Deerfoot, Dec. 22, 1887.

. . . I have contrived at last to make a kind of whole of "Endymion," which had been lying in fragments for many years, but fear I have not made a harmonious statue of it after all.

I have finished the "Epistle to Curtis" after a fashion, well or ill is hard to say. The measure is so facile that one soon loses one's sense of the difference between what sounds like something and what really is something. One needs to brace one's self with a strong dose of Dr. Donne. . . .

TO R. W. GILDER

Deerfoot Farm, Dec. 26, 1887.

. . . My dear boy, if ever you *should* attain to entire utterance of yourself you would be the unhappiest man alive. Be happy in having something to strive after. Possession (unless of the Devil) is nine points of the law, but it is *ten* of disillusion. A happy New Year to you both! I am glad you have been seeing the President.* To me his personality is very *simpatico*. He is a truly American type of the best kind—a type very dear to me, I confess. . . .

TO C. E. NORTON

Deerfoot, Jan. 5, 1888.

. . . I brought up one volume of Singer's "Old Eng-

* Mr. Cleveland.

lish Poets," but 'twas that containing the "Hero and
Leander" of Marlow and Chapman, an old dear of
mine. "Thealma and Clearchus" I left behind because
I didn't want it—nor do I now. The weight of its dulness left a crease in my memory which will never out
any more than that of a dog's-ear in a book. But besides this, a conviction remains from that laborious reading (what a reader I was! I am far fallen from such
grace now) that the book could not have been written
by a contemporary of Spenser, as Walton said it was.
The language was altogether too modern—curiously so
even for 1683, when, as I find, Walton published it.
And this singularity (of modernness) is very notable in
the style of the "Complete Angler" too. I have little
doubt that Walton himself wrote "Thealma and Clearchus," though I can well fancy a coroner writing it, or
sitting on it and bringing in a verdict of "Found Dead."
That Walton should have laid it at the door of his (con-
nubial) great-uncle is, after all, a comparatively innocent
supercherie. If Walton wrote only the verses in praise
of angling printed in the "Complete Angler," how explain Donne's verses to him—unless on the supposition
that the opinions of one's friends about one's verses are
ninety-nine parts friendship to one of judgment? I,
who am just printing mine, am upset by the thought.
Or was there another I. W.? I know of none.

I am wondering more and more if my poems are
good for anything after all. They are old-fashioned in
their simplicity and straightforwardness of style—and
everybody writes so plaguily well nowadays. I fear
that I left off my diet of bee-bread too long and have

written too much prose. A poet shouldn't be, nay, he can't be, anything else without loss to him as poet, however much he may gain as man.

But this is getting as long as the Epistle to the Corinthians (which had to be cut in two), and is not near as entertaining. But I always write my longest letters when I have something else to do. It seems so like being industrious. 'Tis a temptation of the Devil. . . .

TO R. W. GILDER

Deerfoot Farm, Jan. 16, 1888.

. . . If the Landor article be not yet printed I should like to make a correction therein. When I wrote it I sought in vain for a note I had made (when my memory was fresh) of what he said to me about "Old Daddy Wordsworth," as Thackeray used irreverently to call him.* I have now lighted on it, and this it is:

"Mr. Wordsworth, a man may mix poetry with prose as much as he pleases, and it will only elevate and enliven; but the moment he mixes a particle of prose with his poetry it precipitates the whole." If my version in the *Century* differs materially from this, I should be glad to have this take its place, for I don't like a lie even in the milder form of inaccuracy. If I have got it nearly right in the *Century* I shall be glad, because it will partly persuade me that my memory is not so ruinous as I supposed. . . .

---

* "Old Daddy Wordsworth," said Thackeray, "may bless his stars if he ever get high enough in heaven to black Tommy Moore's boots."

TO THE MISSES LAWRENCE

Deerfoot Farm, Jan. 30, 1888.

. . . I am very busy in my old age, if I may call my seventieth year so (on which I enter in twenty-three days), when I feel as young as I ever did. I have been printing a new collection of my old poems, some of them already published in magazines (to help boil the pot for the day), and some out of yellowing portfolios. I shall send you a copy in due time, and you must toss up which shall read it first — for I assume a natural eagerness in both of you. Then I am revising my "Works" for a uniform edition in type so clear that I shall be able to read them myself should I ever have the wish. I have already read over one volume of my prose, and am astonished to find how clever I used to be. I give you my word for it, I was entertained by the reading.

We have been having the coldest weather for many years—cold and clear as a critique of Matt Arnold's. Night before last our thermometer (a very serious one and not given to exaggerations) marked forty-six degrees of frost on the honor of Fahrenheit. I like it, and if you could see the long stretch of snowy peace (with no track of the interviewer's hoof in it) I look at from my windows, you would think that Winter had his compensations. When you *do* have snow in London, it has lost its innocence and looks as if it had come out of the slums. . . .

TO MRS. LESLIE STEPHEN

Deerfoot Farm, Feb. 20, 1888.

. . . This is the first time you ever said anything to me that made me uncomfortable. But when you tell me that my lovely little goddaughter has been supplied with an autograph-book, an instrument of torture unknown even to the Inquisition, you make me shiver. Albums they used to be called and, after exhausting the patience of mankind, hope to continue their abominable work under an alias.

Stammbücher the Germans call them (who, cunning in the invention of bores, invented this also), and I rather like the name, because *stamm* has an imprecatory sound and rhymes honestly with the d—n that rises to one's lips when one sees a specimen. However, I will write in Virginia's, that she may have the pleasure of wondering one of these days how her mother ever could have loved so dull a fellow. . . .

TO C. E. NORTON

Deerfoot Farm, Feb. 21, 1888.

. . . I haven't had much of a week. My wits are sluggish as cold molasses. I have to wait for a thaw like my neighbor the brook here, who is in fine vein this morning, as contemptuous of dams as a Universalist. I never could get any good by Johnson's recipe of "setting doggedly about it." Perhaps I don't take a strong enough dose. . . .

TO THE SAME

Deerfoot Farm, March 11, 1888.

. . . I have been having a very blue week—unable to do anything that I ought to be doing, and of no earthly use (of heavenly there is no question) in the world. . . . But yesterday I received a certain amount of self-satisfaction in a foolish way. I had been reading about Alcott, and was reminded that forty years ago I wrote something about him myself. I read it, and found that, though I could now amend it here and there, I had said gayly pretty much what people are saying seriously now, and this pleased me. Therefore I write to you as my literary executor, to say the second of " Studies for Two Heads " was a sketch from the living Alcott. It must have been written before 1850. Read it and see how you like it. Lord, how easily I used to write!—too easily, I think now. But I couldn't help it. Everything came at a jump and all of a piece. In reading this over again, I doubt if my pencil hesitated once in writing it or made a correction afterwards. Perhaps this is why I never value what I have done till long enough after to have forgotten it (as in this case), and then sometimes, but not often, I am goose enough to be pleased!

. . . Heigh-ho! everything is beginning to seem long ago to me now and everything grows dreamy—but I shall wake now before long. I think it is partly that I can't realize myself here in Southborough. I don't get wonted. I walk to the post-office or over the hills, and though I have every evidence that earth is solid under my feet, yet it crumbles away at every step and leaves me in dreamland. *Is* there anything solid outside the mind? Or is one a little *cracked* now and then? Sometimes in my lonely lunes I fancy it, and then Fact gives me a smart rap on the head and it rings clear again. . . .

TO T. B. ALDRICH

Deerfoot Farm, March 19, 1888.

. . . I liked your little poem about Brownell both for its own sake and for being what Lessing used to call a *Rescue*. But this is not my reason for writing. What I meant to tell you about was one of those coincidences of which so much is made nowadays. Yesterday morning I found myself all of a sudden thinking of Brownell (though I couldn't for my life remember his name) and of those fine Norse-hearted poems of his. I fell into the same line of thought with you in your poem—though mine didn't achieve such gracious curves as yours. Now, I can't recollect that I had thought of Brownell for years, nor could I excogitate any suggestion, by association or otherwise, that should make me think of him then. I was on my way to take down a volume of Dyce's " Middleton " from the shelf when he (anonymously, too, as I have said) dropt in. So sudden and unforewarned was it that I thought it very odd at the time and tried in vain to account for it. The man himself came back to me vividly as I saw him some twenty years ago at our Saturday Club. He had a single touch of vulgarity about him—he dyed his hair (or beard, I forget which—perhaps both). But he was so modest that one soon forgot it as one does a uniform, though a little disconcerting at first. So I said to him, " I remember your face perfectly well, but can't recall your name, and I remember, too, how your great guns used to *jump*—wasn't that the word ?"

Well, in the evening came your poem and gave me the label for my poet. I really think it was rather odd. 'Twas better to remember his poems, though, than his name, wasn't it ? But don't you go to rescuing anybody else, for I might not again verify the proverb that *les beaux esprits se rencontrent*, and my story of how far off your coming shone would be spoiled. . . .

TO C. E. NORTON

Deerfoot Farm, March 27, 1888.

. . . I haven't had a very blessed week. If I could manage the gymnastic feat of jumping off my own shadow, I should do well enough. But it is difficult. And yet I fancy that they who accomplish it are the only ones who have a chance at being happy or reasonably successful. I am such an ill-conditioned mixture of folly and common-sense as makes me despair sometimes. My Folly whispers me, " Now do something really good, as good as you know how," and so I do something, and it isn't so good as I know how. Then comes Common-sense and says, " Why in the dumps? It makes no odds in the end." Very true, but the end may be a good way off, and meanwhile? . . .

Well, I shall hope to see you on Saturday, and I

hope the weight will be lifted for a while. But I am to speak in New York, and that depresses me. What can I say that I and everybody else hasn't said fifty times before? And then my way of saying things doesn't answer for the Philistines, and they are the important people after all. . . .

TO THE SAME

Deerfoot, March 29, 1888.

. . . I was a little consoled yesterday by getting a letter from ——, which she had sagaciously addressed to " Scarborough, Maine," on the cover of which the postmaster of that ilk had written, " No such party known here." How —— ever found out there was such a place and where it was I can't imagine, but although the P. M. *did* call me a " party," there was a kind of comfort in thinking of a place where I had never been heard of. I am thinking of migrating thither and beginning life anew as an honest burgher whose soul has never ventured into a region above buttons.

But by Jove! there's a bluebird warbling, God bless him! 'Tis the best news this many a day. . . .

TO THE SAME

Deerfoot, March 30, 1888.

. . . I was seeing things all night long; they were all beautiful and bright. One night I saw Michael with his scales, and made a poem of it next morning which rescued me from a prose article I was trying to write for a young fellow in Chicago. I sent him the verses (which cost me but half an hour) instead. You will see and like 'em too, I hope.

I am persuaded that the D—l has been abroad in great wrath, but not because his time is short unhappily. I am thankful for the immense ballast of common-sense I carry. It sinks me too deep in the water sometimes for my keel to plough air as a poet's should, but it keeps my top-hamper steady when the wind blows as it has lately.

"Timon" wasn't a bad medicine. The text is one of the worst among all the plays. 'Tis wrapt in smoke, but with awful gushes of flame now and then as from a world on fire. . . .

TO MRS. EDWARD BURNETT

2 Radnor Place, Hyde Park, W.,
May 13, 1888.

. . . London has been very pleasant this week—I mean the weather; not a raindrop since my last letter. And I find a childish pleasure in the vision of splendor it offers me. I like the difficulty I find in crossing the drive-way in Hyde Park for the throng of equipages. I like to see so many people capable of luxuries that are beyond my reach. I wonder whether I should like it as well if I couldn't afford to hire a hansom? I half think I should. It is very odd to be snatched from my cell at Deerfoot and caught up by this whirl of breakfasts, luncheons, teas, dinners, and "goings-on." I am sure I like Deerfoot best, and can't quite make

II.—23

it clear to myself why I am here. Yet you would be pleased with the warmth of my welcome. . . .

It is so fine to-day that I can't help wishing I were in Kensington Gardens, where the new leafage brightens into blossoms against the smoke-blackened trunks, and the thrushes are singing as if they would never be old. It is odd to see the battered old trees there come out in their new spring fashions like dowagers who dress young. I shall be walking across presently. . . .

TO THE SAME

2 Radnor Place, Hyde Park, W.,
June 24, 1888.

. . . You know that my correspondence is apt to have gaps in it, like a saw with which some enterprising boy like Francis has been experimenting, and I felt sure that you would explain this last one by my journey to Bologna.* That, indeed, was the immediate cause of it. The heat was of the best quality, and I felt a good part of the time as I suppose a dissolving view must when it is fulfilling its destiny. But the consequence of that and of the fatigues I underwent was in long last a fit of gout from which I am just recovering. Luckily for me it came to a head gradually, and I was able (with the kind aid of my fellow-travellers Professors Ramsay and Ferguson, of Glasgow) to make the journey of thirty-one hours without break from Milan to London. I look back upon it now with

* To be present as a delegate from Harvard, at the celebration of the eighth hundredth anniversary of the University of Bologna.

amazement when I think that I am on the edge of seventy. Had I stopped on the way I should be there now, for I have been flat on my back since I arrived here eight days ago. . . .

TO THE SAME

2 Radnor Place, Hyde Park, W.,
July 8, 1888.

. . . The gout hardly tolerates any distraction on the part of those it visits, and the material for a letter accumulates slowly. I hold my cup patiently under the faucet, I shake the cask, and it is odds if a draggling drop fall now and then. I don't think that one's meditations on the Universe are exactly the material for a letter or likely to prove so entertaining, not to say profitable, as Swift's on a broomstick. The outward world may be an illusion of the senses—one is often tempted to think it such; but solitary confinement without even so much as Bruce's spider, or Silvio Pellico's mouse, soon teaches one how dependent on it we are for mental enlivenment. The silk-worm and the spider are the only creatures which can spin their own insides to advantage; and the former is nothing to the purpose, since he spins 'em only to exclude himself from the world, while the latter can profit by his gift of nature only when he finds coignes of vantage on which to hitch the web that is to catch his flies for him. This was Montaigne's method, and the connection of his essays is never logical, but is dictated by the accidental prominence of corners of his memory to which he can attach the thread of his discourse. But an essay is not a letter, as you have discovered by this time. The meaning of all this is that my life has been wholly without incident for the last three weeks. To-day is marked by an event of grave importance. I have had my boots on and mock at my crutch. . . .

TO MISS E. G. NORTON

2 Radnor Place, Hyde Park, W.,
July 12, 1888.

. . . Your letter was even more welcome than you could have expected, for it brought a vision of your gracious presence to me while I was prostrate with gout and specially in need of such consolations. It was very nice of you to think of me and to show me that you did in such a charming way. . . .

I occupied my enforced leisure in reading the comedies of Eugène Labiche, which greatly amused me. Since I have been getting better I have read the lives of Archbishop Trench and of W. E. Forster. I knew them both, and the books interested me accordingly, especially the latter. It is pleasant to read about men whom one can respect so much, however one may dissent from some of their opinions. . . .

TO LESLIE STEPHEN

Whitby, Aug. 22, 1888.

. . . I like Whitby as well as ever, weather or no, but find it harder than ever to be jolly. I feel that I am going down-stairs at last, and am not even consoled by the *esprit d'escalier*. But I have found the drawing-room pleasant, on the whole, and liked the people there. . . .

TO MRS. LESLIE STEPHEN

Whitby, Aug. 23, 1888.

. . . I am rather lame to-day because I walked too much and over very rough paths yesterday. But how could I help it? For I will not give in to Old Age. We started, a dozen of us, at half-past ten, as agreed on the day before. The clouds were heaping ominously in the N.W., and soon it began to rain in a haphazard kind of way, as a musician who lodges over one lets his fingers idle among the keys before he settles down to the serious business of torture. So it went on drowsily, but with telling effects of damp, till we reached Falling Foss, which we saw as a sketch in water-colors and which was very pretty. We had left our wagonette at Little Neck, where we were to lunch, and walked thither to meet it by a foot-path along the valley of the stream. This was a very up-and-down business, and especially slippery from clayeyness of soil, especially to me who had on tennis shoes for the ease of my feet, the india-rubber soles of which lent themselves gladly to all the sliding passages of the performance. I was unable to maintain that sedateness of gait which Dante commends as essential to dignity, but escaped without a tumble by dint of much impromptu gymnastics.

Thunder-storms loitered about over the valley, like 'Arries on a bank holiday, at a loss what to do with their leisure, but ducking us now and then by way of showing their good-humor. However, there were parentheses of sunshine, and, on the whole, it was very beautiful. After lunch, being assured that the footpath (two miles and a half in the Yorkshire dialect) from Little Neck to Sleeghts was much easier, I resolved to attempt it. It turned out harder than we expected, owing to slipperiness, and we had to cross the swollen stream three times, leaping from unsteady stone to stone as we could. Episodes of thunder-storm as before all the way. We got in at last; I with my feet giving me twinges like toothache at every step. The sun came out and the hills were glorious all about us for the last half-hour of walking. If you could have seen the golden heaven that deepened in the little mill-pond just before we arrived at Sleeghts! 'Twas like the heart of a poet, no bigger than another's, but capable of holding so much! I don't regret my walk.

It is sunny and soft to-day, and I shall crawl out to bask a little, like the other pensioners of nature. It will not be long now ere I head for St. Ives. . . .

P. S. Pardon this letter. As I think back over it, I fear it must be like one of the business passages of the " Excursion." . . .

TO THE SAME

2 Radnor Place, London, Sept. 29, 1888.

. . . I have not been seriously at work on anything, but only entangled in the briery intricacies of George Meredith, like the poet of the "Romaunt of the Rose," and like him consoling my scratches with the assurance

that there was a consummate flower hidden somewhere
among them, of which one gets enchanting glimpses
now and then.   I am now reading Mrs. Green's " Henry
II." with great edification.

But I am dissolute also.   Last night I went to the
Court Theatre, and saw, I am bound to say, one of the
stupidest pieces of vulgarity that ever pleased a British
public.   Ah, if I were only capable of judging English civilization as American is judged, what a sermon
mightn't I preach !   But I forbear.   No, I won't give in.
I still insist that Britain produces a saint now and then
as fair as if they had stepped down from an old painted
window.

We have been having snivelling weather, but to-day
is sunshiny, and I am going to the private view of the
" Arts and Crafts " Society—a hopeless attempt, in my
opinion, to reproduce the happy inadvertence of mediæval art by deliberate forethought.   But I shall be glad
to see the Burne-Jones windows. . . .

TO MISS SEDGWICK

2 Radnor Place, Oct. 3, 1888.

. . . We are in the beginning of our foggy season, and
to-day are having a yellow fog, and that always enlivens
me, it has such a knack of transfiguring things.   It flat-
ters one's self-esteem, too, in a recondite way, promoting
one for the moment to that exclusive class which can
afford to wrap itself in a golden seclusion.   It is very
picturesque also.   Even the cabs are rimmed with a
halo, and people across the way have all that possibility

of suggestion which piques the fancy so in the figures
of fading frescoes. Even the gray, even the black fogs
make a new and unexplored world not unpleasing to
one who is getting palled with familiar landscapes. . . .

TO F. H. UNDERWOOD

London, Nov. 3, 1888.

. . . I had recollected that you had asked me if I
would read what you had written about me, and could
not be quite sure whether you had asked me by word
of mouth or by letter. You know my shyness about
such things, so I shall only say that what you said gave
me as much pleasure as at my age one is able to take in
such things. One's old self becomes with time a kind
of third person, in whom one takes a certain friendly
interest, with no incursion of that partisanship which is
apt to disturb any discussion of one's actual self —
though less, I would fain think, in my own case than in
most. I fancy I might have accomplished more if I
could have contrived to take a greater interest in myself and my doings. Perhaps not, for I should have
been more conscious. . . .

TO C. E. NORTON

2 Radnor Place, Hyde Park, W.,
Nov. 11, 1888.

. . . It is noon, and I am writing by candle-light.
If I look over the way I can just see the houses
vague as the architecture of Piranesi. But I like fogs;
they leave the imagination so wholly to herself, or just

giving her a jog now and then. I shall go out into the Park by and by, to lose myself in this natural poesy of London which makes the familiar strange. It is as good as travelling in the interior of Africa, without the odious duty of discovery, which makes the strange familiar. There is an ominous feel about it to which I never get wonted, as of the last day, and I listen with a shudder sometimes for the *tuba mirum spargens sonum*. I am still so much of a Puritan that the English words would shock me a little, as they did the other day at ——'s table, when I blurted them out to a parson's wife in my impulsive way, and made her jump as if she had heard the authentic instrument with her accounts but half made up.

There is nothing new here—there seldom is, and this is what makes it so comfortable. The Parnell Commission, like a wounded snake, drags its slow length along with an effect of bore silently and sootily pervasive as the fog of which I was just speaking. Unless some sudden Chinese cracker of *révélation intime* should go off, the world in general will have forgotten it ere it be over. I think Gladstone has at least effected so much— that he has brought Irish and English together on a common ground. Surely this is good so far as it goes, but how long the Irish will allow any ground on which they get a footing to remain common is to me at least problematical. I for one am getting tired of seeing *our* politics playing bob to *their* kite.

The Sackville squall has amused me a good deal, bringing out so strangely as it did the English genius for thinking all the rest of mankind unreasonable. One is reminded of the old story of the madman who thought himself alone in his sanity. I seldom care to discuss anything—most things seem so obvious—least of all with the average Briton, who never is willing to take anything for granted and whose eyes are blind to all side-lights. Yes, there is one thing they always take for granted, namely, that an American *must* see the superiority of England. They have as little tact as their *totem* the bull. I have come to the edge of my temper several times over the Sackville business — always introduced by them. "All Europe is laughing at you, you know," said Sir —— —— to me genially the other day. "That is a matter of supreme indifference to us," I replied blandly, though with a keen temptation to pull a pair of ears so obtrusively long. But with all that there is a manliness about them I heartily like. Tact, after all, is only a sensitiveness of nerve, and there is but a hair's-breadth between this and irritability. . . .

P. S. Fancy! I shall have reached David's limit in three months.

TO MRS. EDWARD BURNETT

2 Radnor Place, Hyde Park, W.,
Nov. 12, 1888.

. . . Alas! in this world we do not cast off our hair shirts. At best we turn them or put on clean ones that haven't lost their bite by wear. . . . If one is good for anything, the world is not a place to be happy in— though, thank God, there are better things than being happy. . . .

TO MRS. JAMES T. FIELDS

68 Beacon Street, Jan. 21, 1889.

. . . It is very kind of you to offer me books, and I
thank you heartily. But alas! it is not books—it is I
that am wanting. I read as a swallow peruses the pool,
with briefest dips at the surface. I suppose I shall
feel the wind in my sails before long. At present I
am becalmed. In some corner of the sky there must
be a breeze waiting. Or am I (as some teach) a machine? and has a grain of sand blown in somewhere?
Never mind, I am much obliged to *you*. . . .

TO MRS. EDWARD BURNETT

1608 K Street, Washington, Feb. 13, 1889.

. . . Philadelphia was very dinnery, of course, with
lunches and Wister parties thrown in. Nothing could
have been more agreeable than my host and hostess
the Weir Mitchells, and everybody was kind. . . .

Here I am busy dining and receptioning again, but
not now for the first time do I find that I am not the
stuff of which lions are made. I feel as if I had on a
false mane which might blow off at the first gust. Like
Bottom "I no lion am, nor yet no lion's dam." But
the shaking up I get does me good.

Yesterday afternoon Ned* and his chum gave me
a tea which was very pleasant, and which Mrs. Cleveland honored with her presence. She is very pretty
and gracious and bears herself very well.

* Mr. Burnett, who was at this time a Member of Congress.

I met the President and her at dinner with the Endicotts. He was very cordial, and there is a look of sentiment in his eyes in odd contrast with the burliness of his person. It is odd to be in a capital again and to renew the familiar round of official receptions with unfamiliar faces and ways. I have been struck with the fine figures and heads of the senators. They are really imposing, and seem to have been sifted out by a kind of natural selection. This morning, after a call on Mr. Bayard at the State Department, I called on Mrs. Cleveland at the White House. She was again very pleasing in a very pretty morning-gown. . . .

TO C. E. NORTON

1608 K Street, Washington, Feb. 15, 1889.

. . . I fear I never had that lively interest in folks that becomes a wise man—I mean *folks* in general. I somehow get to the end of them so soon that they begin to bore me sooner than they should.

I have seen some interesting people, nevertheless, and have been lucky in my hosts (the Mitchells and S. G. W.), who are always good company and hold out, having native springs in them, and not being merely taps of the general system of milk-and-water works. Ward is wonderfully young and like his former self. Hanging before me as I write are two landscapes of his in pastel, as good in their way as anything of the kind I ever saw, and his interest in good things is as lively as ever. Mrs. Ward, too, is little changed since I last saw her, and together they give me a queer feeling that I have come back to a place where we called a halt twenty years ago, and that in retracing my steps I have abolished the years between.

I have seen Bancroft twice and found him as vivid as ever. In answer to a question of mine he told me the odd fact that he learned German of Sidney Willard, who knew the language well, but must have been his own teacher, for he knew nothing of the pronunciation, so that Bancroft, when he arrived in Germany, had only to learn that in order to speak easily.

I have made also a very pleasant acquaintance in Mr. McCulloch, who called on me, a dear old man of eighty-five, rosy and fresh and gentle, looking more like an emeritus professor of philosophy than like a financier. . . .

TO MRS. JAMES T. FIELDS

68 Beacon Street, Feb. 23, 1889.

. . . A rain of flowers came down on me yesterday as on a virgin-martyr, and the hard seventieth step of my climb was velveted with them. They were very sweet, but such gracious words from you two (to me, too) were even sweeter. That two such charming women *—since there are two of you I can say what I like without impertinence—should think of me so kindly makes all *man*kind a matter of indifference.

I shall hope to see you this afternoon, but may be circumvented. If I should be so lucky as to come, and you should observe a pinch of condescension in

* Mrs. Fields and Miss Jewett.

my manner, you will bear with it when I tell you that I was listening to my own praises for two hours last night*—and have hardly yet got used to the discovery of how great a man I am. A poison, you know, may be distilled from laurel leaves, and I think the very smell of them goes to the head. But, after all, *every*body isn't seventy, and there is a certain promotion from the mob in that! . . .

TO MRS. LESLIE STEPHEN

68 Beacon Street, Feb. 27, 1889.

. . . I have been forging over the reef of my seventieth birthday into the smooth water beyond without much damage to my keel, so far as I can discover. Even had I been wrecked I should have saved your box, as Camoëns did his Lusiads. 'Tis a beauty, and I shall fill my pipe from it with a sense of virtue as if I were doing something handsome. How adroitly indulgent you women are. If you can't cleanse us of our vices, you contrive to make them so far as possible becoming.

I was dined on my birthday, and praised to a degree that would have satisfied you, most partial even of your sex. But somehow I liked it, and indeed none but a pig could have helped liking the affectionate way it was done. I suppose it is a sign of weakness in me somewhere, but I can't help it. I *do* like to be liked. It gives me a far better excuse for being about (and in everybody's way) than having written a fine poem does. *That'll* be all very well when one is under the

* At a dinner in his honor at the Tavern Club.

mould. But I am not sure whether one will care for it much. So keep on liking me, won't you?

It is very droll to be seventy. Don't scold me for it—I'll never do it again; but I don't feel any older, I think, and I am sure I don't feel any wiser, than I did before. 'Tis a little depressing to be reminded that one has lived so long and done so little. When I measure the length with the achievement there is a horrible overlapping, but I shall expect a certain deference. Whatever condescension I show will be multiplied by seven instead of six, remember, and precious in proportion. . . .

TO MRS. S. WEIR MITCHELL

68 Beacon Street, Boston, March 9, 1889.

Dear Mrs. Mitchell,—I am not so clever as you show yourself to be in the size of your sheets of paper, which reminds me of that prudence one learns in Italy of ordering one ration (*una porzione*) for two persons. Nor, though I have so many letters to write, and using as I do a more generous sheet, can I divest myself of the feeling that there is a kind of inhospitality in leaving my fourth page blank. Am I flattering myself, as we generally do when there is a choice of motives, by assuming that we act from the better? and is this feeling but a superstition derived from those heathen times (before yours) when a single postage was $18\frac{3}{4}$ cents (written in red ink, as if in the very life-blood of the correspondent), and one felt that one didn't get an honest pennyworth unless one filled every scribable corner of his foolscap? Now, you think I mean by this that I should have answered your note sooner had I as tiny quarto as your own to write upon. But nothing of the kind. It was because I remembered that I had promised you something. . . .

I have been doing my best to be seventy, and have had a dinner, and all kinds of nice things were said about me, and it was very pleasant to think that people were so kind. But I feel that they were trying to make it up to me for having been guilty of some sort of gaucherie, as when one knocks over a stand with some frail thing on it that can't be replaced, and is condoled with, "It's not of the least consequence." Well, I have made up my mind never to do it again. But really I am quite ashamed to find how well people think of me, and yet I can't help liking it too. I feel as if it some-how justified my friends.

I often think of my pleasant week with you in Wal-nut Street. I have now two memories of Philadelphia, antithetic one to the other—the Quaker one of forty-five years ago, and that of yesterday so very unlike it, and both so good. How far away seems and is the first, for it is extinct as the dodo. It was very sweet in its provincial valley of self-sufficientness and contentment. It had a flavor beyond terrapin. But the telegraph has cosmopolitanized us in spite of ourselves; the whole world has but one set of nerves, and we all have the headache together. And, after all, Europe has the ad-vantage of us still, for it has been endowed with the gift of prescience and hears what happens here before it has happened. Do what we will, they get the elder brother's portion. But I am droning.

And I had taken my passage for the 27th April, and now they insist on my being in New York on the 30th to speak for Literature. I had twice refused, for I think I am fairly entitled to my share of silence now; but they set Holmes at me, they set Eliot at me, and I am almost afraid I shall give in. I console myself by stating and thinking that length also has in it an element of majesty.

Well, I must leave you a small mercy of blank paper yet, for I fly to the Cunard office to see if I can make some arrangement that will comport with my martyrization. Would I had the proper spirit that Borachio showed when they told him to come out and be hanged.

With kindest regards to Dr. Mitchell and your daughter and the MacVeaghs (of whom I had too short a glimpse here) and Marguerite, and with remembrances to whoever remembers me,

Affectionately yours,

J. R. LOWELL.

TO S. WEIR MITCHELL

68 Beacon Street, April 2, 1889.

Dear Mitchell, — Your letter of St. Valentine's day would not have waited so long for an answer had the address on the cover been in your own handwriting. As it was, I too hastily concluded the missive to be from an autograph hunter, one of those perverse persons who seek for a sign and to whom no sign shall be given. I tossed it among a heap of others on the top of a revolving bookstand at my elbow, and there it lay all these weeks without any sign of ill-humor. But yesterday, as I reached for a book, one letter disengaged itself from

II.—24

the rest and fell on the floor at my feet. I picked it
up, observed that it had never been opened, again took it
for an autograph beggar, and was about to toss it back
among its fellows, when it struck me that it was too thin
to contain a stamped envelope. So I opened it, and
there was your valentine. The thing struck me as odd.
There was a heap of letters, this one was not on top,
and yet was the only one that struggled forth and fell.
How explain these mysteries? Chance is a mighty
clever fellow.

I was deeply interested in your pamphlet. I think
it lays most of the ghosts, perhaps not all. I believe
them all (so far as they seem to be objectively visible)
figments of the brain. But my doubt is whether there
must not have been some preceding impression of the
nearness of that person whose eidolon seems to be seen
in order to produce the image. Given that impression,
the imagination sees that person (with all the accidents
of gait, gesture, dress even) as the eye had been accustomed to see him when in the body. (I am thinking of
a German ghost which paraded in a bottle-green coat
with brass buttons.) To be sure this perhaps is only
proposing an alternative explanation of phenomena better, at least more simply, accounted for by your cases.
I have long believed my own visions to be *all my eye*,
though I cannot remember that they were ever followed
by headache. Those could be shut out by closing the
lids; but what of those I see with my eyes shut, that
come and go and change without my will, or even in
spite of it? Is everything one has ever seen laid away
in the eye as a photographer stores his negatives?

And is there something analogous in the mind's eye, the memory?

I was particularly struck with the case of the lady who observed that the movements of her sister's image were governed by that of her own eye. What a happy example of the difference between lookers and seers, between the ordinary and the scientific habit of mind.

By the way, have you sent your pamphlets to the psychical-research men? To William James, for example. To me a physical marvel is as interesting as a spiritual one, though in a different way. Pardon my garrulity, busy man that you are, and, with kindest regards to Mrs. Mitchell, be sure that I am

Faithfully yours,

J. R. LOWELL.*

TO THE SAME

Boston, May 16, 1889.

My dear Mitchell,—I am vainly trying to work my correspondence up to date before I sail day after tomorrow. I have been thoroughly fagged with an introduction to the "Complete Angler," which I had pledged

---

* Note by Dr. Mitchell:

"My sending the essay alluded to arose out of a long talk about ghosts, which took us deep into the night twice during the fortnight spent with us in 1889. Mr. Lowell told me that since boyhood he had been subject to visions, which appeared usually in the evening. Commonly he saw a figure in mediæval costume which kept on one side of him. The last vision he had was while staying at an English country-house. After dinner, in the drawing-room, he saw a figure in the dress of a mediæval scholar. The form was very distinct. It beckoned to him, and, determined to see where it would go, he followed it out on to the terrace, where of a sudden it disappeared."

myself to finish ere I went. But I must write a line of thanks for the book which came this morning. I have stolen time to read so much as would enable me to tell you how much I like it (the "Dream Song" is exquisite) —almost more than the other, and that is saying a great deal. It is rather hard on us old fellows to wait so long and then push us from our stools. I am half minded to study medicine if that's what does it.

With kindest regards to Mrs. Mitchell,

Cordially yours,

J. R. LOWELL.

TO R. W. GILDER

68 Beacon Street, May 16, 1889.

. . . When I saw you last I told you I had disappointed you, and so I had, and quite rightly too, though you denied it as you were bound to do. I don't mean that the speech * was bad as speeches go, to judge by the latest quotations, but I delivered it as if I thought it was. The truth was that they made me write it out before I was ready, and that tempted me to try committing it to memory and I couldn't, and I had no entire copy and that bothered me. Then I was disheartened by the size of the house. The sort of things I am apt to say are not exactly to be bawled, and without bawling I might as well have expected to fill the Cave of Kentucky. I felt as Jack Ketch must after the Star Chamber was abolished and the fine crops of the plentiful

* In response to the toast, "Our Literature," at the banquet in New York, given in commemoration of the hundredth anniversary of Washington's Inauguration.

Prynne and Bastwick years were gone, when he looked about on the harvest of ears ripening for his sickle, but denied to its hungry edge. There were the ears (long or otherwise), but I knew they were beyond my reach. I slumped into my temperament.

However, I did not cry over it. I was too busy. I have been writing an introduction to the "Complete Angler," and a poem which I have had in my head for a good while, and which buzzed so the moment my brain went a-Maying that I had to let it out. I wonder whether you will like it. I rather hope you may.

You will be glad to hear that I hope to have a home of my own again when I come back in the fall. I think it probable that I can arrange to live at Elmwood with my daughter. I couldn't without her. 'Tis worth trying. . . .

TO MRS. W. K. CLIFFORD

2 Radnor Place, Hyde Park, W.,
June 11, 1889.

Dear Mrs. Clifford,—You ask me as many questions as if you were a Royal Commission, and two of them— "Do I know you?" and "Do you know me?"—are simply unanswerable, though I think I might answer one of them after a fashion by saying that I never knew a single woman in my life—each of them being so various (I won't add the poet's other epithet) and so apt, like Darwin's insects, but more quickly, to put on whatever self-protective color of sympathy suits their immediate purpose or need.

Somewhere in Scripture (in Proverbs, I think, attributed to Solomon, who had an unrivalled experience in this branch of natural history) a great many disagreeable things are said about women, but I do not remember that " putting their foot in it " is to be found in the indictment. But you have managed to do so—just the smallest foot in the world, of course. You say you had " forgotten " me last winter. Precisely what I supposed. *Habeo confitentem deam !* Why couldn't you have said " neglected " and saved my pride ?

As for the weather, you put your case very prettily, but so far as I am concerned I always make my own. My weather is purely subjective. When I say I make my own I mean that it is made for me, but in my own workshop and in my own little theatre.

Typewriters quotha! They are as bad as postal-cards. Both of them are unclean things I have never touched. Typewriting is hard to read also, harder even than you. I am sure I could never say what I would if I had to pick out my letters like a learned pig, and on a wooden key-board too. But what is all this to the purpose? What I mean to say is, that I will come Wednesday afternoon. . . .

Faithfully yours,

J. R. LOWELL.

TO MRS. EDWARD BURNETT

Whitby, Aug. 4, 1889.

. . . I came hither two days ago and was received with enthusiasm by the Misses Galilee, my landladies. 'Tis my third year with them, and they vow they will never let my rooms (the best in the house) so long as there is any chance of my coming. I like it as much as ever. You know the view from my window by Chadwick's little sketch. I never weary of it. The Abbey says to me, " The best of us get a little shaky at last, and there get to be gaps in our walls," and then the church-yard adds, " But you've no notion what good beds there are at my inn."

We made a tea-party yesterday afternoon to Rigg Mill, where dwell a dear old couple named Harrison. He talks a pure Yorkshire that delights my soul. The mill runs no longer, but the stream does, down through a leafy gorge in little cascades and swirls and quiet pools with skyscapes in them, and seems happy in its holiday. It is a very pretty spot and belonged to the monks once. . . .

TO MRS. LESLIE STEPHEN

Whitby, Aug. 11, 1889.

. . . The Abbey looks across over the red roofs into my window and seems to say, " Why are you not at church to-day?" and I answer fallaciously, " Because like yourself I have gone out of the business, and, moreover, I am writing to a certain saint of my own canonization who looks amazingly as your St. Hilda must have looked (as I fancy her), and the thought of whom has both prayers and praise in it." The Abbey doesn't look satisfied, but I am—so the Abbey may go hang ! Besides, am I not honoring the day with a white shirt and well-blackened boots ? and when I presently go out shall I not crown my head with a chimney-pot hat ? which, rather than the cross, is the symbol of the Englishman's faith—being stiff, hollow, pervious to the rain, and divided in service between Babylon and Sion.

This is my ninth year at Whitby, and the place loses none of its charm for me. It is better than Cornwall, except inasmuch as Cornwall has St. Erth's in it, where sometimes one has beatific visions. I find a strange pleasure in that name too, so homely and motherly, as if some pope had suddenly bethought himself to canonize this dear old Earth of ours so good to us all, and give the body as well as the soul a share in those blessed things. My happiness is so much at the mercy of obscure sympathies and antipathies that perhaps I am less at ease among a Celtic population (though I fancy them more refined) than among these men of Danish stock with whom I own kinship of blood. But you are enough to leaven the biggest batch of Celts that ever was baked, so I am coming to you as soon as I leave Whitby, or shall it be later? . . .

Whitby is coming more and more into the great currents of civilization. We have a spasmodic theatre and an American circus that seems a fixture. Last year there was a delightful clown who really looked as if he couldn't help it, and was a wonderful tumbler too. How the children would have liked it! One other amusement is the Spa, where there is a band of music bad enough to please the Shah. It is brilliantly lighted, and at night it is entertaining to sit above and watch the fashionable world laboriously diverting themselves by promenading to and fro in groups, like a village festival at the opera. The sea, of course, is as fine and as irreconcilable as ever. Thank God, they can't landscape-garden *him.* I think I have confessed to you before that our colors are not so southern as yours. On the land they are as good as they can be in range, variety, and fickleness. . . .

TO C. E. NORTON

Whitby, Aug. 18, 1889.

. . . You are a little severe in your judgment of English society. Buffalo Bill has been taken up by a certain layer of society, but not, I should say, by society in its better sense. The —— has debased a considerable circle, the circumference of which is spreading, as in stagnant pools a circle once started will. There is a partial truth in what you say about society here losing its fastidiousness, but this is mainly true of the ——'s set, and those who are infected by it or wish to be of it. I have not met B. B., but Colonel Colville told me (you know him, I think?) that " B. B. was one of the finest men he ever saw and of princely manners." Moreover, he is really a Somebody and the best of his kind. But I think the true key to this eagerness for lions—even of the poodle sort—is the dulness of the average English mind. I never come back here without being struck with it. Henry James said it always stupefied him at first when he came back from the Continent. What it craves beyond everything is a sensation, anything that will serve as a Worcestershire sauce to its sluggish palate. We of finer and more touchy fibre get our sensations cheaper, and do not find Wordsworth's emotion over a common flower so very wonderful. People are dull enough on our side of the ocean-stream also, God wot; but here, unless I know my people, I never dare to let my mind gambol. Most of them, if I ever do, look on like the famous deaf man at the dancers, wondering to what music I am capering. They call us superficial. Let us thank God, dear Charles, that our nerves are nearer the surface, not so deeply embedded in fat or muscle that wit must take a pitchfork to us.

I am fairly contented here, almost happy sometimes, nay, should be often, could I jump off my own shadow. I know no expedient to get rid of it but Peter Schlemihl's, and alas, nobody, not even the D—l, thinks mine worth buying. 'Tis a beautiful place, with associations that touch me deeply when I am conscious of them, and qualify my mood insensibly when I am not. I have done some reading in Lope de Vega, but am not drawn to him or by him as to and by Calderon. Yet he is wonderful, too, in his way. . . .

TO MRS. EDWARD BURNETT

Whitby, Aug. 20, 1889.

. . . To-day it is raining (as it rains here) with a gentle persistence, as if to convince one by degrees that it is the proper thing to do. I think of the burthen of the old ballad,

> "The rain rins doun through Merryland toun,
>   Sae does it along the Po."

I fancy the old fellow who made it was trying to con-

sole himself for a rainy day like this by making believe it was raining even in Italy, too, all the time.
But we have had good weather on the whole, and the
moors are born again in the purple. I went to Aislaby
Moor yesterday and lay on my back on the springy
heather, making the bees very wroth. They queru-
lously insisted that the heather I covered was the very
heather they had been saving for that morning. But
they did not push things to extremities with me. I
couldn't help wishing the children had been there, they
would have been so happy in that wilderness of bloom.
They would have thought, as everybody does, that the
blossoms a little farther on were finer than those about
their feet. . . .

TO THOMAS HUGHES

Whitby, Aug. 28, 1889.

. . . Whitby is as good as ever, and has now another
pleasant association in recalling you and Mrs. Hughes.
We go to the old moors and the old mills as usual,
though our weather has been a little wrong side out
a good deal of the time. Yesterday we had a thrill-
ing experience in being taken (as we suppose) by the
hostile fleet. At any rate, three men-o'-war first came
in—very unlike the noble creatures that landed royal
Charlie—and fired three heavy guns at us, and as we
have no visible means of support, I take it we surren-
dered and that I am now a prisoner of war. I am
glad I saw those guns fired, for the smoke behaved in
a very strange and beautiful way, first rising a little in

a dense cloud and in a semicircle of lingering Staub-
bachs, completely veiling the villanous-looking mon-
sters that belched them forth.

As they didn't put us on parole, Mrs. —— and I
went to Scarborough—an expedition I had promised
her these nine years, which I thought it hardly safe
to put off any longer at my age. We had a fine day,
and enjoyed ourselves highly. I had always wished to
see the place since I read "A Trip to Scarborough,"
of which I remember now nothing more than the name.
We went up to the Castle (which had a superbly impreg-
nable aerie before the invention of gunpowder), where
we saw the volunteer artillery encamped, resolved to
save Scarborough from the fate of Whitby or die. But
the fleet never came, and the band did its best to keep
up the spirits of the men under this disappointment.
We saw them drilling with the stretchers, which had a
grewsome look, and heard the far-off grumble of a sea-
fight which was going on somewhere behind the haze.
We had the satisfaction of communicating to one of
the officers the fall of Whitby, which hardly seemed to
sadden him so much as it ought—so little do rival
watering-places feel each other's misfortunes. Then we
went to the Spa, lunched at an eating-house as good as
it was cheap, and then sat watching the crowd. They
all had the air of second-hand gentility trying very
hard to make itself believe it was first-hand. It wasn't
shabby gentility, but the profusely new thing which is
far worse. It takes several generations to make clothes
unconscious. But the place was gay and as many-col-
ored as Joseph's coat, and I liked it for an hour or two.

Particularly I liked the little open traps with one horse
ridden by a postilion with silken jerkins and caps of
the brightest hues. I sat with immense satisfaction
behind one whose jacket (stripes red and white) recalled the flag of my country. On the whole we had
a successful day, and on the way home one of the most
surprisingly original and beautiful sunsets I ever saw....

Affectionately yours,

J. R. Lowell.

TO MRS. LESLIE STEPHEN

Whitby, Sept. 11, 1889.

... For the last few days we have been having American weather, except for the haze which softens and civ-
ilizes (perhaps I should say, artistically generalizes) all it
touches, like the slower hand of time. It does in a
moment what the other is too long about for the brev-
ity of our lives. How I do love this unemphatic landscape, which suggests but never defines, in which so
much license is left to conjecture and divination, as when
one looks into the mysterious beyond. And how the
robins and some other little minstrels whose names I
don't know keep on pretending it is the very fresh of
the year. I think few people are made as happy by
the singing of birds as I, and this autumnal music (unknown at home), every bush a song, is one of the things
that especially endear England to me. Even without
song, birds are a perpetual delight, and the rooks alone
are enough to make this country worth living in. I
wish you could see a rook who every morning busies

himself among the chimney-pots opposite my chamber window. For a good while I used to hear his chuckle, but thought he was only flying over. But one day I got out of bed and looked out. There he was on the top of a chimney opposite, perambulating gravely, and now and then cocking his head and looking down a flue. Then he would chuckle and go to another. Then to the next chimney and *da capo*. He found out what they were going to have for breakfast in every house, and whether he enjoyed an imaginary feast or reckoned on a chance at some of the leavings I know not, but he was evidently enjoying himself, and that is always a consoling thing to see. Even in the stingy back-yards of these houses too, wherever there is a disconsolate shrub a robin comes every morning to cheer it up a bit and help it along through the day.

Since I wrote what I did about the weather (one should always let the Eumenides alone) it has begun to rain, but gently, like a rain that was trying to discriminate between the just and the unjust, and sympathized with those confiding enough to leave their umbrellas behind them (I hate to expose *mine* any more than I can help, for reasons of my own). So the rain let me get back dry from the beach, whither I had gone for a whiff of salt air and a few earfuls of that muffled crash of the surf which is so soothing—perpetual ruin with perpetual renewal.

I wonder if your moors have been as gracious as ours this year. I never know how deeply they impress me till long after I have left them, and then I wonder at the store of images wherewith they have peopled my mem-

ory. But what is the use of my asking you any questions when you tell me you could not read my last letter? Was it the blue paper with its ribs that made a
corduroy road for my pen to jolt over, I wonder, or my
failing eyesight, or—and this is saddest to think of—the
dulness of the letter itself? Is this better? I am trying to write as well as I can for my dear and admirable
friend, but what would you have? How should one
write letters worth reading who has so many to write as
I? But never mind. The true use of a letter is to let
one know that one is remembered and valued, and as
you are sure of that, perhaps I need not write at all!
No, the true use of writing is that it brings your friend
to you as you write, and so I have your sweet society
for a while, and you need have only just as much of
mine as you choose to give yourself. . . .

TO MRS. W. E. DARWIN

Whitby, Sept. 13, 1889.

. . . The charm of this place and the kind-heartedness
of the weather have Capuaed me here longer than I
meant.

There is no use in trying to tell you how beautiful
our moors have been — pensively gorgeous like the
purple mourning that used to be worn for kings—as if
they were still commemorating the lovely funerals of
the chieftains whose barrows crown their summits.
And our Abbey—didn't I see it a few nights ago with
the moon shining through its windows till one fancied
it lighted up for service with corpse-lights for candles,

and heard the ghostly miserere of the monks over their ruin?   And then its fantastic transformation by the sea-mists!   Do you wonder that I linger?

I hear the robins singing in your shrubbery and wish you joy of them.   They gladden me every morning from the mangy back-yards of the houses opposite.   What is it Donne calls them?   "The household bird with the red stomacher," or something prettier.   I am doubtful about "household."*   But what would you have of a memory as tumble-down as the Abbey yonder? . . .

TO MRS. EDWARD BURNETT

St. Ives, Sept. 23, 1889.

. . . I am very well—really so absurd a septuagenarian is seldom met with—and my stay at Whitby, where the weather grew to be almost weakly good-natured at last, did me good.   A poem even got itself written there (which seems to me not altogether bad), and this intense activity of the brain has the same effect as exercise on my body, and somehow braces up the whole machine.   My writing this was a lucky thing, for when I got back to London I found a letter from the New York *Ledger* enclosing a draft for £200 for whatever I should choose to send.   So I sent them what I had just written, pacifying my scruples with the thought that after all it was only my *name* they were paying for, and that they knew best what it was worth to them.   The

---

* Lowell's recollection of the verse was correct.   It occurs in Donne's " Epithalamion on Frederick, Count Palatine of the Rhine, and the Lady Elizabeth being married on St. Valentine's Day."

letter, by great good luck, had been overlooked and not forwarded to Whitby as it should have been. Had I got it before my poem got itself out of me, I should have been quite disabled and should have sent back the draft. . . .

TO C. E. NORTON

St. Ives, Sept. 24, 1889.

. . . *Amor che nella mente mi ragiona* has often bid me write to you, and I should certainly have done so, even without the added prompting of your letter, which came to me just as I was starting for my visit here. I am at best a poor correspondent, and at worst no correspondent at all. I make a feint of excusing myself (since one could never get on with one's faults so complacently if one could not palliate them) by reminding myself that I grew up in the ampler days of quarto, nay, folio letter-paper, and of postage that inspired reflection. I can't get over the feeling that less than four pages is niggardly in point of friendship and spendthrift in point of postage. Moreover, I am far past the period when I was a constant novelty to myself and eager to communicate it to all and sundry. I envy the careless profusion with which a younger generation scatters its hasty notes as fish their spawn, while I, a serious barn-door fowl, am inclined to cackle when I succeed in laying my single eggs at decorous (increasingly decorous) intervals. Things don't happen in one so often as they once did.

I also read " Fitzgerald's Correspondence " with great interest and satisfaction. I quite agree with you that

II.—25

they are among the best we have. I fancy he took
enough pains with them to make them as easy as they
are. They were his only means of communication with
the outward world, of *translating* himself as it were into
the vulgar tongue. He was a scholar and a gentleman
—I change the order of the words because I fancy a
distinction and a pleasing one. I agree with you as to
the general sanity of his literary judgments—though he
would not have been so agreeable as he is without a
few honest prejudices too. We are so hustled about
by fortune that I found solace as I read in thinking
that here was a man who insisted on having his life to
himself, and largely had it accordingly. A hermit, by
the bye, as he was, has a great advantage in forming
secure conclusions. Another charm of the book to me
was that it so often reminded me of J. H.

I spent my usual month at Whitby and indeed
stretched it to six weeks, the weather grew so oblig-
ing. I did very little, but felt remarkably well, which
at my age is perhaps as wise an employment as another.
I read a little of Lope, a little of Dante, and a good
deal of Milton, convincing myself of what I had long
taken for granted, that his versification was mainly
modelled on the Italian and especially on the " Divina
Commedia." Many if not most of his odd construc-
tions are to be sought there, I think, rather than in the
ancients. I read something of Byron, too, with an odd
feeling of surprise that the frame-work of the fire-works
(*feux d'artifice* says more) which so dazzled my youth
should look so bare. I read some Old French, having received about a dozen volumes of the "Anciens

Textes" that were due me.   Mainly dull—nothing like the "Galerant" of last year.   I dread falling under its spell again when I go back to Elmwood and the old associations, for I can't see exactly what good it has done me or anybody else.   The average result of my Whitby seems to be that the moors and shy footpaths round about it are dearer to me than ever.

After getting back at last to London, where I halted a day to copy and correct a poem which I forgot to say was one of my Whitby results, I went down for a visit of two or three days in Hampshire.   On my way up again I stopped a few hours at Winchester, where I had the advantage of going over the Cathedral with the dean.   The Norman transept seemed to me the best of it—so massive that it gives one the impression of being a work of nature, like a cliff in which the fancy pleases itself with tracing marks of architectural design. . . .

TO THE MISSES LAWRENCE

2 Radnor Place, Hyde Park, W.,
Oct. 2, 1889.

. . . I am looking (they tell me) younger than ever, which is almost indecent at my time of life when I consider the Psalmist.   However, I don't much mind being young.   'Tis the other thing I dread, and I hope I sha'n't have much of it.   Thus far the earth seems to me as beautiful as ever, and the new song of the birds in spring renews me with the renewing year.   The grasshopper is not yet a burthen, and as for the ceasing of desire, I think the fewer we have the more likely they are to be gratified. . . .

TO MRS. W. K. CLIFFORD

2 Radnor Place, Hyde Park, W.,
Oct. 18, 1889.

. . . Old poets need encouragement far more than young ones, for with youth and inexperience they sometimes lose their better muse. Art may be won, but inexperience once lost can never be recovered. . . .

Well, good - by till next spring, if next spring shall come to me. . . .

XI

1889–1891

RETURN TO ELMWOOD. — DECLINING HEALTH. — VISIT FROM LESLIE STEPHEN. — THE END.

LETTERS TO MRS. LESLIE STEPHEN, R. W. GILDER, JOSIAH QUINCY, THE MISSES LAWRENCE, W. D. HOWELLS, THOMAS HUGHES, S. WEIR MITCHELL, MRS. W. K. CLIFFORD, LESLIE STEPHEN, E. L. GODKIN, MISS KATE FIELD, C. E. NORTON, MISS E. G. NORTON, EDWARD E. HALE, MRS. F. G. SHAW, E. R. HOAR, MRS. BURNETT.

TO MRS. LESLIE STEPHEN

Elmwood, Nov. 9, 1889.

. . . It is a very strange feeling this of renewing my life here. I feel somehow as if Charon had ferried me the wrong way, and yet it is into a world of ghosts that he has brought me, and I am slowly making myself at home among them. It is raining faintly to-day, with a soft southerly wind which will prevail with the few leaves left on my trees to let go their hold and join their fellows on the ground. I have forbidden them to be raked away, for the rustle of them stirs my earliest memories, and when the wind blows they pirouette so gayly as to give me cheerful thoughts of death. But oh, the changes! I hardly know the old road (a street now) that I have paced so many years, for the new houses. My old homestead seems to have a puzzled look in its eyes as it looks down (a trifle superciliously methinks) on these upstarts. " He who lives longest has the most old clothes," says the Zulu proverb, and I shall wear mine till I die.

It is odd to think that the little feet which make the old staircases and passages querulous at their broken slumbers are the second generation since my own. I try to believe it, but find it hard. I feel so anomalously young I can't persuade myself that *I* ever made such a rumpus, though perhaps the boots are thicker now.

The two old English elms in front of the house haven't changed. The sturdy islanders! A trifle thicker in the waist, perhaps, as is the wont of prosperous elders, but looking just as I first saw them seventy years ago, and it is a balm to my eyes. I am by no means sure that it is wise to love the accustomed and familiar so much as I do, but it is pleasant and gives a unity to life which trying can't accomplish.

I began this yesterday and now it is Sunday. You will have *not* gone to church five hours ago. I have just performed the chief function of a householder by winding up all the clocks and adjusting them to a *striking* unanimity. I doubt if this be judicious, for when I am lying awake at night their little differences of opinion amuse me. They persuade me how artificial a contrivance Time is. We have Eternity given us in the lump, can't believe in such luck, and cut it up into mouthfuls as if it wouldn't go round among so many. Are we to be seduced by the superstitious observances of the earth and sun into a belief in days and years ? . . .

TO JOSIAH QUINCY

Elmwood, Cambridge, Mass., Dec. 10, 1889.

Dear Mr. Quincy,—I regret very much that I cannot have the pleasure of joining with you in paying respect to a man so worthy of it as Mr. Cleveland.*

Let who has felt compute the strain
  Of struggle with abuses strong,
The doubtful course, the helpless pain
  Of seeing best intents go wrong.

We, who look on with critic eyes,
  Exempt from action's crucial test,
Human ourselves, at least are wise
  In honoring one who did his best.

Faithfully yours,

J. R. LOWELL.

TO R. W. GILDER

Elmwood, Cambridge, Mass., Dec. 22, 1889.

. . . I should have been glad to preside at the breakfast of the Copyright League, but I really couldn't. Such things worry me nowadays more than you could easily conceive. They take more life out of me than I can afford to give. Kept in this shelter, my candle seems to have some stuff left and shortens at a hopefully moderate rate; but set it in a flurry of air and the deuce is in it, it so swales and runs to waste. . . .

---

* At the banquet of the Boston Merchants' Association, where ex-President Cleveland was the chief guest, on December 12th.

TO THE MISSES LAWRENCE

Elmwood, Cambridge, Mass., Jan. 2, 1890.

. . . Here I am again in the house where I was born longer ago than you can remember, though I wish you more New Year's days than I have had. 'Tis a pleasant old house just about twice as old as I am, four miles from Boston, in what was once the country and is now a populous suburb. But it still has some ten acres of open about it, and some fine old trees. When the worst comes to the worst (if I live so long) I shall still have four and a half acres left with the house, the rest belonging to my brothers and sisters or their heirs. It is a square house with four rooms on a floor, like some houses of the Georgian era I have seen in English provincial towns, only they are of brick and this is of wood. But it is solid with its heavy oaken beams, the spaces between which in the four outer walls are filled in with brick, though you mustn't fancy a brick-and-timber house, for outwardly it is sheathed with wood. Inside there is much wainscot (of deal) painted white in the fashion of the time when it was built. It is very sunny, the sun rising so as to shine (at an acute angle, to be sure) through the northern windows, and going round the other three sides in the course of the day. There is a pretty staircase with the quaint old twisted banisters—which they call balusters now, but mine are banisters. My library occupies two rooms opening into each other by arches at the sides of the ample chimneys. The trees I look out on are the earliest things I remember. There you have me in my new-old quarters. But you must not fancy a large house — rooms sixteen feet square and, on the ground floor, nine high. It was large, as things went here, when it was built, and has a certain air of amplitude about it as from some inward sense of dignity.

Now for out of doors. What do you suppose the thermometer is about on this second day of January? I was going to say he was standing on his head—at any rate he has forgotten what he's about, and is marking sixty-three degrees Fahrenheit on the north side of the house and in the shade! Where is that sense of propriety that once belonged to the seasons? This is flat communism, January insisting on going halves with May. News I have none, nor other resources, as you see, save those of the special correspondent, who takes to description when events fail. Yes, I have one event. I dine to-night with Mr. R. C. Winthrop, who remembers your father very well nearly sixty years ago.

I have all my grandchildren with me, five of them, and the eldest boy is already conspiring with a beard! It is awful, this stealthy advance of Time's insupportable foot. There are two ponies for the children and two dogs, bull-terriers, and most amiable creatures. This is my establishment, and four of the weans have had the *grippe*. I remember it here in '31, I think it was. You see I make all I can of age's one privilege —that of having a drearier memory than other folks.

I forgot one thing. There are plenty of mice in the walls, and, now that I can't go to the play with you, I assist at their little tragedies and comedies behind the wainscot in the night-hours and build up plots in my fancy. 'Tis a French company, for I hear them distinctly say *wee*, *wee*, sometimes. My life, you see, is not without its excitements, and what are your London mice doing that is more important? I see you are to have a Parnell scandal at last, but I overheard an elopement the other night behind the wainscot, and the solicitors talking it over with the desolated husband afterwards. It was very exciting. Ten thousand grains of corn damages!

Good-by, and take care of yourselves till I come with the daffodils. I wish you both many a happy New Year and a share for me in some of them. Poets seem to live long nowadays, and I, too, live in Arcadia after my own fashion.

Affectionately yours,

J. R. L.

TO W. D. HOWELLS

Elmwood, Jan. 10, 1890.

. . . And now let me say something I have been wishing to say this great while. I have seen some of the unworthy flings at you in the papers of late. I know you will not feel them more than an honest man should. But I have indignantly felt them. You are one of the chief honors of our literature, and your praises are dear to us all. You know I don't share some of your opinions or sympathize with some of your judgments, but I am not such an ass as not to like a man better for saying what *he* thinks and not what *I* think. Though I thought those Chicago ruffians well hanged, I specially honored your courage in saying what you did about them. You can't make me fonder of you, but I am sure you will make me prouder of you.

And so I am

Always affectionately yours,

J. R. LOWELL.

TO S. WEIR MITCHELL

Elmwood, Cambridge, Mass., April 4, 1890.

Dear Doctor Mitchell,—Just after getting your note I was put to bed (where I ought to have been sooner, only I wouldn't), and found myself, almost before I knew where I was, under the charge of a nurse and with two doctors in consultation over me. I have had a hard time of it, and was much pulled down. But I had a very present help in the constant encouragement and kindness of my old friend, Dr. Wyman, who even went so far as to watch three nights running at my bedside, and he in his seventy-ninth year. For a fortnight now I have been mending, and have had no return of acute symptoms. Yesterday I was able to dress and get downstairs for the first time, and one of the first things I had on my mind to be done soonest was to thank you for your kind note, and to say that the printing of the poems will begin soon—as soon, I believe, as I shall be in condition to read proofs without too much fatigue.

With affectionate regards to Mrs. Mitchell,

Faithfully yours,

J. R. LOWELL.

TO MRS. W. K. CLIFFORD

Elmwood, Cambridge, Mass., April 9, 1890.

Dear Mrs. Clifford,—It was very good of you to be anxious about me, and I wish I could drop in to ask you for a cup of coffee and thank you in person. That *would* be delightful, but my gratitude must find vent in ink, which sometimes runs cold in spite of us. Pen in hand, one hasn't always the courage of one's feelings. Spoken words may be as warm as one likes— there is always air enough about to temper them to the right point. . . .

I have been really ill—six weeks on my back in bed, whither I refused to go till I could sit up no longer. I couldn't conceive of anything but Death strong enough to throw me. And he did look in at the door once, they tell me, when I was worst, but changed his mind and took his ugly mug elsewhere.

I have now been mending for nearly three weeks and begin once more to have legs and things. But I had grown very weak and am still very easily tired. I have been out of doors thrice, once to bask for an hour in the sun on the veranda, twice to crawl about a little— the last time for nearly a hundred yards, one of the triumphs of pedestrianism. I am bidden to recline as much as possible and am on my back now in a *chaise- longue*. The doctors say I must on no account vent- ure across the water this summer, and I myself haven't the courage, for I have had rather a sharp warning that I am over forty—which I never believed before. When you see me again I shall be an old man—that was a slip, I meant to say "elderly," but it is out now and I must make the best of it. I shall be little better than a tame cat. You will stroke me in a pause of your talk with some more suitable person, and I shall purr.

I couldn't endure my deprivation did I not think my renunciation this year would insure my coming the next. Only by that time, I fear, you will have forgotten me and wonder who I am when I call. Please don't if you can help it. And yet, if you have to make an effort, I shouldn't quite like that either. But I mustn't write any more, for my head begins to grumble, and already has the stitch in its side. Write when you happen to think of it.

Faithfully yours,

J. R. LOWELL.

TO THOMAS HUGHES

Elmwood, Cambridge, Mass., April 20, 1890.

Dear Friend,—What a good old-fashioned Scripture-measure letter was that of yours! It annihilated penny-posts and telegraphs, and grew to a quarto sheet as I read with all the complicated creases of its folding. Pleasant indeed was it to hear such good news from your Deeside hive, which through the boys bids fair to be a true *officina gentium*, peopling our Western emptinesses with the right kind of stock.

And so our bright and busy-minded —— is married, and happily too. After mature deliberation with the help of a pipe, I don't think her husband's not smoking is a fatal objection. A—— would tell you that Napoleon didn't, and Goethe and several other more or less successful men. I consent, therefore, on condition that he stuff his pockets with baccy for his poor parishioners when he goes his rounds ; they know how good it is and how they " puff the prostitute (Fortune) away," or snuff up oblivion with its powdered particles. I remember an old crone whom I used to meet every Sunday in Kensington Gardens when she had her outings from the almshouse and whom I kept supplied with Maccaboy. I think I made her perfectly happy for a week and on such cheap terms as make me blush. She was a dear old thing, and used to make me prettier curtsies than I saw at court. Good heavens, of what uncostly material is our earthly happiness composed—if we only knew it ! What incomes have we not had from a flower, and how unfailing are the dividends of the seasons !

I can't help having a sneaking sympathy with ——, as I think I once wrote to Mrs. Hughes. Philosophy and liberty are excellent things, but I made the discovery early in life that they had one fault—you can't eat 'em, and I found it necessary to eat something, however little. For the celibate (if his father have a balance at his banker's) they will serve, but on no other condition and at best not for long.   —— tried it, and do you know what Mrs. —— once said when somebody asked " if her husband didn't live with his head always in the clouds ?" " Yes, and I'm sometimes tempted to wish he'd draw his feet up after it !" But his were the dreams of middle-age and senescence. Those of youth are sometimes the best possession of our old age. . . . Association with so generous a nature as Auberon Herbert's would do any man good—unless, to be sure, they give up for the moment making themselves good to quarrel about the best way of making other people so. I have known that to happen. But never mind; the desire to sit in the *siege perilleus* is a good thing in itself, if it do not end in sitting there to watch the procession of life go by, papa meanwhile paying a smart fee for young Hopeful's excellent seat.

Speaking of these things reminds me of Howells's last story, "A Hazard of New Fortunes"; have you read it? If not, do, for I am sure you would like it. A noble sentiment pervades it, and it made my inherited comforts here at Elmwood discomforting to me in a very salutary way. I felt in reading some parts of it as I used when the slave would not let me sleep. I don't see my way out of the labyrinth except with the clue of co-operation, and I am not sure even of that with over-population looming in the near distance. I wouldn't live in any of the Socialist or Communist worlds into the plans of which I have looked, for I should be bored to death by the everlasting Dutch landscape. Nothing but the guillotine will ever make men equal on compulsion, and even then they will leap up again in some other world to begin again on the old terms. You will be glad to hear that Carl Schurz (a good judge), who had several talks with the new emperor both as crown prince and after, thinks that he is intelligent, means business, and knows what he is about. As emperor he has done away with some of the old fusses and feathers. Once he sent for Schurz, who was ushered at once into the cabinet of the emperor, with whom he was left alone, and who pushed an easy-

chair towards the fire for him, seating himself on a
hard stool. Bismarck, by the way, said a good thing
to Schurz with which I am growing into sympathy—" I
am beginning to think that the best half of life is before seventy."

I am glad to be remembered by your fair neighbors,
and wish my image in their minds could, in the nature
of things, be as charming as theirs in mine. Tell them
that my power of seeing faces with my eyes shut is a
great blessing to me, since it enables me to see two
such (let their glasses fill up the blank) ones whenever I
like. I have just taken a look at them. Love to Mrs.
Hughes. Thanks for her kind note.

Affectionately yours,
J. R. LOWELL.

I am still doing well, but have to be very careful.
The doctor won't hear of my going abroad this year.
Alas!

TO LESLIE STEPHEN

Elmwood, April 21, 1890.

Dear Leslie,—I have just got your letter and write
to say that your coming would be a great joy to many,
and above all to me. But what I wish to urge is that,
if you *can* come, I hope you will come as early as you
can, because everybody here, except me, runs away in
summer, and there are a few whom I should like you
to see and who would like to see you. Norton's going
would make no odds, because you would seek him at
Ashfield, though I shall keep you as long as I can.

I remember well our parting at the corner of my lane, and how strangely moved I was. It has mingled with and distinguished my affection for you, and I shall forget it only when I forget everything.

I sha'n't be able to walk with you, but, by the time you get here, I suppose I shall be allowed to drive, and we can see Beaver Brook and the oaks again together. Wellington Hill (where you started a fox) I could not attempt.

You *must* come. It will do you good and me too. By the way, what do you think was the first [book] I chose to entertain me after I got downstairs? Your " History of Thought in the Eighteenth Century." I read it over again with unqualified satisfaction. More love to Julia and to the weans. I am tired.

Affectionately yours,
J. R. Lowell.

TO MRS. W. K. CLIFFORD

Elmwood, Cambridge, Mass., April 27, 1890.

Dear Mrs. Clifford,—It is the evening of a drizzly Sunday. I have just been helping my second grandson in his Greek exercise (with an uneasy apprehension that he would find out he was a better Grecian than I), and now lay down " Redgauntlet," in which I am deeply interested, in order, so far as a letter may, to maintain your interest in me. . . .

Yes, I have read Kipling's stories, and with real pleasure. I read them while I was still in bed and under the spell of opium, and so was adopted into their Orien-

II.—26

talism. Some of his verses, too, I liked, especially the
Omar Khayamish at the head of the last chapter. I
find something startlingly vernacular in Oriental poetry (which I know only through translations, mainly
German), as if I had lived some former and forgotten
life in the East. How potent is this Oriental blood—
in Napoleon, in Goethe, in Heine, Victor Hugo, in
Browning, to go no further back! In Montaigne probably; in Dante possibly. I am not so sure that I like
the West-Oestliche as Goethe exemplified it. But I have
hopes of the volume Mr. Kipling seems to promise us
in that last chapter, but I hope he will drop his Hin-
dostanee pedantry. 'Tis as bad as Mrs. Gore's French
used to be. Be truer to your sex, my dear. He is not
Burne-Jones's nephew, but Mrs. Burne-Jones's, and his
book constantly reminded me of Phil. Burne-Jones, by
whom I set great store. How good he was to the children when I stayed with him at Talland House! I
adore that kind of goodness afar off, for I haven't it myself. They tell me I had it once, and perhaps I shall
get it again before long in my second childhood.

I am doing well, thank you. When I get up in the
morning I feel about thirty, but when I go upstairs to
bed I seem to carry a Nestorian weight of years. This
I shall get over when I am allowed to take exercise.
What I can't get over yet is apprehension. My malady came upon me so without warning that I live in
hourly dread of ambushes. Still, I should like to drop
in at 26 Colville Road and fence with you a little. I
don't think you would find *much* difference. Good-by;
write when you remember me. No, not that exactly,

but oftener. Is that a bull? I don't mind if it bring me Europa. Our Spring is just beginning, and the buds are peeping to see if it be really she at last. I am encouraged by finding that my sap still stirs with the rest. There must be some life in my roots yet. Give my love to the two girls.

Faithfully yours,

J. R. LOWELL.

TO THE MISSES LAWRENCE

Elmwood, Cambridge, Mass., May 3, 1890.

. . . Septuagenarians are allowed to talk about themselves, a license, I am inclined to think, which they are beginning to abuse, if one may judge by the number of autobiographies, reminiscences, and things we have had of late. It must have been through a well-founded dread of such garrulities that the ancient Scythians put an end to their old people before these had a chance to become public nuisances. It is whispered that they feasted on them afterwards, but this is doubtful. What is certain is, that no toughness of digestion would have been competent to what their memoirs would probably have turned out to be.

As I say, I have no news because I am not yet permitted to go about and gather the stale stuff we call so. My "Court Journal" is a record of the comings and goings of birds and blossoms. My births, deaths, and marriages are new moons, sunsets, and the pairing of innocent winged creatures. Two days ago I was much excited by the first appearance of a summer

yellow-bird, one of the most graceful of our songsters.
Yesterday a sparrow-hawk perched in one of my trees,
and a bird with a gleaming white waistcoat, that made
him twice as big as he really was, and a purple necktie.
Have you never seen people whose costume lent them
a fictitious greatness? I will not go higher than a lord
mayor for an example. You see that morals flit about
among my boughs as thick as sparrows. And, by the
way, the English sparrows which we carefully imported
are grown as great a nuisance as rabbits in Australia.
They are beyond measure impudent. If you take off
your hat to wipe your brow, they have built a nest in
it before you are ready to put it on again, and then
dispute possession with you. They seize all unoccu-
pied territory, as I won't say who sets them the example of doing. They build in a twinkling half a dozen
nests over one's front door, and if one evict them and
tear down their homesteads as thoroughly as if they
were Irish tenants, the nests are there again next day with
young in them, which the birds borrow as beggars do to
excite compassion. If they let fall nothing worse than
oysters (or whatever it was that the osprey dropt on the
bald pate of Æschylus), one wouldn't mind. They
bully our native birds out of their lives, as British
officials used to bully us poor provincials in the good
old times. What is there in your island — but no,
I won't generalize on so narrow a foundation, as if I
were an English traveller in America. To tell the
truth, I rather like them, and they amuse me immensely, the cock-birds are such insufferable coxcombs. In
our sunny and clear air they are by no means the chim-

ney-sweep-looking creatures you are familiar with in London, but have almost a brilliant plumage.

So you have been at Avignon (Babylon) and Arles (did you observe how pretty the women are?) and Orange (did you think of Guillaume au Court Nez?) and the Pont du Gard. But you say nothing of Vaucluse and its living waters, one of the most beautiful things I ever saw, though a little brackish with Petrarch's tears— not very, for they had more sugar than salt in them. I first saw the Pont du Gard in '52, and next in '72. The same man was in charge and we made a laughing bargain that I should come again after another score of years. And I am already within two years of my tryst. You never saw in the south of France a day more lovely than this. One must make a cloud in one's own mind (as modern poets do) if one would have a cloud, and the breeze is like the waft of one's mistress's fan, cooling and fragrant at once. Time leans on his scythe and rests. . . .

TO MRS. LESLIE STEPHEN

Elmwood, May 4, 1890.

. . . We are beginning to look very pretty here in our new spring dresses, and all my pear-trees with fresh flowers in their bonnets. But, alas, how my trees and shrubs have pined for me in my absence. And they have been shamefully broken, too. For my part, I feel the pain in the limb of a tree as in one of my own. But I am sure they all know me, and will take heart again now that I am come back. They are not quite reconciled with me yet, and I wish I could show you

to them as one of the arguments for my absence. That
would bring them all round.

The birds are here again in reasonable numbers, but
my orioles not yet. They build a pendulous nest, and
so flash in the sun that our literal rustics call them fire
hang-birds. . . .

TO MISS KATE FIELD

Cambridge, May 15, 1890.

Dear Miss Field,—I have had too long an experience
of the providential thickness of the human skull, as well
as of the eventual success of all reasonable reforms, to
be discouraged by the temporary defeat of any measure
which I believe to be sound. I say "providential" because the world is thereby saved many a rash experiment in specious legislation. Were it otherwise, the
Huon's horn of inconsiderate enthusiasm would lead
us a pretty dance among the briers. Unfortunately
there is, as usual, an exception to this general rule, for
the sutures of the political cranium are so loosely knit
as to leave a crevice through which considerations of
ephemeral expediency find a too easy entrance. Such
considerations, it should always be remembered, are
most liable to disastrous recoil.

I grant that our hope has been long-drawn-out, but
since material for it (as for every hope that has a moral
base) has been constantly supplied, it has never become
too attenuated to bear the strain put upon it. It is seventy-one years since Irving wrote: "You observe that
the public complain of the price of my work; this is the

disadvantage of coming in competition with republished English works for which the publishers have not to pay anything to the authors. If the American public wish to have a literature of their own, they must consent to pay for the support of authors."

(And why not, I may add, if we consent to pay Senator Jones for the support of a silver mine?)

It is fifty years since Irving wrote: " How much this growing literature may be retarded by the present state of our copyright law I had recently an instance in the cavalier treatment of a work of merit, written by an American who had not yet established a commanding name in the literary market. I undertook as a friend to dispose of it for him, but found it impossible to get an offer from any of our principal publishers. They even declined to publish it at the author's cost, alleging that it was not worth their while to trouble themselves about native works of doubtful success, while they could pick and choose among the successful works daily poured out by the British press, *for which they had nothing to pay for copyright.*"

This was in 1840, and in the same year Mr. Clay's bill was defeated. We have been fighting for the same cause with the same weapons ever since, and apparently with the same result.

But for all that we have made progress. We have secured public discussion, and a righteous cause which has done that has got the weather gauge of its adversary. I am too old to be persuaded by any appearances, however specious, that Truth has lost or can lose a whit of that divine quality which gives her immortal advantage over Error. The adversary has cunningly intrenched himself in the argument that there can be no such thing as property in an idea, and I grant that this is a fallacy of which it is hard to disabuse the minds of otherwise intelligent men. But it is in the form given to an idea by a man of genius, and in this only, that we assert a right of property to have been created. The founders of our republic tacitly admitted this right when they classed the law of copyright with that of patents. I have known very honest men who denied the public expediency of such a right in both cases, but I cannot understand either the logic or the probity of those who admit the one and deny the other. This right is visible and palpable in a machine, invisible and impalpable in a book, and for this very reason the law should be more assiduous to protect it in the latter case, as being the weaker.

But, after all, every species of property is the artificial creature of law, and the true question is whether, if such property in books did not exist, it would be wise in our own interest to create it. The inventions of Whitney, of Fulton, and of Morse added enormously to the wealth of the nation. Have not those of Edwards and Irving and Cooper and Emerson and Hawthorne and Longfellow (to speak only of the dead) added also to that wealth and in a nobler kind? Or is not moral credit, then, worth something too? Is it not, indeed, the foundation on which financial credit is built and most securely rests?

The foreign right to property of this description stands on precisely the same footing with the domes-

tic right, and the moral wrong of stealing either is
equally great. But literary property is at a disadvantage because it is not open, gross, and palpable, and
therefore the wrongful appropriation of it touches the
public conscience more faintly. In ordinary cases it is
the thief, but in this case the thing stolen, that is invisible. To steal is no doubt more immediately profitable
than acquisition by the more tedious methods of honesty, but is apt to prove more costly in the long run.
How costly our own experiment in larceny has been
those only know who have studied the rise and progress of our literature, which has been forced to grow as
virtue is said to do—in spite of the weight laid upon it.

But even though this particular form of dishonesty
against which we are contending were to be always
and everywhere commercially profitable, I think that
the American people is so honest that it may be made
to see that a profit allowed to be legitimate by us
alone among civilized nations—a profit, too, which goes
wholly into the pockets of a few unscrupulous men—
must have something queer about it, something which
even a country so rich as ours cannot afford.

I have lived to see more than one successful appeal
from the unreason of the people's representatives to
the reason of the people themselves. I am, therefore,
not to be tired with waiting. It is wearisome to ourselves and to others also to go on repeating the arguments we have been using for these forty years and
which to us seem so self-evident, but I think it is true
that no reformer has ever gained his end who had not
first made himself an intolerable bore to the vast ma-

jority of his kind. I have done my share in my time
to help forward such triumphs of tediousness, but you
will not thank me for essaying it again in the sprightly
columns of your paper.*

Faithfully yours,

J. R. LOWELL.

TO THE MISSES LAWRENCE

Elmwood, Cambridge, Mass., July 6, 1890.

Dear Dual-mood,—It is Sunday morning and as fair
as George Herbert's, a happy bridal of Earth and Sky
presaging a long felicity of married days—all honeymoon
that isn't sunshine. Yet I can't help hoping that some
spiteful fairy has hidden a seed of storm somewhere
in the *trousseau*, for we have had no rain these three
weeks, and our turf is beginning to show symptoms of
jaundice. The partiality of the solar system (due, no
doubt, to the insular prejudices of Sir Isaac Newton)
gives you a five hours' start of us; so I suppose you have
both been to church by this time, and have put away
your prayer-books with a comfortable feeling that you
have played your parts in maintaining the equilibrium
of the British Constitution and have done with religion
for a week. With us there has been a divorce of Church
and State, and the children are given over to their own
guidance.

Why must you be so cruel as to flout me with the
nightingale when you knew (or was it *because* you knew?)
we hadn't him? I am not sure we would have him if

* This letter was published in *Kate Field's Washington*.

we could, for, in spite of the poets, who naturally try to make the best of him, he has a bad character among you as a *somnifuge,* and I have heard no music so ill-spoken of as his save only that of the barrel-organ. Even his flatterers seem savagely happy in thinking that he sings with his breast against a thorn and suffers some proportion, inadequate though it be, of the misery he inflicts.   In any case you need not give yourself airs, for our nights will never want for music while we have the mosquito.   What is your nightingale to him, whether for assiduous song or as a prophylactic against inordinate and untimely slumber? He would have prevented the catastrophe of the Foolish Virgins —not that I liken you to those—God forbid! On second thoughts I am not sure that I don't, after all, for I have been sometimes tempted to think that I liked them better than the wise. 'Tis a question of gold spectacles.

I have no news except that my smoke-trees have vapored into rosy clouds that carry on the tradition of sunrise all through the day to the sunset. Sweet-peas, too, are in blossom, and honeysuckle, but, alas, I haven't seen a humming-bird this summer. I never before knew a summer without them.

Your London world seems a great way off, for I am gone back to my old books, and live chiefly two or three centuries ago, sometimes much farther back. I find no nicer creatures than you there.

My grandchildren grow apace and my eldest grandson goes to college this year. My contemporaries drop faster and faster about me, but one gets used to it as the leaves to the falling of their fellows and playmates in autumn. I am not conscious yet of any loosening of my stem. But who ever is?

Affectionately yours,

J. R. LOWELL.

TO C. E. NORTON

Elmwood, Cambridge, Mass., Aug. 23, 1890.

. . . Tied by the leg as I am, I should envy the spryness with which you are skipping over the hills and seeing them golden with the June grass—as good as heather in its way. But I am by nature so stolidly content with seeing the things I have seen all my life, and find such a comforting sympathy in them, that I am on the whole satisfied to sit on the veranda and enjoy a vegetative life with my trees, with Panks and Gobble for company. Gobble is getting to be as interesting a little soul—for I am sure he has one—as I ever saw, and the patience of his father with him, letting him bite his ears, tail, legs, or what not, just as he has composed himself for a nap, is worth many a sermon to me.

The newspapers haven't told you our most important event. The crickets have come, and are trilling away, each on his own hook and without unison, like an orchestra tuning their fiddles. This means that the curtain is going to rise for the entry of autumn. I find no sadness in it—cheer rather. It is *my* season of the year now, and I heard my crickets long ago, only they creak in the joints instead of the grass.

I have finished my "Areopagitica"* business after a
fashion, that is, I sent it off yesterday, and am now
beginning to think of what I might have said and
meant to say. This is an old phenomenon, but I suppose it only means that the Muse is a woman and
saves all she wishes to say for a postscript.

Anyhow, I was well tired of the thing (it has two
clever things in it), and so after posting it I gave myself a good bath in Calderon. He always entertains
and absorbs me after everybody else has given it up.
I am quite conscious how much sameness there is in
him, and yet there is endless variety too, and if his
horizon be not of the widest, heat-lightnings of fancy
are forever winking round the edges of it. Partly, perhaps, the charm is in the language and the verse, which
slips along thoughtless as a brook. There are greater
poets, but none so constantly delightful. His mind is
a kaleidoscope, at every turn making a new image of
the same bits of colored glass—cheap material enough,
but who cares? Not so cheap either when one comes
to think of it, for these are fragments from painted
windows, deepened in hue with incense fumes and
thrilled through and through with organ and choir.
Well, it is a comfort that there *used* to be poets, at
any rate, only it is despair to see how easily they did it!

Pongame le reugo á los pies de Peter's Hill, and tell
the park-like trees there that I shall never cease to
love them. And take off your hat for me to Monad-

---

* An Introduction to an edition of the "Areopagitica," printed
by the Grolier Club, of New York, in facsimile of the first edition.

nock, the most high-bred of our mountains. There must be something rarely fine in the Ashfield landscape, it has stamped itself so on my memory. I see it more clearly than many more familiar.

Dr. Wyman has just been in, and still forbids my walking. I grin and bear it. . . .

TO MISS E. G. NORTON

Elmwood, Cambridge, Mass., 7tember 7, 1890.

Dear Lily,—Do you observe my date? You would infer wonders from it as from a seventh son's seventh son. But I pray you in advance to do nothing of the kind, for my letter is predestined to dulness. And it is this consciousness, not infidelity, that has kept me silent so long with your dear letter on my table and on my conscience too. I have been dronish all summer. I don't mean lazy, but derive my adjective rather from the drone of a bagpipe, which is as oppressive to everybody else as it seems inexhaustibly delightful to the manipulator of it. I am struck, on after-thought, with the infelicity of my comparison, for I am not eager to bestow myself on the rest of mankind. Much rather am I incommunicable as a jelly-fish on the sands—did you ever essay conversation with one? Southampton Water would give you a chance. I fancy you making the experiment and whisking away with a pretty flutter of scorn in your skirts and a " Good-by, Uncle James; I give you up as a bad job!"

What would you have? The birds have ceased to sing, and I drag out my long days on the veranda with

no company but that of Panks (my dog), who generously shares his dumbness with me and looks up at me
as who should say, "You are become unspeakable as
one of us, poor old fellow; I pity you!"

I said the birds had ceased, but I was wrong. The
screech-owl is in season, and every night yodels mourn-
fully about the house like a banshee. How they used
to scare me when I was a boy! And even now I don't
feel quite secure in the silenter watches of the night.
But the crickets have come, too, and are cheerful
enough in their monotonous way. I venture to think
they have told me the same thing before. But that
makes them all the more like human society.

I haven't the least notion where you are, and have
to invent epicycles for you, as old astronomers for the
moon, to account for your aberrations and fix you for
a moment in the right spot for my fancy. So I shall
suppose you at Basset, which must be delightful at this
season, if Aquarius have set his watering-pot in the
corner at last. Are the robins and finches cheery in
the garden? Our ancestors brought hither with them
laws, language, and other engines of oppression; why
did they leave those behind? Yet we are not wholly
comfortless. A robin forgot himself yesterday and sang
once, but stopped short with a twinge of conscience,
like a child that catches itself feeling happy in church.
Meanwhile we are having pears.

Your latest sensation is Newman's death. A beautiful old man, as I remember him, but surely a futile life
if ever there was one, trying to make a past unreality
supply the place of a present one that was becoming

past, and forgetting that God is always "I am," never "I was." He will be remembered chiefly by his "Lead, kindly light," which is as far from poetry as I hope most hymns are from the ear to which they were addressed. Else would it be shut to all our petitions. . . .

Your affectionate
UNCLE JAMES.

TO S. WEIR MITCHELL

Elmwood, Cambridge, Mass., Sept. 24, 1890.

Dear Mitchell,—The other day I wrote to my publishers asking them to send you a copy of my new edition *Hommage d'Auteur*. They replied that you were already a subscriber for a large-paper copy, an *Edition de looks*. This is a cross too heavy for my strength, and accordingly I beg that you will permit your subscription to be transferred to me and accept the copy, not as a requital for many obligations, but as a record of my affection and respect.

I am elated by the chance to step into your shoes, which, under any other circumstances, would be a world too wide for me, but under these will not wobble unpleasantly. You must not deny me this; indeed, I shall so far presume upon your friendship as to direct Messrs. Houghton & Mifflin accordingly.

I cannot do much, for I get more easily tired than before my illness. I had a slight relapse in the latter part of June, and this was in one sense an encouragement, for it was soon over and without any of the anguish I had before. But it has left me with an irksome feeling that my malady may be lying in wait for me around the next corner, and floor me again at any moment. This is not a frame of mind auspicious for any continuous or fruitful work.

I beg you to make my affectionate regards acceptable to Mrs. Mitchell, and remain

Always faithfully yours,

J. R. LOWELL.

TO THOMAS HUGHES

Elmwood, Cambridge, Mass., Oct. 1, 1890.

My dear old Friend, — With the cooler weather of autumn (and it is the most fountain-of-youthy I know of) I am beginning to feel like my old, or rather my young, self again. When you write next it must be in words of one syllable, and with everything adapted to the apprehension of a boy. Since my illness I have been under the weather, but a week ago this meteorological incubus was suddenly lifted away and life was lightsome again.

I wish you could share my day with me. It is simply what a day should be that has a good conscience— nothing left in it but a well-manner'd sunshine and the mere pleasure of being. I can't bear to think that our politicians should have any share in it. It was meant for better men. However, it may make them think there is a God in heaven, and that he visits earth sometimes in his mercy.

This morning I read that the Tariff Bill is passed— the first experiment a really intelligent people have

II.—27

ever tried to make one blade of grass grow where two grew before, by means of legislation. A reaction is sure to follow, and what I fear is, that their excesses may make it so sudden as to be calamitous. It is a comfort to think that nations, if they have any stuff in them, survive even folly.

I have felt so sluggish and unwieldy this summer that I have found it hard to write even a letter, and all that I have done is a short preface to an exact reprint of the first edition of Milton's "Areopagitica." It will be a pretty book, and I shall send you a copy. If the preface do not attract you, there is good pasture in the text. It is published by a club of book-and-binding lovers—the Grolier.

My eldest grandson enters college this year, a shocking anachronism, for I could swear I wasn't forty this very morning—not a day older for love or money—and the sun shining in on me as I write seems to say, "Strike off another [decade] and done with it." The only thing that makes me doubt is helping Joe with his Greek. I seem to have got farther away from it than my years would warrant. And the absurd quiddities with which the grammarians have made the language indigestible nowadays! If the Greeks had had to think of all these things when they were writing, they couldn't have managed it at all. . . .

Why did Balfour make martyrs of all those fellows who were making fools of themselves to his advantage? But, as I have always said, "the stars in their courses fight against you in the Irish question."

TO MRS. LESLIE STEPHEN

Elmwood, Oct. 7, 1890.

. . . A cold north-easter is blowing and drizzling and whatever else the D—l prompts it to do. I have just touched off the heap of wood that has been waiting in the chimney all summer, and it is blazing and crackling merrily. I put under a modest veil of French the fact that *aussi j'ai allumé ma pipe*, and there you have me. . . . I entirely sympathize with you in your tenderness about Thoby, for I have a grandson who goes off to a boarding-school to-morrow. He doesn't look as if he were a bit sentimental, but his heart is so full that it spills over in tears at the least jar. And *such* tears! as big as those of Jacques's stag! I never saw any with so much water in them. Whether the salt be in proportion is another matter. They drop silently upon his expansive waistcoat to rebound in spray. They are of the Roman fashion—they could not have filled their lachrymatories else. And Gobble, my puppy, whom Leslie will remember, was he not carried away howling to a boarding-school where he is to be taught dogmatics! Yes, dear friend, I weep with you, tear for tear. They are grandfather's tears, to be sure, and not worth so much as a mother's, but they will serve at a pinch. I continue as well as when I wrote. After growing younger every day for a fortnight, I have resolved to draw the line at forty and intrench me there for the rest of my days. 'Tis an age that does not carry me beyond the circle of a woman's interest, and so will do very well. You won't be putting cushions behind me or tame-catting me, if you please. A man of sense ought never (ought he?) to get a hair's-breadth beyond fawty. Shall I send you my photograph?

Joe has just come in with his Greek lesson for to-morrow, so if I get a little higgledy-piggledy you mustn't mind. When he finds a difficulty he consults the oracle, who is no longer so glib in that tongue as in that of Dodona, and cannot like that save his credit by an amphibolous answer. (The oracle uses that adjective with design, to make you think him not quite so shady in his Greek as he pretends.) 'Tis an excellent exercise for me, and my lichens are getting a little rubbed off, revealing unsuspected Attic inscriptions underneath. My embarrassments are increased by the new-fangled pronunciation, so unlike that of the ancient Grecians of my time. Fancy their calling εἰμί (I'm I) *amee!* The world certainly *is* going to the bad heels over head. I had long supposed it, but this convinces me.

I was wrong about the hydrangea. It doesn't turn blue, but pale-green, like the sky sometimes after sunset, or like a bit of green cheese from the new moon. It is I that turns blue sometimes, but I sha'n't any more, now that I'm fairly forty. It was looking forward to that which depressed me. One really doesn't feel any older after one gets there, as you will find out one of these days. . . .

TO R. W. GILDER

Elmwood, Cambridge, Mass., Oct. 9, 1890.

My dear Gilder,—You recall very happy days with

your "Conversations" and things. *Dio mio*, how full
of hope and confidence I was, how young, in short! I
was twenty-three when I wrote the prose, and many of
the verses are even younger. Mabel's mother designed
the illuminated covers before we were married.

But, thank God, I am as young as ever. There is an
exhaustless fund of inexperience somewhere about me,
a Fortunatus-purse that keeps me so. I have had my
share of bitter experiences like the rest, but they have
left no black drop behind them in my blood—*pour me
faire envisager la vie en noir.*

You must know, then, that after a summer of helpless inertia, I got up one morning about a fortnight ago
as if nothing had ever happened—not even a birthday
later than my fortieth. I haven't the smallest notion
how it was done, what Fountain of Youth I drank in
dream, but so it was. May it only last!

I don't know De Quincey well enough to write anything about him. I have not read a line of him these
thirty years. I never write about anybody without
reading him through so as to get a total impression,
and I have not time enough to do that in his case now.
The only feeling I find in my memory concerning him
is, that he was a kind of inspired *cad*, and an amplifica-
tion of that with critical rose-water wouldn't answer
your purpose.

But I begin on "Parkman" to-morrow. My bugbear
in respect of him has been that I wrote two or three
short things about him from twenty-five to thirty years
ago, and can't say them so well again. Do you think I
might quote a sentence or two from my former self? I
may be driven to it. . . .

I am almost afraid to say how well I am lest the Liers in Wait should be listening, but meanwhile it is delightful.

Affectionately yours (both),

J. R. LOWELL.

From the *Universal Eavesdropper:*

"ANECDOTE OF JAMES RUSSELL LOWELL.

"Passing along the Edgeware Road with a friend two years ago, their eyes were attracted by a sign with this inscription, 'Hospital for Incurable Children.' Turning to his companion, with that genial smile for which he is remarkable, Lowell said quietly, 'There's where they'll send *me* one of these days.'"

TO THE MISSES LAWRENCE

Elmwood, Cambridge, Mass., Oct. 12, 1890.

. . . Φίλτατα ἀμφότερα — which, being interpreted, means, I believe, My dears both—I was on the point of writing to ask how you did, or what I had done that you should be silent so long, when your welcome letter came to relieve me of my doubts. It was as full of the warm South as the beaker Keats wished for, and of names that set one's fancy dancing. I hope, now you are so near, that you will go to Venice—'tis the only city that deserves to be called *she*. Perhaps this feminine charm of hers works less strongly on those of your sex, but you will be foolish virgins if you don't call upon her when you have so good a chance. Except London, Venice is the one place I care to see again, and I still hope it if I live. She

always receives me like an old lover, put upon a footing of friendship, of course, yet with a secret between
us that sets me apart from ordinary friends. And yet
would she ever forgive me if I accepted the position
as if there were no risk in it?

And so you have seen and heard avalanches? I am
not sure that I don't like best the silent white flash
so far away that one doesn't hear the thunder. Snow
has no business to make a noise any more than a young
maiden has. When it falls, it seems as if the great silence Up There were filtering down upon us flake by
flake. When it joins in the mob of an avalanche it
belies its own nature, and ought to be ashamed of
itself. Besides, I needn't go to the Alps in search of
this wonder, for I am familiar with the tame, domestic species, the cat of this tiger, here when the deep
snow loosens and slides from the roof at night in a
thaw, and wakes me just soon enough to hear the last
throb of its muffled thunder.

And the Lago Maggiore, too, how has it been vul-
garized by the rows of hotels that prink themselves
along its shores and stare into its mirror with eyes as
dull as those of tourists! Not that I don't think fond-
ly of *two* tourists, and should be glad to have been
with them there. And did you climb up into the
empty noddle of San Carlo Borromeo and put more
cleverness into it than was ever there before?

Well, well, *we* are looking rather pretty here, and
think ourselves well worth seeing in our new autumnal
fashions. Our autumn beats the porphyrogeneti, for
he is born not only in the purple, but in every other

color that is brilliant, and in gold too, if you come to
that. *Per Bacco!* I think Nature grows more and more
beautiful and companionable as one grows older, and
the Earth more motherly-tender to one who will ask
to sleep in her lap so soon. But, in the nature of
things, I am happy to think you won't reach this point
of view for a long while yet.

I do little else than read of late, and have been re-
reading Rousseau. I went to him to look up something, grew interested, and went on for weeks. He is
(or seems) many ways a very complex character, and
one feels as if the two poles of the magnet were somehow mixed in him, so that hardly has he attracted you
powerfully, when you are benumbed with as strong a
shock of repulsion. He is always the victim of a fine
phrase—a monstrous liar, but always the first dupe of
his own lie. I don't know why I am telling you this,
and I can't tell you any more, you will be glad to hear,
for one of my grandsons is studying his Cicero at my
side, and asks me so many questions that I am puzzled as to whether Catiline or Jean Jacques were the
greater rascal, or Cicero a greater liar than J. J. However, you will acknowledge that I seldom put such
stuff into my letters, but good wholesome nonsense
rather, keeping my seriousness to bore myself with.

You will be glad to hear that I am suddenly begun
to be much better—Heaven only knows why, unless
it be that I was fairly tired of being good for nothing.
If ever you see me again within any reasonable time,
you will be shyer of me, I am grown so young. You
won't be able to treat me as if I were shelved among

the seventies any more. But I will try to be as old as I can. . . .

Good-by.
                        Affectionately yours,
                                GIACOPO IL RIGIOVINATO.

TO R. W. GILDER

Elmwood, Cambridge, Mass., Nov. 10, 1890.

My dear Gilder,—You probably have been expecting to receive ere now my little piece about Parkman. I have been trying at it, but my wits nowadays are like a cow trying to bite a pumpkin (did you ever see that illustration of *magnis excidit ausis ?*) and can't seem to git no kind o' purchase on anything. My illness has wrought some subtle change in me which I feel, but can't explain. I live in a state of nervous apprehension, like timid folk when burglars are about, or an Irish landlord when there is a hedge within gunshot. I was getting over it when I last wrote to you, but since then I have had two attacks—the last yesterday — which both, to be sure, passed away without any serious consequence, but left me depressed and disheartened again. I know it is foolish, but I can't help it as yet. By and by, when I have made up my mind that my malady is something I must reckon with for the rest of my life, I shall take it more easily.

I am rather languid to-day after the enemy's raid, but I shall always have energy enough to send my love to Mrs. Gilder and you.

                        Faithfully yours,
                                J. R. LOWELL.

TO EDWARD EVERETT HALE

Elmwood, Cambridge, Nov. 11, 1890.

Dear Edward,—M. Guizot asked me, " How long do you think the American Republic will endure?" My answer was, " So long as the ideas of its founders continue to be dominant." I quoted this in an address before the New York Reform Club in 1888. Of course I condensed it. In my conversation with Guizot, I naturally explained that by " ideas " I meant also the traditions of their race in government and morals.

Faithfully yours,

J. R. LOWELL.

TO MRS. LESLIE STEPHEN

Dec. 4, 1890.

. . . I am not half what I was this time last year. For the first time in my life I am on ill terms with the weather, which indeed has been of late as unaccountable as Sarah Bernhardt, without her motive of advertising itself. Yesterday morning the mercury stood at 1° below zero of Fahrenheit. At two o'clock it had risen only to 10°, blowing hard from the N. W. At five the wind went round to the east and it was raining. In the night it took a miff at something, whisked back to the N. W., and is now a gale, with the glass sinking as rapidly as a disappointed child's heart. . . . To-day, however, I have the sun, which is always a consoler, but if you could hear the wind. The surges break thunderously in my chimneys, and the house whines and whistles like the cordage of a ship in heavy weather. ——

Here I was suddenly called away by hearing a blind slam in the third story, threatening my window glass. I found three swinging loose. Such are the cares of a house-keeper with sixty windows on his conscience. How often I recall the saying of Montaigne that a loose tile on his roof gave him far deeper concern than matters of real import.

I am sitting in the sun as I write, and letting him bake me like a pot in the furnace. I hope he may give me (poor earthen vessel) a firmness of consistency to resist the brazen fellows against whom I am jostled by the current of life. I spend most of my time in my chair, for I am denied any exercise that would count. I don't miss it as much as I thought I should, but miss it, nevertheless. Were it not for ——'s sharp eye over me, I should break through all rules and take my chance. Still, I cling to what hope of life I have left, and tighten my clutch as I feel the end of the rope slipping through my fingers. I don't bother about Death, but sha'n't be sorry if he delays as long as he honestly can. This is all stuff, by the way. I am feeling uncommonly well. . . .

TO THE MISSES LAWRENCE

Elmwood, Cambridge, Mass., Dec. 18, 1890.

. . . You live in the world's capital city, and the only advantage I can see in such centres of over-population is that they supply endless topics for correspondence. Something is always happening there. But what topic has a hermit like me save himself?— supremely interest-

ing at one end of a correspondence; liable to lose flavor
at the other, three thousand miles away. Unless, to
be sure, the hermit be important enough, like St. Anthony, to attract the special attention of the Evil One.
And even then the spectacles provided by the Arch
Tempter were hardly of a kind wherewith to entertain
two demure young women, though dwelling in Babylon.

Shall I tell you of the weather? You have enough
and to spare of your own. No doubt we had a great
storm last night, and my chimneys bellowed like bulls
of Bashan—or rather like those of the Pope, for nothing came of it, and this morning the winds have bated
their breath. Or shall I tell you what I have been
reading? I read old books mostly, and am apt to
think that they tell me a secret or two which they
have saved for me. Of course I shouldn't think of
blabbing, and, besides, how do I know that they don't
say the same thing to everybody? They may be like
women in such matters. And what do you care about
Terence, for example, whom I have just read through
again, when you can go to the French play? I found
him rather amusing for a poor devil who had to do his
writing before America was discovered. And I have
been re-reading South's sermons, and like the handsome way he has of taking everything for granted while
he seems to be arguing its probability. But you can
hear as good at St. Paul's—I was going to say. I had
forgotten Dean Church's death, a great loss to friendship and to literature, one of the few men worthy to sit
in Donne's stall. I am grateful to him for more than
one kindness.

To come back to lighter matters. I have also been reading Charles de Bernard for the I know not what[th] time. I wonder if you know him and like him as much as I do. He is one of the Balzacidæ, no doubt, but he knew the Great World far better than Balzac knew it, and has a far lighter touch. He was waited on, too, by a guardian angel of gentlemanly humor that generally saved him from yielding to the temptation of melodrama as Balzac so often did. I like his shorter stories best, though the devil-may-care artist in "Gerfaut" is a masterpiece.

22d.   Here I found myself such a bore that I put by my letter for a luckier day. To-day is one of triumphant sunshine, which is always medicinal, and then, too, the days have begun to lengthen, which always comforts me, I don't know why, for I do nothing with 'em, and my own are shortening all the while. Moreover, my malady has let me alone for five weeks, and I have every reason to be jolly. The children are all busy and mysterious about Christmas—an anniversary which I am beginning to look on as sourly as my Puritan ancestors did, it has become such a *corvée* of unmeaning presents. It was much merrier when I was young, and got a gift or two that were worth something for their rarity and because they came from nearest and dearest. Nor do people eat so manfully as they used before stomachs were invented. My grandson Frank, to be sure, is a doughty and serious trencherman who, after eating straight through a *menu*, could turn round and eat backwards to the soup again with entire self-possession. He is a stay to me in the general backsliding and my only mitigation of the approaching festival.

You see what a cross old thing I am become! It all comes of living too much out of the world. I fancy hermits are mostly dull. I am sure Parnell's is—I don't mean C. S., but the doctor. As for C. S., I pity him. I don't like to see anybody tumble, and he had qualities as a captain that are not too plenty. McCarthy occupies his throne as the two kings of Brentford might. The Irish half of him will be always consulting the English half, and there will be no single sharp-edged will as before.

Good-by; forgive, but don't forget

Your affectionate and tiresome

J. R. LOWELL.

TO E. L. GODKIN

Elmwood, Cambridge, Jan. 5, 1891.

. . . As for my poor self, I have had no sharp attack since the 16th November, though an unwonted languor and ease in getting tired remind me feelingly that I got a severer wrench last winter than I have been willing to think. At seventy-one, I was far short of my age. At seventy-two, I have overtaken and passed it. But patience, and shuffle the cards!

I am beginning to think that Ireland "is almost damned in a fair wife," but I fancy Parnell will come to the top again, for none of the others have his quality of captaincy. McCarthy is too mushy. But the Devil seems to have a finger in every Irish pie. . . .

TO MRS. R. W. GILDER

Elmwood, Cambridge, Mass., Jan. 12, 1891.

. . . Yes, thank you, I am fairly well—but not what I was. I need no Gil Blas to tell me that—and I would dismiss him if he did, though, all the same. I am no longer an invalid exactly, but a val-e-tu-di-na-rian. 'Tis a noble long word and seems to imply promotion. In short, I am as well as need be, but I can't *do* anything. My spurs, somehow, seem to have been lost overboard in the rough weather of last spring, as Dr. Johnson's were on his tour to the Hebrides. My Pegasus only shakes his ears and won't budge. That's the way I am.

Tell Gilder how much I liked his poem in the *Atlantic* the other week. The "New Day" is still authentically shining on him. 'Tis a good sign and makes you both younger than ever. . . .

TO THE SAME

Elmwood, Cambridge, Jan. 26, 1891.

P. S.

I had hardly posted my answer to your last letter when I recollected with a twinge that I had left a question you asked me hanging like a hook without its eye. (There is a sex in images, you will observe, which can be judiciously fitted to one's correspondent.) You asked me what I thought of Adams's " Dana." Well, I like it. He has been immitigably, but not, I think, obtrusively frank. . . . But the Adamses have a genius for saying even a gracious thing in an ungracious way. The Adams flavor is as unmistakable as that of the Catawba grape.

It won't out of the wine, do what you will. I rather like
it. It reminds me of New England woods. 'Tis the
conscience we have inherited from our Puritan forebears (*ursa novanglica*). There are occasions where it
should appear in evening dress, with the reticences
and connivances which that implies, and perhaps biography is one of them—but I am not sure. I fancy
an honest man easier in his grave with the bare truth
told about him on his headstone. Perhaps we pardon
superiority more readily if we can comfort ourselves
with a knowledge of its weaknesses. Dana had great
powers, but he lacked that touch of genius which com-
munizes, which puts a man on a level with the highest
and lowest of his kind. He had a talent for locking
himself in, with " no admission except on business "
on the door. But he had a courage of perfect proof.
I knew him well from boyhood up. . . . His highest
quality was forensic. He could state a case with a force
and lucidity that belong only to minds of the first rate.
He could convince, but somehow without persuading.
Do you find the real inside of him in his letters? I
think not—and this is a pretty sure test. . . .

TO MRS. L. STEPHEN

Feb. 11, 1891.

. . . I wish you could see my dogs lying before
my fire, each making a pillow of the other and looking round to me from time to time lest I should forget they loved me. Human eyes have generally precious little soul in them, but with theirs there comes

sometimes the longing for a soul and almost overtaking it that is desperately touching. It makes me believe in the story of those poor transmogrified sisters in the "Arabian Nights." I do a good deal of loose reading, too, after a fashion. I lately read Boswell's "Johnson" through again, for the fourth time, and have just finished "Scott's Diary," a refreshingly manly book. I read novels also, a new habit with me—and have to thank your friend, Mr. Norris, for much pleasant disposal of time which I knew not what to do with. I shall begin another story of his the moment I have posted this.

A cold snap is just beginning with us, and the northwest wind is crowing lustily in my chimney. But the sun is shining, and the mere consciousness of that always keeps me warm. It is by imagination that we mostly live, after all. I more and more doubt whether I shall get across this spring. Perhaps I may later, and drop in on you at St. Ives. . . . What could possess Leslie to go to Switzerland, where it is as cold as science, and they have given up Tell? But it is well for him to get away from the Dixery. I hate to think of his giving his life for the lives of fellows of whom we were blessedly ignorant; they were most of them dead or damned, and we hoped we were rid of 'em. . . .

TO MRS. FRANCIS G. SHAW

Elmwood, Feb. 18, 1891.

. . . Your letter was a cordial to me. You are quite right in thinking that I don't like my own things so

II.—28

well as I wish I did. But that doesn't hinder my liking very much that you should like them better than
I do. There is no valid reason why you shouldn't, for
you don't know how much poorer they are than I
hoped they were going to be. . . . I have been a very
miserable creature for a month or more, but things are
beginning to go better with me, and I hope to be young
again with the year—never so young as you, to be sure,
but fairly so for a veteran. . . .

TO THOMAS HUGHES

Elmwood, Cambridge, March 7, 1891.

Dear Friend,—I was just going to write to you when
I was knocked flat by the sharpest attack of gout (save
one) I have ever had. . . .

I am glad you got the books and like them. I
didn't mean by this collected and uniform edition to
write " Finis," though I am not sure my health won't
write it for me. But I have enough uncollected essays of one kind and another to make a volume which
I shall publish in the spring or autumn. I have also
poems enough to fill a small other volume. If the
summer does as much for me as I hope, I suppose
that I shall wet my pen again. . . .

You make my mouth water by what you say of
your fair neighbors, whom I venture to count among
my friends, but neither you nor they must think the
Irish Question settled, or near it. You know how
highly I value Balfour, and I think he has done much
and well, but the Irish trouble is something too deep

for railways or transplantation to cure. It is a case of suppressed gout. *Experto crede*—don't I live in the midst of a population chiefly Irish? It is proof against everything—even against the exquisite comicality of its own proceedings. Boulogne must be in the Grand Duchy of Gerolstein.

You are having daffodils and things ere this. We are still in the depth of winter, if that is to be measured in snow. The view from my windows would gladden the heart of a polar bear. But this will make our spring less unendurable when it comes.

Our politics are going well. The Congress just ended has spent all our surplus and more. This brings us down to hard-pan at last, which will be good for us. . . .

TO W. D. HOWELLS

Elmwood, Cambridge, Mass., April 15, 1891.

My dear Howells,—How could you doubt that I should like anything you wrote—even about myself?* I am, perhaps, less able to judge what you have sent me, because I am less intimate with my own works than with those of other people, but I was altogether pleased that you should have found in them the motive for saying so many pleasant things about me.

Always affectionately yours,

El Viejo.

TO E. R. HOAR

Elmwood, Cambridge, June 1, 1891.

Dear Judge,—I missed you and marvelled, and am

* In the Editor's Study, *Harper's Magazine.*

grieved to hear that you had so painful a reason for not coming. I trust you are more than convalescent by this time, and there is nothing pleasanter to look back upon [than] the gout—unless it be a prison. Even in the very frenzy of its attack I have found topics of consolatory reflection. Is it podagra? I think how much better off I am than the poor centipedes must be. Is it chiragra? I imagine Briareus roaring.

I call *my* gout the unearned increment from my good grandfather's Madeira, and think how excellent it must have been, and sip it cool from the bin of fancy, and wish he had left me the cause instead of the effect. I dare say he would, had he known I was coming and was to be so unreasonable.

My neighbor, Mr. Warner, came in last evening and tells me the doctors pronounce it [your attack] to be inflammatory rheumatism. But from his account of it I am sure it was acute gout. *Experto crede Roberto*, as our old friend Democritus Junior used to say. Three more than intolerable days, and then a gradual relaxation of the vise, one turn at a time, but each a foretaste of Elysium—*that's* gout and nothing else. Our doctors don't know gout. . . .

Don't think because I have had a consultation over me that I am worse. I *have*, to be sure, been very weak lately and scant o' breath, but for a day or two I have felt lighter in the spirit and in the flesh too. Sleeplessness has been my bother, owing to a nervous cough which lies in ambush till I go to bed and then harries me without ceasing. The mere bodily weariness of it is such that I get up more tired than I went to bed.

I am now fighting it with opium, and if I can once break up its automatic action (for such it has become) I shall begin to gain at once, I think. Then, perhaps, I shall be able to get up to Concord, which would do me good in more ways than one.

Day before yesterday I should not have had vital energy enough to write all this, nor resolution enough to write even a notelet, for which *I* thank God, though perhaps you mayn't.

Convalescence is an admirable time for brooding over mares'-nests, and I hope you may hatch an egg or two. Several handsome chicks of whimsey have clipped the shell under me.

Good-by and God bless you. Make the first use of your feet in coming to see me.

Affectionately yours,
J. R. LOWELL.

TO MRS. EDWARD BURNETT

Elmwood, Cambridge, June 14, 1891.

. . . Thermometer 76°, north veranda a paradise, the pale green of the catalpa so beautiful against the darker of the English elms that I can hardly keep my eyes on my paper to write; Joe sitting near me doing his algebra, which he is using, I fear, as a prophylactic against the piety of church-going, and I weakly submitting, in the absence of the domestic despot—such is the *mise-en-scène*. My handwriting *will* run down hill. I suppose because *I* am—in spite of continued watchfulness on my part.

The house goes on quietly enough so far as I can see. . . . Shall I send you " The Moonstone"? I found it very interesting—not such a breakneck interest as Reade's, where one follows the scent of the plot head-long as that of a fox in the hunting-field, but still with an interest keen enough for the arm-chair. I am now in the midst of " Armadale."

I have said all that I know, except that George continues to worry the lawn with his two machines, one of which perfects the roughness left by the other. His air when mounted on the horse-machine puts me in mind of Neptune in the " Iliad." . . .

TO LESLIE STEPHEN

Elmwood, June 21, 1891.

Dear Leslie,—If I have not written it has been because I had nothing good to say of myself. I have been very wretched with one thing and another. And now a painful sensation is taking its turn. I could crawl about a little till this came, and now my chief exercise is on the nightmare. I can't sleep without opium.

Your affectionate letter was refreshing to me, and there was not a word in it to which I did not heartily respond. I thank God for that far-away visit of yours, which began for me one of the dearest friendships of my life. How vividly I remember our parting under the lamp-post when you went away! I beguile the time now chiefly in the reading of novels, and am looking forward eagerly to a new one by your friend

Norris which I see announced. I never read so many before, I think, in my life, and they come to me as fresh as the fairy tales of my boyhood. . . .

All your friends here are well, and each doing good in his several way. . . .

Always affectionately yours,

J. R. LOWELL.

INDEX

Titles of Mr. Lowell's poems and other writings referred to in his Letters are entered in *italics* in the following index.

II.—29

History, its value in a course of reading, i. 91 ; composition of, ii. 222.
Hoar, Judge E. R., i. 404 ; ii. 53, 56.
——, Letter to, **1891**, ii. 435.
Hogarth, i. 257.
Holbein, i. 246.
Holmes, John, i. 341, 346; ii. 45, 80, 98, 154, 176, 199; dinner to, in 1861, i. 313.
——, Letter to, **1856**, i. 250.
Holmes, O. W., i. 144; ii. 13, 141, 301, 308, 369 ; his "Autocrat," i. 288 ; poem at dinner to Prince Jerome Napoleon, 316 ; his "Emerson," ii. 291 ; in England, 314.
——, Letters to, **1858**, i. 288;—**1884**, ii. 291.
Holmes house, ii. 277.
Home, delights of, i. 14.
Homes, characteristic of their owners, i. 284.
Home Rule, 1886, ii. 310, 313, 314, 315, 316. *See also* Gladstone, W. E. ; Irish question ; McCarthy, Justin ; Parnell, C. S.
Homesickness, ii. 252.
Horace, i. 377 ; ii. 162.
Horse-chestnuts, ii. 146.
Hosmer, Dr., ii. 195.
Hospitality, Bostonian, ii. 163.
Houses, should be destroyed when their owners have left them, i. 197; change of occupants, 284.
Howe, Dr. Estes, i. 313.
——, Letters to, **1856**, i. 254, 261.
Howe, Mrs. Estes, Letters to, **1856**, i. 258, 263.
Howell, James, ii. 44 ; his letters, 340.
Howells, W. D., advice to, i. 305 ; letter of introduction to Hawthorne, 305 ; his "Pilot's Story," 306 ; article on Recent Italian Comedy, 338 ; Venetian letters, 338 ; articles in the "Nation," 350, 355 ; article on Curtis, 404 ; his "Gnadenhütten, ii. 13 ; his "My Doorstep Acquaintance," 32; the ideal element in, 44 ; new house in Cambridge, 101 ; his "Lady of the Aroostook," 240 ; his work, 241 ; his stories, 243 ; a professorship of literature offered

to, 269; his "Silas Lapham," 297 ; "The Minister's Charge," 306 ; and the Chicago anarchists, 394 ; "A Hazard of New Fortunes," 399 ; his sketch of Lowell in the "Editor's Study," 435.
——, Letters to, **1860**, i. 305, 306 ; —**1864**, 338 ;—**1865**, 350 ;—**1868**, 403 ;—**1869**, ii. 16, 32, 34, 35, 43 ; —**1870**, 58 ;—**1874**, 121;—**1875**, 137 ;—**1876**, 179 ;—**1879**, 239 ;—**1882**, 268;—**1885**, 296, 297;—**1886**, 306, 307, 319 ;—**1890**, 394 ;—**1891**, 435.
Hughes, Thomas, "Tom Brown," i. 298 ; his portrait desired, 301 ; visit in Cambridge, ii. 63 ; regret at his departure, 67 ; his "Memoir of a Brother," 92 ; attitude towards disestablishment and cooperation, 94 ; not returned to Parliament in 1874, 124 ; his "Life of Fraser," 335.
——, Letters to, **1859**, i. 295 ;—**1860**, 299 ;—**1863**, 332 ;—**1869**, ii. 40 ;—**1870**, 58, 59, 61, 67, 69 ;—**1873**, 92, 102, 110 ;—**1874**, 123, 128 ;—**1875**, 134 ;—**1876**, 173 ;—**1877**, 197;—**1878**, 233;—**1884**, 282; —**1887**, 329, 335 ;—**1889**, 379;—**1890**, 397, 417 ;—**1891**, 434.
Hugo, Victor, ii. 47.
Hull, Isaac, at Faneuil Hall, Boston, ii. 305.
Hull, visit to, in 1859, i. 291.
Human nature, the light and the dark sides, i. 159.
Humanity, ii. 14.
Humor, character of, i. 118 ; by contract, 189.
Hungarian question, i. 173.
Hungarian revolution, letter to the "Advertiser" on, i. 189.
Hunkers, i. 188.
Hunt, Holman, his "Claudio and Isabella," i. 248.
Hunt, Leigh, i. 237, 317.
Hyde Park, London, ii. 198.
Hydrangea, ii. 420.
Hypochondria, i. 350.

Ice, its color, i. 94.
Ice-cutting, i. 95.
Icelanders, i. 312.
Ill-luck, i. 295.

THE END